POWER AND PREJUDICE

POWER AND PREJUDICE;

The Reception of the Gospel of Mark .

BRENDA DEEN SCHILDGEN

WAYNE STATE UNIVERSITY PRESS
DETROIT

03 02 01 00 99   5 4 3 2 1

Library of Congress Cataloging-in-Publication Data

Schildgen, Brenda Deen, 1942–
    Power and prejudice : the reception of the Gospel of Mark / Brenda
Deen Schildgen.
        p.   cm.
    Includes bibliographical references and index.
    ISBN 0-8143-2785-0 (alk. paper)
    1. Bible. N.T. Mark—Criticism, interpretation, etc.—History.
I. Title.
BS2585.2.S269   1998
226.3'06'09—dc21   98-28981

*For Anna
and Sergio*

Contents

List of Illustrations

Preface

Written by a medievalist, this book poaches on the territory of biblical scholars. However, though it is addressed to both literary and biblical scholars, it
engages topics central to the study of the humanities on the eve of the third
millennium of reading the Gospel of Mark. As a study of the history of
scholarship on a particular canonical text, it serializes the forces determining
communal reading habits. I was led to the study of the Bible because of the
crisis in interpretation wrought by the radical critique of structuralism and
historical studies in the last few decades. I was driven to look at the Bible as
a collection of texts that had been subjected to ongoing interpretation, to
uncover whether any "normative" interpretation or hermeneutical practice
could or had been sustained. This study is a tentative look at answering that
question.

Surveying the reception of a particular work over a long time span,
especially when that work happens to be a "canonical" text, confronts the
researcher with a number of questions. How can one read this text? What if
anything should dominate the inquirer's interests—philology, history, social
situations, literary texture? Early readers who wrestled with the issues developed inclusive systems for reading. For example, Origen's and Jerome's
threefold method for textual exegesis (literal, historical, and spiritual),[1] when
understood as philological, historical, and symbolic (theological and literary)
interpretation, provides a model for responses to the Gospels, for in every era
one or more of these approaches has received priority in the interpretation of
the Bible. The *how* or hermeneutics of reading is subject to radical changes

throughout history, whether the fourfold (literal, allegorical, moral, anagogical), threefold (literal, historical, spiritual) methods; the historical-literary-theological approaches of the patristic and medieval eras; the primarily two-fold method of the humanists and reformers (philological-spiritual); the single focus of the rationalists of the eighteenth, and historians of the nineteenth century (textual and historical); or the multiple methods of the twentieth century. There is much to recommend interpretive models from the patristic period. Intellectuals of that period were interested in the "literal" level of the text, but they embraced a polyvalent system for reading though they reined the text in to their single view of the created universe. They avoided the pitfalls of binary reading, whether philological/spiritual, historical/spiritual, or, even worse, single techniques that have emerged from the early modern period forward. But the church fathers had no experience with prose fiction; they didn't understand how the literary surface—that is, the arrangement, the elaboration or abridgment, or the flashback or flash forward, or the length of the sentences—functions to build a dramatic narrative and how its arrangement conveys its interpretation of the events it recounts.

This study also raises questions about periodization. With contemporary debates in mind, for example, I began to worry about dividing this time into conventional periods like the ancient period, Medieval, Renaissance, Enlightenment, and so forth. Did they exist? Was Jacques Le Goff's idea that the ancient world ended with the collapse of the Roman Empire, the Middle Ages spanned from then until the Industrial Revolution, and the modern period emerged in the eighteenth century a more descriptive system?[2]

An examination of this reception history reveals that paradigm shifts do occur.[3] Though often spurred on by a single person's critical questions and the material circumstances to make the challenge possible (whether the availability of resources like ancient languages, manuscripts, texts, or financial support for the scholar's work), these shifts don't happen in months or even years, but over centuries. At the risk of simplifying these observations into fairy-tale trebling, I began to see that the time span could be divided according to these dominant hermeneutics, as for example, the Age of Allegory (from the fourth to the fourteenth century); the Age of Philology (from the fourteenth to the eighteenth century); the Age of History (from the eighteenth to the twentieth century); and now, perhaps, the Age of Hypertext, in which all the subjective interests of readers can be applied to the text (from the late twentieth century). These periods are paralleled by which aspect of Aristotle's rhetorical triad (speaker, speech, audience)[4] has preoccupied inquirers at any given moment—the Age of Author(ity) (130–eighteenth century), when apostolic origins and earlier authors' testimonies held power; the Age of the Text (fourteenth century–nineteenth century), when recovery of an accurate text preoccupied inquirers; the Age of the

Reader (eighteenth century–present), when radical new objective questions energized the inquiries of subject-readers. Because of the nature of the critiques and responses to them over this time span, the history of the text reflects the history of Christianity: Early Christianity (100–1140), Middle and Late Christianity (1140–Industrial Revolution), Post-Christianity (1887–present), remembering that these dates are at best tentative. This overlaps with other political and cultural changes like the Age of the Church (90–1520); the Age of the Monarch (1399/1519–1776/1918); the Age of the Scholar (1348/1449–present); and finally, recalling that Erasmus thought books about the Bible would be saleable items, the Age of the Consumer (1456–present), from the time of the printing press. The early period can be understood as the Age of "spiritualization," when the symbolic significance of the text overtook all other interests. This was followed by an Age of "objectification," when the text was the focus of objective scholarship culminating in accurate texts and historical hypotheses about them; this in turn has been overtaken in the Age of the Reader by a focus on subjective interests, made even more possible by the advent of the hypertext.[5] As all this shuffling shows, there are numerous ways to divide this long time span, although it is clear that shifts do indeed take place and, however they are labeled, they are common to particular periods and conditioned by material developments or circumstances when new approaches to reading the Bible deconstruct established patterns of interpretation.

In this century, partly because of the emergence of modern "scientific" disciplines, new questions have been raised about the biblical texts leading to wholly new hermeneutics. These include sociological, anthropological, historical, political, literary, psychological, theological, as well as philological probings. These are further developed in schools of thought, whether Marxist, feminist, structuralist, post-structuralist, Freudian, Jungian, Lacanian, deconstructive, and so forth. Depending on the discipline of the inquirer, these analyses will lead to further theorizing about the theological, literary, political, social, or anthropological implications of these readings.

Because of our historical knowledge, our own era is uniquely situated to make use of all former approaches, and perhaps this accounts for the stream of diversity in approaches to reading the Bible. An analysis that reviews the history of the responses to a particular literary work attempts to overcome the "immediacy"[6] of the momentary reaction and place all earlier responses into a historical and social continuum. These differences that result from divergent interests and attitudes throughout history do not undermine the convictions of communities of interpreters; nor do they make meaning inaccessible. Rather, they demonstrate historical continuity and a persistence of human interest in texts deemed culturally, aesthetically, and historically foundational. They emphasize the capacity of certain texts to re-present themselves with integrity to different eras when different literary, social, and ideological interests emerge.

Acknowledgments

This study grew from a Master's thesis written at the University of San Francisco. The thesis compared the reception of the Gospel of Mark in the patristic period with the eighteenth century and was titled, "Habits of the Mind: Prejudice and Ideology in the Reading of the Gospel of Mark." Guided by Profs. John Elliott, Hamilton Hess, and Frank Buckley, S.J., the study won the College Theology Society's prize for the best Master's thesis in 1989. That earlier work led to this book, which presumptuously undertakes to analyze the reception of Mark from 130 c.e. to the present. When I begin to think of all those I must thank for their help and encouragement, many come to mind. But foremost among these are my teachers, Profs. John Elliott, Hamilton Hess, and Frank Buckley, S.J. Prof. Elliott, particularly, not only taught me how to read the Bible, as one of my readers he has been most generous in helping me see many deficiencies in this study. Those that remain are mine alone, for he has been the most careful reader and critic of my work. Of course, Prof. Emmy Werner, whose own work is inspirational, constantly spurred me on to finish this study, as also Stanley Jacobsen, whose "free" lunches were actually occasions to encourage me to keep working and to finish. Others have given much encouragement, including Prof. William Kennedy (Cornell), who heard me give parts of this study in a paper delivered at the American Comparative Literature Association in 1991; Prof. Giuseppe Mazzotta (Yale), who read the manuscript many years ago; Prof. Peter Hawkins (Yale), to whom I am also grateful for support; Prof. Brian Stock, who helped me to understand Augustine; and Prof. Hayden White,

15

a generous and provocative reader and critic. Manuscript librarians at the Bodleian, especially Melissa Dalziel; the British Library; the Biliotheque Nationale; Jack von Euw, curator of the Bancroft Pictorial Collection, and Tony Bliss, curator for rare books and manuscripts, at the Bancroft Library at U. C., Berkeley, all were generous with their expertise and knowledge. Finally, Jennifer Backer, editor at Wayne State University Press, whose enthusiasm makes me want to meet all her deadlines; Sandra Williamson, a most creative and meticulous copy editor; my husband Bob Schildgen, best critic and advisor; Prof. Kari Lokke, my most supportive and helpful director in the Comparative Literature Program at U. C., Davis; and Jeanne Hart, who, as secretary in the Comparative Literature Program at U. C., Davis, always asked about how my work on the Bible was progressing.

The Reception
of the Gospel of Mark

"Pius labor, sed periculosa praesumptio"
Jerome, *Epistula ad Damasum, Vulgata*

The history of how the Bible has been read emphasizes more forcefully than the history of any other text how tentative and yet how powerful reading-interpretive habits are. On the one hand, they are the product of changing historical circumstances and interests, and on the other they influence and direct later generations of readers. They reflect reigning political and social attitudes as well as current rhetorical and hermeneutical practice.[1] The biblical text has been subject to corruptions due to transcriptions, translations, and deliberate alterations. Also the habits of reading it—whether based on methodological convictions and prejudice, liturgical practice, styles of arranging the texts themselves (harmonies, *glossa,* synopses, trilingual versions, and annotations, for example), or developments in the material production of "text"—constitute the Bible's ever fluid reception. The Gospel of Mark, because of its virtual absence in this long tradition of response and dramatic rise in reading interest since the eighteenth century, offers a stunning case history of biblical reception.

Because the reader's interests have acquired such importance in recent years, contemporary reception studies focus on how audiences have responded to literary works, whether that audience is a commentator, translator, or writer of a new version of the original text. A number of issues emerge in a reception study involving the Bible: What is the nature of the canon, and how is it that canonicity does not assure attention to all the texts in the Bible? What habits of reading direct the reception of a biblical text? Are these reading habits indications of the dominant concerns of particular periods? What is the role of authority in the reception of a biblical text? Because the Bible is not the exclusive property of a cultural elite, does its reception

---

cross freely between high and popular culture? What does the reception history of a particular biblical text reveal about the history of scholarship? Is the reception affected by shifts in the technology of text production? The Gospel of Mark's reception shows that there is a canon within the biblical canon; that ways of reading or dominant hermeneutical interests in certain periods direct how any text will be received, even or especially "sacred scripture"; that distinctions between high and popular culture have had a profound role in the text's reception; and finally, that the history of biblical scholarship is a story of widely divergent interests and prejudices that have directed and controlled the gospel's fortunes. A study such as this clearly has implications not only for religious studies but more importantly for any discipline in the humanities, including history, philosophy, and literature, for it raises questions about canons, ideological prejudices, rhetorical standards and convictions, and scholarly practices and habits.

Reception theory has been a central preoccupation of critical theorists for the last quarter of a century. In fact, all the major cultural, philosophical, and literary theorists have probed literary reception as an aspect of interpretive controversy, a discussion that has swept over literary discourse. Whereas formerly literary reception was viewed almost one-dimensionally, as we examined how one author was influenced by an earlier one, or one country received the literary tradition of another, the discussions of recent years have enlarged the scope of inquiry to include all responses to an earlier work as part of the work's reception history. Thus, for Gerard Genette,[2] Jacques Derrida,[3] or Michel Foucault,[4] the entire commentary tradition on a work is a "supplement" to the original text.[5] Genette's theory of "transtextualite," in fact, considers everything that puts one text, manifestly or secretly, in a relationship with other texts. Of his several types of transtextuality, he called the commentary tradition on a particular text its "metatextuality," which unites one text to another whether it cites the earlier text or not.[6]

Some theories emphasize the role of individuality in responses to texts, as, for example, reader-response theory. Theorists of this type oppose the idea that meaning is exclusively in the text. Further, these theorists dwell on such individualist responses to literary artifacts, objectifying the text as the "new critics" had done, while making the subject-reader the central artificer in its re-creation.[7] American criticism has occupied itself with this kind of "romantic," individualistic "reception" theory—particularly Harold Bloom, whose "anxiety of influence" seeks to explain the problematic relationship later writers experience with their precursors.[8] Recognizing that social communities create meanings, Stanley Fish expanded the discussion of reception to include the source of the dissonance between the hypothetical originative "meaning" of a text and the community of readers who later interpret it.[9] In contrast to these American scholars, Frank Kermode has explored the relationship between reception and value in an effort to understand shifting interests of readers and the role of literary critics in this continuing cultural enterprise.[10] Literary critics, with widely divergent methods or anti-methods, generally agree that a literary work includes the text, its readers, and all the readers' responses to the text.[11] Rhetorical theory is yet another approach to reception, for since Aristotle it has included speaker, speech, and audience in its methodical approach to "interpreting" speeches (*Rhetoric* I:3).[12] Reception theorists have generally focused only on the audience response to literary works, often excluding questions of intentionality or the intrinsic and extrinsic features of the text that might control or at least rein in free-floating interpretations. Rhetoric—as developed theoretically by Aristotle—though primarily interested in speeches, has included nonetheless a theory of interpretation coupled with its discussion of the production of speech.[13] In contrast, reception studies tend to focus on the nature of the audience's responses to a text, whether "immediate" or over a long time span, and only consider authorial intentionality and the external features of the text insofar as these might help to assess what may have contributed to the nature of the text's reception at a particular moment in time. Few take up the power of authoritative voices in determining the fate of a text, although discussions in recent years that open up canons to interrogation have made prejudice based on gender, ethnic, or other social and cultural bias the culprit in determining selections. As a consequence, reception studies often tell us more about historical interests than about the text itself. But taken together, these historically situated responses contribute to an increased awareness of many facets of a particular text that some periods may ignore or glide over in favor of others.

A biblical text, because its canonicity has assured its place in a culture of doctrinal reading for almost two thousand years, provides a dramatic example of reception and the changes to a text wrought by time. Probably the only comparable Western texts are the *Aeneid* and Homer's epics. Confucius's *Analects,* the *Mahabharata,* and the *Ramayana* are non-Western examples of works subject to systematic and continuous reading. The Gospel of Mark was more or less ignored until the eighteenth century, when the scientific-historical agenda took over biblical studies. The patristic period, epitomized by Augustine, represents one aspect of the story of Mark's reception. It contrasts with the eighteenth century, when scholars with historical interests began Mark's restoration—which also contrasts with the twentieth century, when individual reading, unrestricted by a narrow authoritarianism, has led to the habit of reading and interpreting the Gospels separately. This in its turn has led to an explosion of studies of Mark that probe literary, political, and social questions as well as theological ones, completely overturning the gospel's traditional reputation as a summary of Matthew.

Because this gospel is part of a sacred canon, it poses very interesting questoins for the history of reception. Reception is made problematic because to determine it we must assess readers' subjective responses to literary works. Therefore, in a study of strictly literary reception, we would want to determine what interests in the historical context shape particular renderings or what determined shifts in attitudes or approaches to a particular text.[14] This is not simply an intellectual history question. Potential answers must take into account the material historical situation. For example, who is doing the interpreting? Are they part of an institutional structure that has certain and peculiar intellectual commitments? Are they challenging long-held convictions either about the text or its position in some sort of cultural practice (whether religious, academic, private, or popular)? Has a technology of text production assumed an importance that challenges patterns of response?

With a canonical religious text, however, its status would appear to be predetermined by its canonical status. The biblical canon is closed, in the sense that no texts can be added to it and neither can any texts be removed from it. But this is precisely why the reception of the Gospel of Mark is so provocative: its canonicity did little to promote interest in it. Like some other texts in the Bible, the Gospel of Mark's canonicity was merely a label and did not contribute to its being read or written on. In fact, not until 1969 did it become a regular part of the liturgical lectionary cycle, shared by Protestants and Roman Catholics, although brief parts of it had been consistently read.

One very simple explanation for this lack of interest in Mark is the status of the text itself in contrast to the other synoptics. If one were reading the gospel for the story rather than for the narrative—the distinction that Genette makes to delineate how a story is told from the succession of events themselves—Mark would have little to add to Matthew or Luke.[15] In fact, the agreements among the synoptic Gospels that are used to support the two-source theory[16] highlight precisely why Mark might be neglected if one were reading for contributions to the story line or for unique sayings.[17] Matthew and Mark or Mark and Luke regularly agree with each other. With the following brief exceptions—Mark 3:20, Jesus' family tries to seize him; 4:26–29, the parable of the seed growing secretly; 7:31–37, the healing of the deaf-mute; 8:22–26, the blind man healed at Bethsaida; 9:49, a unique saying, "Have salt in yourselves, and be at peace with one another"; 14:51, the young man fleeing—Mark overlaps with either Matthew or Luke.

In examining the gospel's reception history, I will argue that earlier eras, particularly the patristic period, while tolerating its presence in the canon, found its omissions and sparse, simple style[18] unsuited to the stylistic tastes and ideological interests of the period. So powerful were the authoritative readers of this period that the effect of the patristic neglect of the gospel is apparent even today. When we consider those New Testament stories that have impressed themselves into the Christian imagination and popular iconography, we find they are not specific to the Gospel of Mark. The Annunciation, Mary visiting Elizabeth, "no room at the inn," the scene at the stable in Bethlehem, the three shepherds, the three magi, the wedding at Cana, the young Jesus arguing at the temple, the Sermon on the Mount, Peter cutting off an ear at the garden, the Resurrection, and Thomas putting his finger in Jesus' hand for proof: these are the popular images of the Jesus story not found in Mark. Most practicing Christians could not identify the gospel to which any of these narrative kernels belongs. They are products of a harmonious reading of the Gospels, the kind promoted by Augustine in his *On the Harmony of the Gospels*. Mark's contribution to these stories is negligible. He lacks the entire infancy and childhood story, Mary is insignificant in his version, and he has no post-Resurrection sightings of Jesus. With some detailed differences, the passion events are nevertheless quite parallel in the four versions, so a unique Markan contribution to the general story is hard to identify—although his empty tomb, with the shocked and surprised visitors, has had a considerable cultural impact, a topic that will be discussed in this study.

The "absences" in the Gospel of Mark may well have been responsible for its egregious early reputation. The lapses are linguistic, literary, and narratival. That is, Mark has grammatical errors, it lacks any sophistication in rhetorical style, and, as noted above, it has specific narrative gaps. For example, there is no genealogy, no motivation for Judas, no reconciliation between Peter and Jesus after Peter's denial, no concrete teaching like the Sermon on the Mount or the Lord's Prayer. These absences may well have been disconcerting to early readers, and they were compensated for by the other gospels, canonical and apocryphal, to suit the needs of specific communities; by textual additions (as Mark 16:9–20) to complete the story; and by harmonies. The harmonies created by earlier readers and commentators—e.g., Tatian—overcame these absences and simultaneously altered the unique character of each gospel.

But our own era finds Mark's gaps and silences precisely the source of its interest, as commentators seek to understand these absences literarily or intellectually. The current theory that Mark was the source for Luke and Matthew, who filled in the gospel's gaps, reverses the early Church's obscuring of Mark's contribution with Matthew and Luke. Like the gospel's empty tomb, its ambiguities, paradoxes, and "open-endedness" prove to be precisely what interests contemporary commentators. The gospel's long-term reception points to the role of powerful readers in deciding what will be read, to the exercise of institutional authority in controlling what will be read and how this reading will be practiced, and to how changing cultural and ideological concerns, interpretive methods, and contemporary tastes affect reading interests. It also shows how unusual it is for readers/interpreters to break away from ruling interests, whether as attitudes toward the gospel or in methods and styles of commenting.

Studying Mark's reception in commentaries, translations, liturgical functions, harmonies, *glossa*, synopses, or quotations reveals how the biblical text has been understood in new circumstances and cultural contexts. Long-term histories of reading strategies draw attention to changes in a text's reception: on the one hand, changes in oral versus silent reading, a process that occurred during the Middle Ages, and second, the transformation from accepting authoritative texts without question to creating original responses to them (whether the Bible itself or commentaries on it), a process that many argue began in the twelfth century.[19] Though the text itself may be viewed as "normative" because of its canonical status, its "metatextual" history redefines its "norms" and uses and even recreates its meaning and focus. These formal responses to the gospel underscore the ways of reading that have dominated certain time periods or supported ideological interests. For example, if we picture a sample page of a harmony, a glossed text, an annotation, the polyglot Bible, or a synopsis, we are confronted with the radically different reading patterns of the gospel in times when each of these forms undergirded commentaries. A harmony constructs a linear text, and although it reminds us that we are reading Matthew, Mark, Luke, or John, it produces its story more or less chronologically and eliminates differences. The *glosses* provide interlinear (see fig. 1) or marginal commentary (see fig. 2), translation, or paraphrasing of the primary text, disrupting the reading with an unharmonious reminder of its failure to communicate without the necessary gloss. Annotations (see fig. 3), the product of the philological interests of

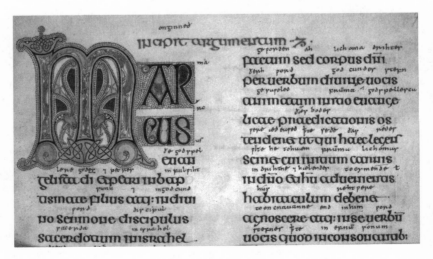

Fig. 1. *Lindisfarne Gospels*, opening of the Gospel of Mark with Anglo-Saxon gloss.

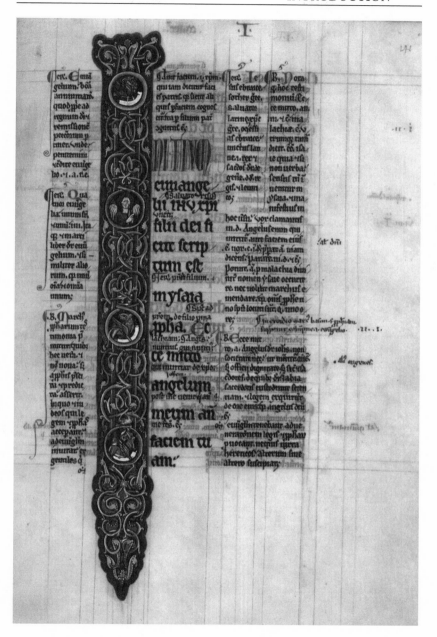

Fig. 2. *Glossa Ordinaria,* opening of the Gospel of Mark with gloss.

IN MARCVM 101

unam aut alteram horã, fed menfes fermè fex. Cogita, quæfo, lector optime, quãtum tædij utilitatis publicæ gratia deuoremus. Neqʒ uero pigebit, fi poft hac per ociũ continget alia cõquirere, quæ poffint opus hoc uel locupletius reddere, uel emendatius, illa quoqʒ in cõʒ munem ufum adijcere. Plufculũ aũt præfidij nobis fuppetebat in Matthæo ex ueterũ cõʒ mentarijs, ut in quē cõplures fcripferũt, Origenes, Chryfoftomus, Hieronymus. In hũc nĩ hil habemus, quod equidē fciam uetuftũ. Nam Theophylactus neotericus eft. & ij comʒ mētarij, qui Hieronymi titulo circũferuntur, ut nõ fint ufqʒquaqʒ reijciendi, tamen nõ maʒ gis fapiunt Hieronymũ, cʒ forba ficum. Cæterũ quo pauciores in hãc fcripferint, illud opiʒ nor, in caufa fuiffe, quod explicato Matthæo, & hũc explicatũ effe putarēt. Iam illud te no lim lateat lector, quod hactenus præfati fumus in Marcum, ad primã huius operis æditioʒ nem pertinere. Cum hæc fit æditio tertia qua decreuimus effe contenti: non quod ullũ fit opus, cui non poffit adijci, quód ue nõ poffit reddi melius, fed quod uideam Sycophanʒ tis nunc ubiqʒ regnantibus dandũ effe locum. ut exiftimem in tam humili, tamqʒ in amœʒ no argumento diligentiam immodicam merito reprehendendam effe.

Initium euangelij.) Et hic Hebræorum more exorfus eft ab ipfo operis titulo, quemad modum Matthæus, cuius epitomen fcripfit Marcus autore Auguftino.

In Efaia propheta.) In Græcorum exemplaribus, quæ quidē ego uiderim, Efaiæ nomē nõ exprimitur, fed tantũ, ὦ προφήταις, id eft, In prophetis. Verũ id apparet mutatum daʒ ta opera à doctis, qui deprehenderant hoc teftimonium è duobus prophetis effe conftaʒ tum, Quæadmodum indicat Hieronymus in libro de optimo genere interpretandi. Siqʒ dem prior pars, nempe illa, Ego mitto angelum meũ ante faciem tuã, qui præparabit uiam tuam ante te, eft apud Malachiam cap. tertio. Quo fanè loco illud obiter annotandũ, Hic ronymũ in eo, quod modo citauimus opere, memoria lapfum uideri poffe, cũ ait, hoc teʒ ftimoniũ haberi in fine Malachiæ. Nam cũ totum huius prophetæ uaticiniũ quatuor capiʒ tibus abfoluatur, & hic locus fit in ipfa ftatim fronte tertij capitis, in medio uerius eft, cʒ in fine. Verũ fufpicor quæ res impofuerit Hieronymianæ memoriæ, nimirum quod in extre mo calce habeatur non diffimile uaticinium, quod & ipfum de Ioanne interpretantur, Ecʒ ce ego mittam uobis Heliam ͵pphetam antecʒ ueniet dies domini. Neqʒ enim mihi fatifʒ facit excufatio cuiufdam, qui putat in fine dictũ effe, quod fit paulo infra mediũ. Cæterum quãcʒ fententiæ fumma confentit, uerba tamen Euangeliftæ nõnihil diffident, tum à Seʒ ptuaginta, tũ ab Hebraica ueritate. Siquidē Hebræa fic reddidit Hieronymus: Ecce ego mitto angelũ meũ, & præparabit uiã ante faciē meã, confentientibus per omnia Septuaʒ ginta, nifi quod Mitto, uerterunt in futurum, mittã, in quo Marcus cõcordat cũ Hebræis. Cæterũ addidit, Tuã, cũ tantũ fit uiam. Et rurfum quod illic eft, Ante faciem meam, hic re fert ante faciem tuã, mutata perfona. Nam apud ͵pphetam hæc uerba uidentur effe Chrifti de fe loquētis, etiamfi mox mutata perfona, de fe tancʒ de alio loquatur: Et fta tim ueniet ad templũ dominator. Contra apud Euangeliftã hæc uerba patris funt loquenʒ tis ad filiũ, Qui præparabit uiam tuã ante te. Iam pofterior pars, Vox clamãtis in deferto, parate uiam domini &c. eft apud Efaiam cap. quadragefimo. Hebraica fic uertit Hieronyʒ mus, Vox clamantis in deferto, parate uiam dñi, Rectas facite femitas dei noftri, In nullo diffentientibus Septuaginta ab Hebræis. Diffentiunt & hic nonnihil Euangeliftæ, fed in uerbis dũtaxat. Nam quod cæteri dixerũt, Rectas facite femitas eius, Ioãnes dixit: Dirigi te uiã dñi. Deinde quod habet Hebraica ueritas, & Septuaginta trãftulerũt: Rectas facite femitas dei noftri, Matthæus, Marcus, & Lucas pofuerunt femitas eius: fiue quod Euanʒ geliftæ rarius dei uocabulũ tribuant Chrifto, ob ͵pphanas & impias illorũ temporũ aures, ut plenius docebimus in Pauli: fiue quod Euangeliftæ, cum Hebraice fcirent, non indige rent trãflatione Septuaginta: deinde cũ ab Hebræis nõ anxie decerperent, quod fcripfit effet, fed quod memoria fuggerebat, defcriberent, uerbis nonnunqʒ diffident, in fententia concordant, id quod pluribus in locis admonuit diuus Hieronymus. Iam illud, quãdo no tum eft ijs quoqʒ qui Græce nefciunt, angelũ fignificare nuncium, non arbitror admonenʒ dum. Fortaffis hic melius uertiffet Nũcium. Deinde hic dixit fimpliciter, Angelũ, fed adʒ dito articulo, τὸν ἄγγελον, ut certũ aliquē angelum, fiue nuncium intelligas defignari: cum omnes alioqui prophetæ nuncij fuerint uenturi Chrifti. At hic unicus ille, & eximius fuit

i 3   nuncius,

(marginal notes:)
Cõmentarij in Marcum falfo infcri pti Hierony mo.

Hieronymus memoria laʒ pfus.

Varietas inʒ terpretum.

Diffonantia Euangelifta rum in uerʒ bis. Chriftus raʒ ro dictº deus

Angelus͵ nuncius.

Fig. 3. Erasmus's Annotations, showing his attention to philological issues and his questioning of earlier philological work, particularly Jerome's.

the humanists in the early modern period, address serious textual, philological, and other critical issues, attacking the proclaimed integrity of the texts.[20]

The humanist polyglot Bible (see fig. 4) had a similar impact by putting the Bible in several languages side by side. The synopses produced in the eighteenth century and later place the four Gospels side by side (see p. 27)[21]; while drawing attention to coinciding texts, they feature difference, ambiguity, and conflict. This is made even more emphatic with the *Synopsis Quattuor Evangeliorum*, also including the Gospel of Thomas and pericopes from other apocryphal gospels.[22]

These ways of arranging the biblical text in fact reconstruct it. They change the actual *gestalt* of the text, for these reconstructions radically alter its appearance and impact. On the other hand, they reflect a textual revision based on interpretive principles or convictions, a process in which the editor, who is also a reader, has adopted a new hermeneutic that changes the way the text appears on the page. This new textual arrangement supports a new hermeneutic and, in turn, solicits new responses from its readers—and indeed potentially elicits new hermeneutics.

These habits of reading press home how diverse learned and unlearned "readings" of the Bible have been over the last two millennia, showing that the seeming definite rhetorical line between writer, text, and commentator often has been elided in this long tradition of commenting on, interpreting, or appropriating its fragments to new intellectual, literary, or other social settings. In different eras with different interests, one or another part of this assumed triad has seized or asserted power and worked to establish the text's central purpose or meaning, whether supported by institutional authority, convictions about superior philological knowledge, or a simple desire to open the text to greater numbers of readers. For example, in the patristic period and also in the medieval period, biblical texts were used to undergird doctrinal teachings, so that even commentaries on specific texts drew support for contemporary or established doctrine. Among philologists—and these can be found throughout the long period of biblical commentary, from Jerome to the present—the accuracy of the text takes precedence over all other interests. Naturally, philologists come into conflict with doctrinalists, as Jerome did in his squabbles with Augustine about how to read the Bible. The philological approach, in which the text asserts its power over theological or orthodox traditions, dominated biblical scholarship from the later Middle Ages to the nineteenth century. Historical and sociological approaches to interpretation, on the other hand, re-create the original author, audience, and situation for the text as the clue to understanding it. This latter variety of biblical scholarship emerged in the last century. This "movement" back and forth from text to reader, past time to present time, one social community to other social communities allows us to let the text say and mean what it only suggests or hints at, while we as readers give authority to formerly

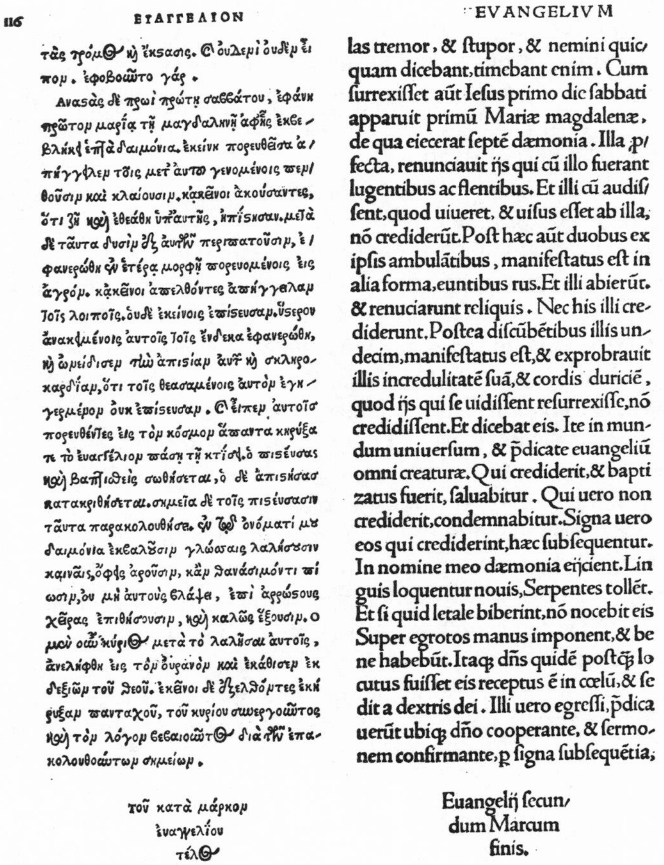

116   ΕΥΑΓΓΕΛΙΟΝ   ΕΥΑΝGELIVM

τὰς τρόμ⸋ καὶ ἔκσασις. ⳨ οὐδενὶ οὐδὲν εἰ
πον. ἐφοβοῦντο γάρ.

Ἀνασὰς δὲ πρωὶ πρώτῃ σαββάτου, ἐφάνη
πρῶτον μαρίᾳ τῇ μαγδαληνῇ ἀφῆς ἐκβε/
βλήκει ἑπτὰ δαιμόνια.ἐκείνη πορευθεῖσα ἀ/
πήγγειλεν τοῖς μετ᾽ αὐτῶ γενομένοις περὶ
θοῦσιμ καὶ κλαίουσιμ,κᾀκεῖνοι ἀκούσαντες,
ὅτι ζῇ καὶ ἐθεάθη ὑπ᾽αυτῆς, ἠπίστησαν.μετὰ
δὲ ταῦτα δυσὶμ ἐξ αυτῶν περιπατοῦσιμ, ἐ/
φανερώθη ἐν ἑτέρα μορφῇ πορευομένοις εἰς
ἀγρόν. κᾀκεῖνοι ἀπελθόντες ἀπήγγειλαμ
τοῖς λοιποῖς,οὐδὲ ἐκείνοις ἐπίστευσαμ.ὕστερον
ἀνακειμένοις αυτοῖς τοῖς ἕνδεκα ἐφανερώθη,
καὶ ὠνείδισεμ τὴν ἀπιστίαν αὐτῶ καὶ σκληρο/
καρδίαμ,ὅτι τοῖς θεασαμένοις αυτόμ ἐγη/
γερμένον οὐκ ἐπίστευσαν. ⳨ εἶπεν αυτοῖσ
πορευθέντες εἰς τὸμ κόσμομ ἅπαντα κηρύξα
τε τὸ ἐυαγγέλιον πάσῃ τῇ κτίσ⸋.ὁ πιστεύσας
καὶ βαπτισθεὶς σωθήσεται,ὁ δὲ ἀπιστήσασ
κατακριθήσεται.σημεῖα δὲ τοῖς πιστεύσασιν
ταῦτα παρακολουθήσει. ἐν τῷ ὀνόματί μυ
δαιμόνια ἐκβαλοῦσιμ γλώσαις λαλήσουσιν
καιναῖς,ὄφεις ἀροῦσιμ, κᾀμ θανάσιμόν τι
ωσιμ,ου μὴ αυτοὺς ἐλάψῃ , ἐπὶ ἀρρώσους
χεῖρας ἐπιθήσουσιμ, καὶ καλῶς ἕξουσιμ.Ο
μυ οὖν κύρι⸋ μετὰ τὸ λαλῆσαι αυτοῖς ,
ἀνελήφθη εἰς τὸμ ουρανὸμ καὶ ἐκάθισεμ ἐκ
δεξιῶμ τοῦ θεοῦ. ἐκεῖνοι δὲ ἐξελθόμτες ἐκή
ρυξαμ πανταχοῦ, τοῦ κυρίου συνεργοῦμτος
καὶ τὸμ λόγομ βεβαιοῦμτ⸋ διὰ τῶ ἐπα/
κολουθοῦμτωμ σημείωμ.

τοῦ κατὰ μάρκομ
ἐναγγελίου
τέλ⸋

las tremor, & stupor, & nemini quic/
quam dicebant.timebant enim. Cum
surrexisset aut Iesus primo die sabbati
apparuit primū Mariæ magdalenæ,
de qua eiecerat septē dæmonia. Illa pr/
fecta, renunciauit ijs qui cū illo fuerant
lugentibus ac flentibus. Et illi cū audis/
sent,quod uiueret. & uisus esset ab illa,
nō crediderūt.Post hæc aut duobus ex
ipsis ambulātibus , manifestatus est in
alia forma,euntibus rus.Et illi abierūt.
& renuciarunt reliquis . Nec his illi cre/
diderunt.Postea discūbētibus illis un/
decim,manifestatus est,& exprobrauit
illis incredulitatē suā,& cordis duriciē ,
quod ijs qui se uidissent resurrexisse,nō
credidissent.Et dicebat eis. Ite in mun/
dum uniuersum , & pdicate euangeliū
omni creaturæ.Qui crediderit,& bapti
zatus fuerit, saluabitur . Qui uero non
crediderit,condemnabitur.Signa uero
eos qui crediderint,hæc subsequentur.
In nomine meo dæmonia eijcient.Lin
guis loquentur nouis,Serpentes tollet.
Et si quid letale biberint,nō nocebit eis
Super egrotos manus imponent,& be
ne habebūt.Itaq; dns quidē postqz lo
cutus fuisset eis receptus ē in cœlū,& se
dit a dextris dei . Illi uero egressi,pdica
uerūt ubiq; dño cooperante, & sermo/
nem confirmante,p signa subsequētia;

Euangelij secun/
dum Marcum
finis.

Fig. 4. Erasmus's polyglot with Greek and Latin text side by side in the New Testament.

The Temptation

Matt. 4.1–11	Mark 1.12–13	Luke 4.1–13

[1]Then Jesus was led up by the Spirit into the wilderness to be tempted by the devil.

[2]And he fasted forty days and forty nights, and afterward he was hungry.

[3]And the tempter came and said to him, "If you are the Son of God, command these stones to become loaves of bread."

[4]But he answered, "It is written, 'Man shall not live by bread alone, but by every word that proceeds from the mouth of God.' "

[5]Then the devil took him to the holy city, and set him on the pinnacle of the temple, and

[6]said to him, "If you are the Son of God, throw yourself down, for it is written, 'He will give his angels charge of you,' and 'On their hands they will bear you up, lest you strike your foot against a stone.' "

[12]The Spirit immediately drove him out into the wilderness.

[13]And he was in the wilderness forty days; tempted by Satan; and he was with the wild beasts;

[1]And Jesus, full of the Holy Spirit, returned from Jordan, and was led by the Spirit for forty days in the wilderness, tempted by the devil. And he ate nothing in those days; and when they were ended, he was hungry.

[3]The devil said to him, "If you are the Son of God, command this stone to become bread."

[4]And Jesus answered him, "It is written, 'Man shall not live by bread alone.' "[a]

[a] *Synopsis of the Four Gospels. Greek-English edition of Synopsis Quattuor Evangeliorum*, ed. Kurt Aland (Stuttgart: United Bible Societies, 1990).

ignored implications and redirect these prompts to new contexts and new intellectual and cultural interests and prejudices. Thus the exegetical habit of commenting, delineating, and probing a text serves as a "supplement" to its silences and absences, at the same time adding to its original suggestiveness and maintaining its literary life.[23] The commentary tradition proves that the original text has served as a stimulus; depending on the community, learned or otherwise, this prompt has pushed the imagination of readers with their various intellectual, artistic, or theological interests. In fact, the division between *res* (thing) and *signum* (sign) is at the center of the whole history of commentary on the Bible. For as Augustine himself argued, *signum* rarely represents a single *res,* and because the *signum* is figurative, its meaning is ambiguous. It is this lack of singular coincidence between words and their implied meaning that undergirds the entire cultural enterprise of reading, writing, rewriting, commenting, and interpreting.[24] The history of interpretation of individual texts certainly corroborates this view.

This history also demonstrates how all understanding inevitably involves prejudice, and although prejudice is not a pejorative term, since the Enlightenment it has been spurned. "Prejudice" does not mean "false judgment," for it can be both negative and positive. These prejudices, which are the tacit exercise of our mental faculties, constitute the "historical reality" of our being.[25] Interests and prejudices include not only doctrinal and ideological convictions but also attitudes about literary decorum and the interpretive methods any reader might employ. It is these prejudices that are sustained in "interpretive communities."[26] The "interpretive communities" who have studied the gospel include those concerned with ecclesiological issues, biblical exegetes, liturgists, lectionary writers and scholars, systematicians, and, in recent times, historians, sociologists, anthropologists, and literary scholars. Intellectual interests informed by the disciplines of all these interpreters have influenced the reception of the gospel. Furthermore, attitudes (i.e., perspectives, interests, and values) toward these concerns have altered throughout history. In addition to the application of theories of interpretation and stylistic standards, the social location of the "interpretive community"—its socioeconomic status, its institutional affiliation, its education and socio-cultural condition—affects the attention or inattention it might be inclined to give to a subject.

Status is a very complex issue involving many variables, including "power," occupational prestige, privilege, income or wealth, education and knowledge, religious and "ritual purity," "family and ethnic group position," and "local-community status."[27] Throughout history, affiliation has also played an important role in designating status: that is, with whom or what does a person associate him or herself? We cannot underestimate the role these characteristics of the reader play in his or her interpretive habits. For example, the powerful readers of the patristic period were Church authorities who were establishing a new religion with new normative texts in the face of what they perceived as godless paganism, heterodoxies, and heresies. The spiraling danger of political, civic, and social collapse of the Roman Empire threatened to destroy the singular truth of this religion and the institution that supported it. In contrast, medieval commentators, who were often members of a religious order that supported their intellectual activity, were building on an established tradition they sought to strengthen and embellish as they continued the proselytizing tradition of early Christianity. In the Reformation, biblical scholars were often patronized by powerful monarchs whose personal interests could not fail to influence the shape and force of their work. Their focus on *sola scriptura* was used as a weapon against perceived ecclesiastical excesses. The recovery of classical Greek and Latin likewise refocused scholars' biblical work to philological concerns.

In the twentieth century, scholars have been patronized by universities that require them to produce original research. Whereas the church fathers sought uniformity in an effort to direct and control intellectual experimentation and tried to impose absolute authority on theological writings, modern scholars patronized by universities have only a marginal influence on religious issues and no ecclesiastical authority. Their work on the Bible is a complex modern leisure activity, for although they are paid to produce their scholarly studies, their choices are less obligatory and prompted primarily by individual interests. But because the rewards for this kind of work are based on the novelty of its contribution, scholars feel compelled to produce original work. Scholars also experience the "anxiety of influence" because they must set out their intellectual territory in an uneasy relationship with all earlier similar work. On the other hand, they cannot be too original, for they must reflect prevailing trends in order to be acceptable to the contemporary "academic marketplace"—which is not so free as contemporary culture often assumes. Like the medieval monk, whose intellectual work had to comply with doctrine and established practice, the modern scholar's work must reflect contemporary trends and current intellectual practice. The combined emphasis on originality, inherited from Romanticism, the patronage of secular universities, the legacy of the humanistic idea of scholarly leisure,[28] and marketplace values, together with the development of modern disciplines, have resulted in the great diversity of creative biblical scholarship in this century.

Although the Bible is a literary text that commands canonical respect but also demands constant reinterpretation, it is not primarily an aesthetic object. Nevertheless, as with literary artifacts, its interpreters are concerned with the circumstances of its construction, its relationship to history and society, and the way the text changes meanings throughout time, depending on current ideologies and attitudes. In the case of the Gospel of Mark, more recent readers have been able to approach the text with a sympathy and interest that it had not heretofore experienced. The gospel's canonicity has not been doubted, and, as a normative document, it has been used to mediate ecclesiological and doctrinal issues. The text was never truly abandoned, but changes in the interests and prejudices of the reading public throughout history have resulted in different interpretations.

In order to understand shifting interpretations and attitudes toward a literary work over a long time span, the historian must determine the context (cultural, intellectual, political, social, and so on) in which the work has been evaluated. The context of a literary work includes the critical assumptions and expectations in the historical periods in which it is read. These assumptions and interests are often tacit; they are the traditions of seeing and understanding that we carry with us unquestioningly. They are based on the interpretive methods applied in reading as well as on the literary and rhetorical values that characterize the reader's or the interpreter's investigative habits.

The current debate and intellectual struggle over the formation of literary canons has focused on the role of extrinsic social and political factors in the selection of favored texts. The recognition that the canon is an "institutional construction" has further undermined the legitimacy of the ideology of tradition,[29] leading some theorists to maintain that texts in the canon are representative of "extraesthetic values,"[30] that is, of the social and political status and values of the "interpretive communities" who select the work. Others insist—as, for example, feminist, Marxist, and social critics—that works reflecting the interests of the ruling economic and political structure are selected for canonization because their value is relative to the values of the choosers. Thus, for instance, African-American, female, and other silenced voices are excluded from the canon.[31]

As with the creation of secular literary canons in Western universities, which represent specific values consciously determined by canon compilers,[32] the biblical canon was created and re-created by exclusive groups of readers who shared similar cultural, ideological, or aesthetic values and institutional commitments. Though the standards or values differ between biblical and literary canon makers, the practice of exclusion exercised by a powerful group of "informed" readers is parallel. Furthermore, whether in the literary or the biblical domain, when an author is considered "inspired" that does not guarantee all of his or her works will receive the same degree of approbation. As Kermode and others have suggested, personal preferences and opinions rule these choices, which aren't always deserved, and these attitudes consign works to a canon or to oblivion.[33] Inevitably there is also a canon within a canon for both religious and literary texts. Within the New Testament, certain documents, though not "more canonical," have been favored by Church custom in lectionaries, as theological proof-texts, and in the commentary tradition. Of the Gospels, Matthew and John have shared the limelight, as have Paul's Letters to the Romans, the Corinthians, and the Galatians, and the Apocalypse of John.[34] Convictions, whether ideological, social, or even aesthetic, and individual tastes, undergirded by specific ecclesiastical or theological interests, create these canons and designate both the privileged and the excluded.

Similarities exist between the creation of a literary canon and the biblical canon, but there are also marked differences. First of all, although the texts were written within the literary tradition of sacred Scripture, none of the books of the New Testament were written with the precise idea of canonicity in mind. But, like literary works in which authors convey a relationship to earlier works that do have "quasi" canonical status, whether through genre or specific allusions to precursor works (e.g., Dante's *Comedy* and Virgil's *Aeneid*, Joyce's *Ulysses* and the whole tradition of epic that lies behind it), the biblical authors also allude to earlier texts with a near-sacred status. For gospel and letter writers of the New Testament, this pattern of allusion or intertextual relationship declares their interconnection with the revered texts of "Israel."[35] Although this rewriting of ancient texts is a central feature of the New Testament authors, their writing was nonetheless primarily prompted by immediate social, religious, and cultural interests.[36] The Gospels and letters are not the works of literary artists seeking fame and recognition but the urgings of a desperate people whose only recourse from loss was the hope offered by their proclaimed "way." The reading habits of early Christian communities over a three-hundred-year tradition confirmed their importance. While the canon had been developing in the first three centuries of Christianity, by the fourth century the Church had selected certain documents as normative. The criteria that gave authority to this selection were "apostolicity, catholicity, orthodoxy, and established usage."[37] These emerged in reaction to heterodoxies of certain groups in the first centuries after the death of Jesus. The spread of Marcionism, which restricted Christian literature to the Gospel of Luke and the letters of Paul with all Judaic characteristics edited out, gnosticism, and Montanism prompted the Church leadership to establish some sort of textual uniformity. Canonicity with authoritative texts were one of the means to this stability.

At the same time, an attempt at strict theological orthodoxy was emerging to counteract the heterodoxy and heresy that marked the intellectual diversity of this period in Church history. The texts included in the canon had to have catholic, that is, universal, appeal and be regularly read in the churches. The value in a canonical codex was the creation of a normative collection of documents by which orthodoxy could be articulated and sustained.[38] The exclusion of the gnostic gospels and other texts reflected the ecclesiastical communities' commitment to a kind of public multiregional universality. The gnostic texts were "secret" in the sense that they were confined to small communities with local interests, in contrast to the "fourfold witness" (Matthew, Mark, Luke, and John) that was widely disseminated throughout the churches of the Roman Empire. The ultimate triumph of the fourfold witness was not a victory for a single point of view; the genius of the collection was that although it excluded many documents, it embraced many different theological viewpoints and other significant socio-historical differences.

On the other hand, the many discrepancies within the "fourfold witness" caused non-Christian detractors to dismiss the Bible as full of contradictions, and this assault led to the development of harmonies and Eusebius's canons or lists of parallel texts among the Gospels (see fig. 5). Exclusion of the many other revered documents labeled "apocrypha" was based on their "secrecy," a word that by the third century was used synonymously with "falseness" and "forgery."[39] Though the winners in the struggle were the suc-

Fig. 5. Eusebius Canons.

cessful majority, their criteria for inclusion embraced tradition to show respect for continuity, universality to demonstrate their democratic convictions, and common knowledge to show their pejorative attitude toward secrecy. In contrast, the claims of the excluded gnostic and apocryphal gospels were precisely their secrecy, isolation, special interests, and esotericism.[40] The fourfold witness in a unified collection became the source document for the developing orthodoxies of the period, the means to re-create consciousness according to the terms of the gospel message and exclude all challenges to the orthodoxy that would prevail. But it was a "flexible framework," for though theological concerns were clearly important to the canonical editors, who sought to present a version of the life of Jesus that communicated to the future readers and faithful, they preserved continuity with the past.[41] Unfortunately, because the fourfold witness was usually read as a single unit, the unique literary characteristics of each of the gospels were inevitably ignored.

This study examines what characteristics of the Gospel of Mark led to its being included in this orthodox canon and then explores the history of its reception. The reception of this gospel in contrast to that of the others demonstrates that while reception is a problem of reading, *what* is being read makes a difference to the analysis or commentary drawn from the text. This study will show that Matthew and John have always been the favorite Gospels for commentators, proving that what is chosen for reading does follow some logic or taste on the part of readers. On the other hand, *how* the text is being read, as well as its contents, directs the reception of the Gospels. The study follows a chronological sequence to discuss the gospel's reception, starting with the patristic period and ending with the twentieth century, while considering specific kinds of reception that are themselves constructs of particular eras. For example, I will discuss commentaries (theological, literary, political, and social), translations, citations, lectionaries and sermons, and harmonies and glosses. Different periods focus on one or another of these reception activities or reading strategies, and this study attempts to examine why certain approaches preoccupied some eras and were ignored in others. Scholarly methodologies (whether theological, philosophical, literary, political, social, and so on); ecclesiological and authoritarian interests; social and historical developments (as the breakdown or emergence of the power of a particular political entity, ecclesiastic structure, or culture), or a major linguistic or philological change, such as the assertion of the European vernacular languages into literary activity in the Middle Ages or the recovery of Greek and Hebrew texts; and rhetorical and literary standards, all have played a significant role in the reception of the Gospel of Mark.

Because Mark is an "absent-presence" in the biblical canon, when it receives attention—a reversal of its commonly received inattention—the forms of the gospel's reception turn out to be indicators of changing historical and cultural forces. These forces are the subject of this book.

Chapter 1

Present but Absent:
Mark as Amanuensis and Abbreviator
(130 to 430)

"Mark was Peter's interpreter."
Eusebius[1]

Two strong comments by central figures in the early Church about the Gospel of Mark directed its reception for a millennium and a half. The first is Eusebius's, quoting Papias's *Expositions of the Oracles of the Lord* (c.130), saying that Mark was Peter's amanuensis. The second is Augustine's, who silenced the Gospel of Mark for almost fourteen hundred years with his assertion that Mark was the epitomizer and abbreviator of Matthew: Mark pares him (i.e., Matthew) down and seems his follower and abbreviator.[2]

The Papias tradition was repeated in a variety of ways by Justin Martyr, who, in his *Dialogue with Trypho* (c.135) refers to the *apomnemoneumata* of Peter as the source of the "sons of Thunder" designation for James and John, a phrase unique to Mark (Mark 3:17). Irenaeus of Lyons (130–200) claimed Mark was Peter's interpreter and disciple (3.1.1).[3] The *Anti-Marcionite Prologue* (c.4th century) and the *Evv. Prologi Vetustissimi* likewise refer to Mark as the interpreter of Peter and describe him as "colobodactylus" (stumpy-fingered),[4] a description used by Hippolytus in the third century. Irenaeus of Lyons, Clement of Alexandria (c.180),[5] and Origen (c.200)—according to Eusebius (260–339)[6]—Tertullian (c.160–c.220) in *Adversus Marcionem* IV, 5,[7] and Eusebius in *Ecclesiastical History* (323) connected Mark to Peter once again (II, XV:1–2), as did John Chrysostom (c.386–98) in his homilies on Matthew.[8] Jerome, in his *Commentary on Matthew* and *On Famous Men* (392),[9] repeated the by then well-established tradition that Mark was Peter's interpreter who recorded what he had heard Peter preach in Rome. This association of Mark with Peter held such authority that it echoed through the Middle Ages and even showed up with the Reformers, such as John Hus, for example—"Mark was ordained by God to write the gospel of the true deeds of Christ, and instructed by Peter, with whom he was intimate"—and John Wyclif's *Concordia evangeliorum super Mattheum*.[10]

In his ardent desire to explain the relationship among the Gospels and counter attacks about the contradictions among them, Augustine, nevertheless, passed over the tradition connecting Mark to Peter in silence and found the gospel an abbreviation of Matthew. When Isidore of Seville (560–636) again connected Mark to Peter but repeated Augustine's statement that Mark abbreviated Matthew, he became the source for subsequent repetitions of this opinion throughout the Middle Ages and Renaissance.[11] Though not always acknowledged as the source of the judgment until the eighteenth century, Augustine's opinion dominated the attitude toward the gospel, although there were more commentaries on it during these centuries than in the patristic era.

This contrast explains Mark's absence and presence, for the gospel was present in the canon but essentially absent from attention. The assumed original association of Mark with Peter, the apostle charged with ecclesiastical authority by Jesus (Matt. 16:18) gave Mark canonical legitimacy according to the standard of the church fathers that demanded "apostolicity" to support a gospel's canonical status.

The Gospel of Mark also met the other major criteria for inclusion in the canon developed by the early canonical compilers to eliminate texts considered esoteric and exclusive.[12] In addition to "apostolicity," these included catholicity and traditional usage. The tradition connecting Mark to Peter was insurmountable evidence for its inclusion, as was the belief that Matthew and John were Jesus' disciples. The community of readers whose responsibility it was to establish the canon valued the weight of the authorial and apostolic genesis of the text. The Councils of Carthage (Hippo, 393 and 397, and Mileve in 402), at which Augustine was a major contributor, listed Mark among the authentic Church documents, but inclusion in this codex of orthodox biblical texts did not guarantee wide attention for Mark's gospel in the patristic era. On the contrary, the gospel is the least discussed or quoted in commentaries and citations, and it appears rarely in the few lectionary sequences that have been re-created from Church records.[13] The criteria of orthodoxy, catholicity, and traditional usage emerged in the first four centuries because of the institutional Church's need to contain, control, and make uniform Christian beliefs, teachings, practices, and texts. The exercise of the literary interests and prejudices of the period reflects this effort to create a universal cultural community with shared beliefs, practices, texts, and interpretations.

This early attention to Mark, which guaranteed its place in the canon, identified the author, the author's sources, especially Peter, or the author's relationship to the other Gospels, in an effort to establish the authority of the text, its position in the canon, and its relationship to the other Gospels. It was recognized as part of the canon of the New Testament c.400 C.E., according to the witness of Athanasius (367), Jerome (384), and Augustine (396–397)[14], and it was included as early as 200 C.E. in the corpus of holy texts. Both Clement of Alexandria (150–215) and Origen (185–254) included the four Gospels and the writings of the apostles with the epistles of Paul in their lists of revered and accepted Church documents.[15]

The abundant evidence about the time and circumstances of the composition of the Gospel of Mark, based on numerous references to his relationship to Peter, demonstrates the importance the Fathers placed on the "authority" of the texts. Like earlier and later canon makers, whether in the secular or religious domains, the Fathers conferred value on the text because of the authority of its writer rather than because of any "intrinsic" merit it possessed. The connection between Mark and the apostle Peter satisfied a cultural and intellectual commitment of the church fathers, because they valued original sources that demonstrated the antiquity and therefore the veracity of current beliefs. For them, authorship and connection to Peter and hence to Jesus was a value that superseded all others. However, as will be shown, inclusion because of this value did not assure literary attention.

In the forthcoming discussion of Mark's reception, I do not discuss the gospels of Luke and Matthew as responses to Mark, despite the currency of the Markan priority theory advanced in the nineteenth century that swept over the synoptic order theory. There is, at the moment, enough serious discussion of the persuasiveness of this theory to show some disagreement about the relationship among the synoptic Gospels.[16] If one were to include them in such a discussion, one could quickly demonstrate, as redaction criticism effectively does, the desire of commentators, translators, and redactors to "master absence," for both gospels fill many of the gaps in the Markan narrative. Indeed, the Matthaean and Lukan reception of Mark made the Gospel of Mark almost unnecessary.

Absence: Argumentum e silentio

Despite the general belief, as evidenced by the many witnesses cited above, that Mark was Peter's interpreter, Mark's gospel nevertheless attracted the least attention of the four during the patristic period. There are no commentaries on the gospel by the major church fathers, with the exception of Jerome's ten sermons on the gospel.[17] Furthermore, Mark is cited infrequently in comparison with the other Gospels, particularly Matthew and John.

Absences and surprising presences of the gospel in the first four centuries of Christianity are exposed by an examination of other commentaries, proof-texts, canonical debates, or lectionary cycles, but the gospel fails to make a strong appearance. When it came to harmonizing, its unique character was obscured as a result of the elision into a uniform narrative rendition; only its inclusion in the Greek Bible and Latin translations guaranteed its presence in a future culture of reading. The references or allusions to the gospel in citations and lectionary cycles in the patristic period point conclusively to the absence of Mark as a major text in the early Church. In addition to theological convictions that harmonized the Gospels, emphasis on the gospel communications as sources of dogmatic formulations at the expense of their narrative features, together with application of interpretive methods, influenced the attitudes of the rhetorically trained Fathers from Irenaeus to Jerome and Augustine. While defending the *lingua rustica* of the Gospels, they chose as their favorites the gospels that most clearly represented their theological and intellectual interests and institutional goals, showing that their reading habits were dominated by specific interests, just as, on closer scrutiny, later authoritative readers have proved to be.

An analysis of the gospel's reception in the period 130–430 demonstrates the nature of the Fathers' specific interests and the attitudes they brought to the Gospels. The first of these, epitomized by Augustine, was the desire to harmonize the four versions. Second was Matthew's pride of place as the first in the collection because of its supposed apostolic connection, its greater detail and completeness, and its references to specific ecclesiastical and sacramental practices that were central to the discussions of the age.[18] Mark's neglect in this period was a consequence of the patristic writers' interest in harmony that rendered his contribution negligible, as well as their desire for clarity in sacramental and ecclesiastical issues, on which Mark is close to silent. Despite the Fathers' capacity to read beyond a literary surface and appreciate the complex symbolisms implicit in many biblical narratives, they lacked the capacity to "read" the surface of a literary narrative in the way that modern readers have been trained to do. Their commitment to apostolicity as a criterion assured equal place in the canon to all the Gospels viewed as "apostolic," but the dating of these Gospels was irrelevant to them—in contrast to the modern era, when such issues have become critical to biblical scholarship. Whether in terms of aesthetic, theological, social, or cultural interests and attitudes, the Fathers recognized in Matthew and John a message and rhetorical manner that was consonant with their own interests and literary standards, in particular contrast to Mark's parsimonious offering.

The Fathers of the patristic period, active in hermeneutical inquiry, whether Greek or Latin, came from economic environments that made it possible for them to pursue a traditional pagan education in rhetoric, one of the only "passports to success" for the free and civilized who were not rich.[19] They received respectable secular educations,[20] studied the great works of

Greek and Latin literature, and, although they were located throughout the eastern and western empires, they were residents of urban areas. Certainly those Fathers who resided in Alexandria and Antioch (Origen, Cyril of Alexandria, Clement of Alexandria, John Chrysostom) had greater intellectual prestige within the Church than those dispersed in the cities of the western Church. On the other hand, connection to the politically powerful cities of Rome, in the case of Jerome, or Milan, as in the case of Ambrose and Augustine, also gave the Fathers status and therefore power within the Church. Whether in the East or West, the Fathers were members of church communities that were united in their intent to establish a universal Church with shared values and beliefs and a harmonious tradition.

One might call the early church fathers members of an "interpretive community." They were developing ecclesiastical standards and theological teachings; they were interested in the universality, harmony, orthodoxy, and continuity of the Church, and in establishing their own authority; and they brought these concerns to the forefront as they consciously developed interpretive methods to be applied to their sacred texts. In addition, they had inherited the legacy of the pagan literary tradition, which they adapted to the new religious culture. Their intellectual methods, however, were not historically conscious in the sense that they were aware that their interpretations were time-bound and a result of their own contemporary cultural circumstances. Rather, they self-consciously imposed a single criterion on their intellectual activities. History for them had been inevitably altered by the Incarnation, which forever had changed how books were to be authorized, read, or interpreted.[21] For Augustine, for example, to read the Scriptures required reflection on the relationship between scriptural words and Christ as Word.[22] "He was interested in the subjective element in the response to texts, but he does not believe in the text's or the reader's self-sufficiency."[23] Because reading the Bible was so closely associated with his conversion (*Confessions*, Bk. VIII), it became for Augustine not the "cause of conversion but the symbol of conversion."[24] His insistence on a self-conscious hermeneutics, however, was unusual. Readers often ignore such self-understanding as a prerequisite to understanding the object of investigation; therefore, as Hans-Georg Gadamer argues in *Truth and Method,* the experience of reading is one of "immediacy."[25] Indeed, the history of reading Mark shows that until the modern period, even when commentators were conscious of their hermeneutics, they often failed to find anything of major significance in the second gospel.

Of the biblical commentators of the era, Origen, who spent his lifetime on exegetical studies and wrote commentaries on almost every biblical document, left no trace of a commentary on Mark.[26] Hilary of Poitiers (c.315–c.367) wrote a commentary on Matthew.[27] Titus of Bostra (d. before 378) had a commentary comprised of homilies on Luke.[28] Ambrose of Milan

(339–397) wrote an *Expositio Evangelii secundum Lucam.*[29] Jerome (c.345–419/420), who also wrote a commentary on Matthew (398)[30] did leave ten sermons on Mark (393). We have three commentaries by Cyril of Alexandria (d.444), one on John (earlier than c.429) that remains[31] and one on Matthew of which fragments remain;[32] 156 homilies and a Syriac version of the sixth or seventh century, which preserves Cyril's commentary on Luke (c.430).[33] Of the Antiochenes, John Chrysostom (c.344–407) has a commentary on Matthew, in the form of ninety homilies (c.390).[34] He also has left eighty-eight homilies on John[35] and seven on Luke. Theodore of Mopsuestia (d.428), who was one of the most brilliant exegetes of the period and produced numerous commentaries, left one on John preserved in Syriac that still exists, and one each on Matthew and Luke, fragments of which remain.[36] Though we have numerous extant sermons of Augustine on the Gospels, a work titled *On the Psalms,* and a commentary (series of homilies) on the Gospel of John (414–416),[37] the Bishop of Hippo (354–430) focused on the agreement among the Gospels, producing *De Consensu Evangelistarum*[38] (c.400) and *Questiones evangeliorum*[39] (on Matthew and Luke, c.399). Victor of Antioch, writing in the late fifth century, noted this absence and compiled a series of comments on the gospel based on Markan references in the commentaries on the other gospel writers by Origen, Titus of Bostra, Theodore of Mopsuestia, Chrysostom, and Cyril of Alexandria.[40]

This brief overview shows that if we were to select the choice gospel in the patristic period on the basis of the commentary tradition, Matthew would certainly take the first place, with John as a strong second. It is noteworthy that whether Greek, Syriac, or Latin, whether located in Antioch, Alexandria, Rome, or Carthage, the Fathers were unanimous in their election of Matthew and John as their favorite Gospels. They were, however, almost silent on the Markan gospel.

Like the rabbis, Christian writers of the patristic period also used citations (proof-texts) and allusions to sacred writings. As a consequence, another source of information about the fate of the second gospel in the patristic era is the number and nature of citations of the Markan text in the many writings of the period. Here the figures are just as compelling as the silent commentary tradition.

References as allusions or citations to Mark begin with Papias's *Expositions of the Oracles of the Lord* (c.130), followed by Justin Martyr (c.135, *Dialogue with Trypho*) and Irenaeus (c.190, *Against Heresies*). In fact, according to citations in the *Biblia Patristica*, from the earliest period to Clement of Alexandria (c.150–215), there are approximately 3,900 references to Matthew, 3,300 to Luke, 2,000 to John, and 1,400 to Mark.[41] These references are not regionally distributed, though patterns of citations are parallel among all the writers, whether African, Asian, or European. But the balance among the Gospels in this period was more favorable to Mark than in the following century.[42] Clement of Alexandria has two very intriguing connections to the Gospel of Mark, the first of which is his *Quis dives salvetur?*[43] and the second his Letter on the Secret Gospel of Mark,[44] which I will discuss in the next chapter. In the third century, excluding Origen, Matthew became the overwhelming source for quotations (approximately 3,600), in contrast to Luke (around 1,000), John (approximately 1,600), and Mark (around 250). Origen mined Matthew for almost 8,000 references, in contrast to almost 5,000 for John, 3,000 for Luke, and a mere 650 for Mark.[45] This pattern of Matthean preeminence continued throughout the patristic period, with John the second choice. Mark is quoted by both the Greek and Latin Fathers about one time for every seven to ten or more of Matthew or John. This is true for Basil of Caesarea (c.329–379), Gregory of Nazianzus (c.330–c.390), Eusebius, and Gregory of Nyssa (c.335–394). Among the Latin writers, Hilary of Poitiers and Ambrose, for example, the overwhelming choice was Matthew. Augustine was even more severe. In many of his works (*On the Holy Trinity*,[46] or in doctrinal treatises and moral treatises), we find few or no references to Mark. In the *Confessions*, likewise, there are few references[47]— approximately five in the *City of God*,[48] in contrast to one hundred of Matthew in the *Confessions* and thirty-five in the *City of God*. This pattern continues throughout his works. In his extant sermons on the Gospels, he quotes Matthew approximately 250 times, John 170, Luke 150, and Mark fifteen. The actual count of the citations, however, shows that if there is a stepchild in the canon, Mark is the one about whom the Fathers spoke most infrequently. Also, and more importantly, it demonstrates that the biblical texts were not read as narratives in themselves but as sources for proofs of doctrinal and ecclesiastical positions. In this enterprise, Mark was a weak contender.

Like the pattern of citation, the lectionary in the first centuries of the Church shows that the Gospels most frequently chosen were John and Matthew, with Luke represented about half as many times as the two favorites, and Mark infrequently.[49] Although these lectionary sequences are incomplete and somewhat hypothetically reconstructed, the evidence is persuasive that Matthew and John were the gospels most frequently read and that Mark—with the exception of Mark 16, which had a prominent place in the Easter reading cycle of the western rites—was for the most part ignored. Because of the special status of Mark in the Alexandrian Church, pericopes unique to the gospel may have been read, as they are to this day in both the Coptic and the Orthodox rites, during Lent.[50] But for the forthcoming sixteen hundred years, until Vatican II, in fact, Mark was essentially excluded from the Roman liturgy.[51]

The virtual absence of Mark in the first centuries of Christian writing demonstrates that despite the gospel's presence in the canon, it was not treated equally with the others, let alone with any special deference. The creators of the canon, the authoritative community of readers who determined a text's orthodoxy, using their own excluding criteria, chose Mark for inclusion. Using different criteria, this same community of Greek and Latin rhetorically trained church fathers, who recognized the gospel's canonicity, nevertheless chose to ignore it. In the next chapter, I will discuss the attention given to the gospel in the patristic period and advance some theories about what motivated this interest.

CHAPTER 2

The Gospel of Mark
in the Patristic Period

When asked my status, I replied I was a Christian. And He who
sat upon the judgment seat said: "You lie. You are a Ciceronian,
not a Christian. Where your treasure is, there lies your heart
also."

Jerome, Letter 22[1]

Although serious differences existed among them, Church authorities
in the early years of Christianity shared the common goal of establishing normative texts and methods for their interpretation. They
were building an authoritative textual tradition ruled by specific convictions
to which this community had submitted itself. As a new social phenomenon,
growing in the shadow of the declining military power and political domi-
nance of the Roman Empire, and witnessing the collapsing social and political organization of the Empire, the Christian Church struggled for unity,
orthodoxy, and universality. It replaced Roman structures of political and
military control with ecclesiastical ones, as it formed a socially constructed,
interpretive community with its own vested interests.

The Fathers undoubtedly exercised several different intellectual interests in the acts of reading, interpreting, or clarifying biblical texts. Preemi-
nent among these was the need to establish universal creedal formulations
based on the biblical foundation and the authority of tradition. Also, as readers, they brought interpretive methods and rhetorical standards, concerns
about completeness of information or articulateness of the narrative, and
genre expectations, among others, to their tasks. In all these respects, the
Gospel of Mark did not conform to literary expectations. As intellectuals
trained in the high culture of the Roman Empire, the Fathers brought their
education with them as they entered into the life of the Church, forging new

intellectual syntheses of Greco-Roman learning with the Judeo-Christian experience.

As shown in the last chapter, the attention given to the Gospel of Mark in the years between 130 and 430 included comments about the circumstances of the Gospel's composition and the identity of its author, and his association with the apostle Peter, which established the gospel's presence in the canon. And yet it enjoyed only a relatively absent presence. Although no commentary on Mark survives from this period, other forms of attention were conferred on the gospel. Though receiving less attention than that given the other Gospels, particularly to John and Matthew, Mark's gospel received attention through translation, harmonies, proof-texts, sermons, and liturgical practices. The uses of the Markan gospel reveal specific formative interests on the part of the Church scholars of the period. These included the need for standardized central texts, a harmonious single "evangelium," standardized sacramental and liturgical practice, and standard methods for reading and interpreting.

On the other hand, the paucity of interest in Mark's gospel points to the dominant interests and standards brought to bear on the texts. First, if Church intellectuals were looking for a complete story of Jesus, Mark was deficient in contrast to Matthew and Luke; in fact, Matthew and Luke overlap with Mark with few exceptions. Second, to bolster doctrinal formulations, Mark's gospel had less to offer than Matthew and Luke, who provide support for doctrines like the Trinity and the Incarnation or the emerging practice of sacraments like baptism. Third, in terms of rhetorical standards and expectations, Mark did not satisfy the rhetorically trained Fathers. Thus the reception in terms of actual citations in the period draws attention to the Fathers' careful reading that was directed by the ecclesiastical concerns of the times. But the relative inattention demands further investigation into the Fathers' hermeneutical methods and how these might reflect the "prejudices" of their era.

The works on the Bible in this period were products of powerful bishops centered in Rome, Carthage, Alexandria, and Antioch. Patronage of this type assured that the works represented the reigning ideologies and methodologies supported in the episcopal centers of authority. The bishops who ruled from these seats of authority had been trained to the highest standards of literary culture, the cultural property of the elite social strata of the times. But they shepherded a religion whose social convictions contradicted the values of that culture and whose sacred texts lacked the "sublime" eloquence of their literary training.[2] What convictions and concerns the Fathers' treatment of the Gospel of Mark reveal I will explore in the first part of this chapter; in the second I will focus on what their responses suggest about their reading habits, interpretive commitments, and stylistic prejudices.

Mark's Place in Patristic Readings of the Gospel

I. HARMONIES

To counter the criticism that the Bible included contradictions between Jewish Scriptures and the sacred corpus of Christian works, but also
within the Christian texts themselves, in the early centuries the Fathers
sought to harmonize the Gospels with each other and with authoritative
teachings. Pagan critics like Celsus, orthodox ones like Gaius, and anti-Sem-
ites like Marcion dwelt on the contradictions among the Gospels.[3] To overcome this apparent disharmony, early writers focused on showing their
agreements while at the same time ignoring the specific narrative or stylistic
character of each gospel. A major response to Mark's gospel in this early
period was the effort to harmonize it with the other Gospels. Marcion's
abortive editing of Luke and the Pauline corpus to create a "Christian" document[4] was in its way an attempt to confront the diversity represented by the
many extant gospels of the time, of which over fifty fragments and references
remain.[5] Another more successful attempt was the *Diatessaron* (c.170), probably written first in Syriac, a version which "quickly became the standard
gospel text, a position it would hold for centuries."[6]

The writer of this first harmony was a Syrian named Tatian, who became a student of Justin Martyr in Rome. Briefly encountering the world of
Greco-Roman philosophy and theology, he found in Christianity universality and simplicity expressed in the directness of the Christian message and
what he took as its radically ascetic values.[7] Although an enormous number
of harmonies are extant, particularly dating from the twelfth–fourteenth centuries, the quest for Tatian's original text has been an ongoing and frustrated
scholarly endeavor. The original is therefore a matter of hypothesis based on
existing manuscripts. In a twelfth–fourteenth century Arabic version, assumed to link back to earlier versions, we find that without leaving out any
uniquely Markan expressions, Tatian's text features first John, then Luke,
and third Matthew prominently. Like Marcion, he retreated from the Hebraic origins of the Gospels, which explains why he excluded Matthew's
genealogy for Jesus; he also adhered to some gnostic views, which no doubt
lay behind his preference for John's opening, with its reference to the
"logos."[8]

An effort to create a single historical version of the life of Jesus, Tatian's harmony is arranged sequentially, moving from line to line to represent
all the Gospels' contributions in terms of "content" or "sense" rather than in
parallel columns, as in the synopses developed in the eighteenth century.
Such an arrangement of the text reveals the author's effort to make his reading of all the works conform to a single, linear sense. The harmony attempts
to erase differences and fashion a seamless garment of the story with patches
of the old, though the pieces may be of the same color but of different

materials. For example, it begins with John's opening (John 1:5), moves to Luke's story of Elizabeth (Luke 1:5–25), followed by the Annunciation to Mary, the meeting with Elizabeth, and the birth of Jesus (Luke 1:26–80); then to Matthew's visit of the wise men, Joseph's dream, and the flight to Egypt and return (Matt.: 2:1–23); and then back to Luke's story of Jesus' childhood (2:40–52). Mark finally appears in the collation after the baptism, when the spirit "drove" (*ekballein*) Jesus to the desert (Mark 1:12), testifying to Tatian's awareness of a unique Markan expression. Indeed, his use of Mark shows that he had identified specific Markan signs, for the next reference is to Mark 1:15, Mark's original first words for Jesus, "The time has arrived." By starting with John and following with the events related to Jesus' birth, the harmony eliminates Mark's startling opening *in medias res,* for Mark's beginning is never mentioned. Similarly, by ending with John 21:25, which follows Matthew's ending at 28:20 to go forth and baptize all nations, Luke's ascension, and Mark's longer ending at 16:20, he erases Mark's empty tomb and absent Jesus conclusion.

Tatian's collation reveals his theological convictions: a desire for homogeneity not provided by the four Gospels, his affection for John and Luke, and his commitment to a biographical-historical version of Jesus' life. In conflating the gospel versions, Tatian showed that he did not read the gospels as separate and distinct literary works with their own purposes and unique audiences. Rather his "harmony" edits the events of the four Gospels to emphasize a theology of unity among them. Though it respects the integrity of the words in the extant four Gospels, the *Diatessaron* created a version of the story unbound by time or circumstance but "true" for the present and the future. It therefore belongs to the early Church's habit of seeking to establish a stable but inflexible foundation on which would rest textual conformity and uniformity. Comparable versions to Tatian's appeared throughout the European Middle Ages in Latin[9] as well as in the modern European languages, showing the widespread interest in a uniform gospel story.[10]

The social and political climates of the times must certainly have influenced these reading habits. When Augustine wrote *De Consensu Evangelistarum* (399), even though Christianity had "triumphed" politically—in the sense that the persecutions had ended and the Roman Empire was ruled by Christians—nonetheless he faced the vituperative attacks of various non-Christian and gnostic sects of the time, one of whose primary criticisms of Christianity was its failure to produce a text without blatant contradictions. This now familiar assault on the Bible, in the second–fifth centuries, forced Christian writers into the defensive position of arguing for the harmony of the Gospels. Writers of the period were creating a universal religious community, and tolerance for diversity within and outside that community was contrary to that goal. Furthermore, interpretive methods as developed by Origen in *De Principiis* and Augustine in *De Doctrina Christiana* became necessary not only to bolster methods of interpreting texts but for political reasons as well. These interpretive methods provided the means to show the connection between the Hebrew or Greek versions of Jewish Scripture and the emerging New Testament Church, and therefore they demonstrate the continuity of the church of Israel in the New Testament with the patristic era, the antiquity of the Christian Church, and its continuity with the Hebrew past. Augustine's *De Doctrina* also functioned as a way to teach priests how to read the Bible, for scriptural study had a fundamental role in the economy of salvation.[11] As Brian Stock writes of the *De Doctrina*, the Christian community is conceived as "a body of readers, either as clergy or as cultured laypersons."[12]

Working on the *De Trinitate* and the *De Consensu Evangelistarum* at the same time, Augustine set out in the former to delineate the central Christian doctrine of the Trinity, and in the latter to dispel "pagan" attacks on Christian texts. Identifying the fourfold gospel witness in the singular as *evangelium* ("Among all the divine authorities contained in sacred scripture, the gospel (*evangelium*) stands supreme") (1,1, passim), Augustine's *De Consensu* argues against those who attacked the Gospels on the grounds that they did not represent the writings of Jesus and that the divine records were contradictory.[13] In Book 1, Chapter 2, Augustine advances his two-source theory to explain the intertextual relationships among the Gospels, proposing that Mark was almost entirely dependent on Matthew:

> For in his narrative he gives nothing in concert with John apart from the others: by himself separately he has little to record; in conjunction with Luke, as distinguished from the rest, he has still less; but in concord with Matthew, he has a very large number of passages. Much too, he narrates in words almost numerically and identically the same as those used by Matthew where the agreement is either with the evangelist alone, or with him in connection with the rest."[14]

A careful reader, in the sense that he recognized the overlapping texts, he gave Matthew priority and dismissed Mark almost perfunctorily: "separately, he has little to record." Proposing an inter-gospel relationship putting Mark on the receiving end rather than on the initiating end no doubt contributed to Augustine's position on Mark's lack of importance.

Furthermore, his harmony sought to bring conflicting testimonies into agreement. He achieved this by "inclusion" and "omission," defending the integrity of the combined account he had constructed by conflating the versions and using the criterion of "unity of sense" rather than unity of the letter to accommodate the various ways in which the same event might be recorded. The differences in sequential order, Augustine suggested, could be explained by the recollection of the individual gospel writers. The tone in the *De Consensu* is defensive, as Augustine argues against an assumed challenge from his audience. In Book 4, he takes on all those passages that are unique to Mark, Luke, or John, concluding "that not one of these evangelists contains anything at variance with other statements in his own Gospel, or inconsistent with the accounts presented by his fellow-historians." Taking up pericopes found in Mark but not in Matthew, he writes, "This particular statement [Mark 4:31] . . . Mark has in common with Luke." "But it raises no . . . difficulty," or "there is no discrepancy between them." He concludes, "Mark introduced nothing of a kind to make it necessary for us to institute a special comparison between it and any other statement, or to conduct an inquiry with the view of dispelling any appearance of discrepancy."[15]

The *De Consensu* also suggests how Augustine, at least in this project, was reading the Gospels. Knowing little or no Greek, his Bible was the *Vetus Latina* translation.[16] Although he had mastered its textual characteristics, he was nevertheless reading for the content of the narrative (i.e., the linear events of Jesus' life) and for the emphasis of each writer that revealed a unique theology. Noting that each gospel has a specific theology, he focused on specifically Johannine, Matthean, and Lukan insights: Matthew presents a kingly Christ, Luke a priestly Christ, and John a divine Christ. Mark imitates Matthew. Matthew and Luke attend to Jesus' active life. John, whom Augustine called the "most eminent of the four evangelists," attends to Christ's representation of the contemplative life,[17] revealing Augustine's personal ideal and the specific interests he brought to the texts. But he was not interested in "the content of the form,"[18] that is, the content or meaning implicit in the way the writers narrate their story. Seeking the "presence" in the texts, that is, the theological meaning locked within, and reading only the lines that advance a theology of Jesus' life while ignoring the literary techniques weaving Mark's story together, Augustine egregiously dismissed Mark as an epitomizer. Though a very sensitive reader with a highly sophisticated theory of interpretation (as shown in *De Magistro, De Doctrina Christiana,* and the *Confessions,* among other works),[19] Augustine in his biblical interpretations often deliberately goes beyond what the words can actually support, for he takes hints and stretches them to mean what will fit within his own theological construction.[20] He lacked the interpretive skill of Philo, Origen, and Jerome, but what Augustine brought to the text was his special combination of "meditative reading, exploration of the self, and first-person narrative."[21] He insisted that if the interpretation of a passage did not lead to love of God and love of neighbor, it had been read incorrectly. Since he could barely read the original Greek, in contrast to Jerome and John Chrysostom, he missed many of the specific literary qualities of the Markan Greek text.

Tatian's harmony, Eusebius's ten canons of the four Gospels,[22] and

Augustine's *De Consensu Evangelistarum* all show very careful reading of the four Gospels in the sense that they note all or most of the similarities and discrepancies among them. But the primary concern of these authors is to prove the unanimity of the entire corpus. By making all the deviations among the Gospels conform to a single version, they created a uniform story and conflated the differences. While endeavoring to overcome differences and diversity as represented in the different accounts of the life of Jesus, they also were attempting to create a unified and uniform Church with as little variety in ecclesiastical belief and practice as possible. They were so successful in their attempt to unify the gospel stories that to this day the religious imaginations of Christians and non-Christians alike share the version of Jesus' life represented in the harmonized gospels. Eusebius's ten canons featuring resemblance and correspondence among the Gospels (see fig. 5, p. 32) and Augustine's agreement show that their principal concerns were to eliminate differences, merge versions, and produce a universal Christian story.

The addition of verses 9 to 20 to Chapter 16 of Mark in early editions of the gospel—a pattern that continues up to the present—is another aspect of the attempt to create a harmonious synchrony among the Gospels. The gospel's disconcerting conclusion, its empty tomb and absent Jesus and the fear of the women,[23] have been subjected to constant addition, so that even to this day most readers of the Bible do not know that according to most ancient authorities the gospel ends at 16:8. Augustine, at pains to harmonize all the gospel versions of the "resurrection," used Mark 16:9–20 along with Matthew's, John's, and Luke's versions to show there are no discrepancies among them.[24] Again, the provocative conclusion, like Mark's startling opening, disappears with the harmony. This modification of the ending suggests how important both synchrony and clarity about the Resurrection were to early readers, interests that prompt all but the most philologically committed readers. All the major early witnesses—Clement, Origen, Eusebius, and Jerome—excluded the longer ending, as does the current standard Greek edition. In contrast, most harmonies, breviaries, and translations have included it, often without any editorial clarification.

This act of harmonizing, evident in the early centuries of the Church, highlights the differences between the reading habits of the early Church writers and readers and biblical scholars of the Enlightenment. The former sought a consistent story and message, parallelism, and similarity. The eighteenth-century synopses of the Gospels exploded this veneer of uniformity into difference and contrast. But the primary interest in the first three centuries of the Church was to create unity and homogeneity and establish an orthodox tradition.

The editing and translation of texts is yet another aspect of the Fathers' interest in universality and uniformity. Philological concerns, particularly as they affected editions and translations of the Bible in the first four centuries of the Church and then later in the Middle Ages and Renaissance, have been of such significance to the history of Christianity that this subject will be treated in a later chapter. Here, of course, philological questions highlight discrepancies and differences that cannot be easily dismissed. Because Jerome left a number of documents delineating the attitudes he brought to the acts of translation and editing, we have some solid information about his theoretical approach to his Bible translation project.[25] The interest in translation in this period was motivated primarily by the same sentiments that encouraged harmonies and authoritative decisions on doctrine. Church leaders needed a standard text to undergird their ecclesiastical authority. In chapter 4 I will discuss Jerome's translation/edition as one of many philological approaches to the Gospel of Mark from the fourth through the sixteenth centuries. At this later point, new authoritative vernacular bibles took the place of Jerome's Latin text.

II. Mark in the Lectionary

Though no fixed lectionary emerged in the first centuries of the Church, liturgical scholars believe the Easter readings were the first to become "fixed and invariable."[26] This fact is most interesting for the fate of the Gospel of Mark, because it took a prominent role in at least two Easter rites of the early Church: the Alexandrian and the Roman.[27] In another move toward greater harmony, uniformity, and universality—specific goals of the post-Constantinian church—by the fourth century a degree of standardization had emerged in the lectionary cycle, possibly in connection with the Council of Carthage's (397) sponsorship of an official canon of readings. It was a bishop's prerogative to choose the readings in these formative years of the Church, but numerous witnesses suggest the readings included selections from the Old Testament prophets, the apostle Paul, and the Gospels.[28]

There is no evidence that the Markan gospel was read at all at Rome until the second century when a second Easter liturgy, to occur on Easter after the vigil of the previous night, was added. Mark's selection for this early morning liturgy is interesting because although the synoptic gospels are very close regarding the Resurrection narrative (Matt. 28:1–8; Mark 16:1–8; Luke 24:1–12), Mark has some particularly original features. First, besides emphasizing that it was early in the morning, the narrative draws attention to the behavior of the three women who come to the tomb (they are talking among themselves about the huge stone and how to move it, they are amazed by the young man at the tomb, and they are frightened by the empty tomb)(16:1–8). The dramatic possibilities unfold in the narrative itself. In addition to the fact that it seems like an earlier scene—in contrast to John, where the visitors to the tomb meet Jesus (John 20:1–13), or to Matthew

(Matt. 28:1–10) and Luke (24:1–35), who follow the morning scene with encounters with Jesus later in the day—this episode no doubt contributed to its being chosen for the early morning liturgy. One of Augustine's Easter sermons also includes Mark, but with the longer ending (Mark 16:1–16), which sequentially would move the events to Easter Monday.[29] Since the Christian *pascha*, the day of the Resurrection, was the one feast always celebrated in the early Church, Mark played an important early role. This *pascha* ritual was probably linked to a baptismal ceremony, with Mark 7:32–37 (the curing of the deaf man) used when the candidates were touched.[30] This decision to give Mark such a prominent position in the Easter liturgy had a profound impact on cultural history: the medieval drama grew out of this Easter liturgy, a development of the popularizing of the Bible in its medieval uses, which will be discussed in the next chapter. As the chosen reading for Easter morning, some portion of Mark 16:1–20 received widespread attention. It was read on one occasion during Easter week, whether Easter Sunday morning, or Monday, or Friday, although usually for Easter day it was Mark 16:1–8. This is true for a number of rites, including Augustine's African rite (based on his lectionary), the Roman, the Neapolitan, the Anglo-Saxon, Gallican, and Mozarabic rites.[31]

Another noteworthy liturgical use of Mark is the liturgy of the Alexandrian patriarchate, named after Mark, although this liturgy does not have any references peculiar to the evangelist.[32] Tradition cited in Eusebius held that Mark as emissary of Peter went to Alexandria.[33] The use of Mark in the Alexandrian paschal liturgy, however, may also explain two uses of Markan material by Clement of Alexandria (153–217), even though Mark was not Clement's favorite source for proof-texts. The first of these is in Clement's treatise, *Quis dives salvetur?* This discussion elaborates on his longest quote from any of the Gospels, Mark 10:17–31, which he reproduces with numerous omissions and changes. This led one early writer to conclude that he was quoting from memory, had a very poor papyrus, or adapted Mark under the influence of Matthew's text.[34] The second of these is in his *Letter on the Secret Gospel of Mark*, where we find references to the same and connected passages of Mark. Together, these references show that Clement was for some reason very interested in this section of Mark. The letter locates the pericopes it quotes from the Secret Gospel as adjacent to 10:34 and 46. The material in Mark 10:13–45 is not unique to Mark in the synoptic accounts, for there are parallel versions in either Matthew (19:20–28) or Luke (18:15–34). Mark's version, however, is more emphatic, twice stating how difficult it is for the rich to enter the kingdom of heaven but insisting on the potential reward of eternal life for those who convert—a very fitting theme for a baptismal ceremony. It was probably used liturgically in Clement's church at the *megala musteria*, the reinterpretation of resurrection as initiation, and vice versa, with the entire paschal ceremony, including baptism.[35] The mysteriousness of the Markan version of the Resurrection, with its early morning atmosphere and empty tomb, perhaps lies behind its selection for such a prominent place in two different Easter rites, but Clement aligns Jesus' Resurrection with this earlier promise of eternal life. Whatever reasons underlay their selection, these references show that although Mark was essentially ignored in the lectionary cycles, the gospel played a prominent role in the Easter liturgy.

Despite Mark's importance in the paschal liturgy, where he was chosen because of his distinctness, it is Matthew and John with Luke a distant third who appear most frequently in the lectionary cycles. Mark was read perhaps once for every sixteen readings of Matthew and John. The lectionaries of Peter Chrysologus, Maximus Taurinensis, and Leo the Great all feature Matthew prominently.[36]

III. CITATIONS OF MARK

The limited number of references to Mark as proof-texts or in sermons among the early writers nonetheless reveals a pattern of citation that further illustrates the interests of the Fathers. The geographical location of the writers in general does not appear significant, for uniformity of opinion on Mark existed in the early Church from Syria to Africa and Europe. Textual witnesses connecting Mark to Peter and Rome appear in diverse environments and seem unrelated to a specific regional conviction, with the exception, of course, that Mark was also associated with Alexandria.

References are used to support convictions about the sacraments or doctrines (marriage, priesthood, the Trinity, for example) or about interpretive methods. Like the focus in harmonies, translations, and liturgy, these references also support the central concerns of the early Church regarding uniformity of texts, doctrine, liturgical practice, and interpretive method.

References to Mark usually involve passages unique to him, that is, not present in the other synoptics, and these proof-texts follow convention in that they are used to prop up an argument. These quotations are moved to the literary context of the commentator's own work, often without concern for the context from which they were removed. In their new setting, they are employed to reinforce arguments. For example, Irenaeus in *Adversus Haereses*, to support his polemical treatise, either cites or refers to Mark more than one hundred times, in contrast to twice as many references to Matthew.[37] The Gospel of Mark presented a problem for Irenaeus because, as he writes, the gospel made it possible to misunderstand the relationship between Jesus and the Christ: "Those who separate Jesus from the Christ and wish this 'Christ' to remain 'impassable,' so that Jesus alone would have suffered, give their preference to the Gospel according to Mark; but if they read with the love of truth, they have the possibility to correct themselves."[38] He sees Mark as less decisive on the divine nature of Jesus than the other Gospels and, in this passage at least, suggests that those reading the gospel should guard themselves with specific preconceptions against the possibilities the text itself suggests. Furthermore, against those who were trying to distinguish Jesus' humanity from his divinity, he writes, "And to the one who says, 'Good Teacher,' the Lord showed that God is truly good, and replying to them, 'Why call me good? Only one is good, the Father in the heavens,' "[39] thus using Mark to emphasize Christ's goodness as central to his argument about the interrelationship of Jesus as man and the Christ. Threatened by the gnostic interpretations of Mark, Irenaeus's references in these instances are against Mark's seeming "low" Christology, which he perceives as inconsistent with the doctrinal interests of many Church authorities. But at the same time, he is attentive to the nature of the Markan theology that he refocuses to support the emerging high Christology.

Tertullian (145–220), who criticized Greek philosophy and learning ("What has Athens to do with Jerusalem, the Academy with Christ?") on the grounds that Christianity and paganism were incompatible,[40] repeats Irenaeus's pattern of using the gospel to support his own theology, quoting Mark approximately 250 times. The passages were apparently selected for their uniqueness and their polemical value. In *De Monogamia,* for example, Tertullian cites Mark 1:30 in order to use the existence of Peter's mother-in-law in his discussion of monogamy and its tradition in the Church: "Thus are the witnesses Our Lord had in his childhood; there was no other in his adulthood. I find only Peter married, since he has a mother-in-law, but I presume he was monogamous because of the church founded on him."[41] Like Irenaeus, Tertullian extracts Markan statements to support a contemporary concern—in this case, the argument for celibacy—but he must explain away the fact of Peter's mother-in-law in the Gospel of Mark to support this early Church interest in a celibate priesthood.

Turning to Origen, the scant 650 references to Mark in his monumental corpus of philological and commentary work appear primarily in his commentaries on Matthew and John, but again his citations, like those of others, confirm contemporary issues. These include convictions about doctrinal issues like the Trinity and, more particularly, biblical support for theological points. Origen has a number of favorite Markan passages, as for example, Mark 4:11 and 10:18. Origen uses Mark 4:11f.—Jesus' own explanation of how to interpret his parables, where he allegorizes the parable of the sower, in his own discussion of interpretive method in many of his treatises (*Against Celsus, De Principiis, Commentary on Matthew, Commentary on John*), arguing in favor of allegorical reading principles that he ties to Jesus' own interpretive methods.[42] The second, Mark 10:18—Jesus' remark that "None is good save God the father"—a citation that Irenaeus took up for the same reasons, occurs frequently in both the *Commentary on John* and *De Principiis,* and Origen must explain how this does not contradict trinitarian theology.

The homilies of Jerome and Augustine on Mark highlight the differences in their approaches to the gospel. These Fathers fought bitterly over how the Scriptures might be interpreted and translated (i.e., from the *Septuagint* or the Hebrew, collations of which drew attention to serious discrepancies). Both were trained in Ciceronian rhetoric, but Jerome, the philologist, defended the same kind of interpretive veracity he applied to secular literature.[43] Augustine's passionate interests were in the clarification of Church teachings, the codification of Christian doctrines and ecclesiastical practices, and the elimination of heterodoxies in an age of Christian intellectual controversy and political and social collapse. For him the teachings of the Church were difficult to follow but simple in what they expected. In his reading of the Gospels, he too often seeks to bring the texts into line with his own theological presuppositions. His limited work on Mark follows this pattern. In his extant sermons on Mark (Sermon 95 on Mark 8:5; Sermon 96, on Mark 8:34; Sermon 97 on Mark 13:32; Sermon 223 on Mark 16:16), he uses the gospel as the starting point to develop his own opinion. For example, on Mark 13:32 and the coming Day of Judgement (in Sermon 97), he writes, "The advice, brothers, you have just heard Scripture give, when it tells us to watch for the last day, every one should think of as concerning his own last day; for when you judge or think the last day of the world to be in the future, you sleep with concern for your own last day."[44] He moves from this point to his own convictions about the ideal of asceticism and abdication of worldly value: "Let us not love the world. It overwhelms its lovers, it does not lead us to the good."[45] In the sermon on the miracle of the seven loaves (95), he ignores several symbolic and social implications of the story and applies his own brand of allegorical interpretation, using the Markan passage to elaborate on contemporary ecclesiastical convictions, the seven works of the Holy Spirit, the Church under the four evangelists, and the seven baskets of leftovers as the perfect Church: "The seven loaves signify the sevenfold working of the Holy Spirit; the 'four thousand men,' the Church established on the four Gospels; 'the seven baskets of fragments,' the perfection of the Church" (95).[46] Further on into his homily, the discussion shifts to Matthew 22:11, and again he applies an allegorical interpretation, arguing for the universal Church, a trinitarian theology, and his own *caritas/cupiditas* (charity/ cupidity) moral system. This is Augustine's style: to use the biblical reference, in this case Mark, as the starting point for a moral or ecclesiastical discussion and then move to his central theological concerns.

As a philologist first, engaged in editing, translating, and collating the Hebrew, Greek, and Latin versions of the Bible, Jerome showed more attention to stylistic and linguistic elements in the Gospels than did his contemporary Augustine. His ten homilies begin with a specific Markan reference and explore its immediate meaning, expand to the surrounding pericopes, and apply the passage to contemporary circumstances. Although he supports his arguments with references to other biblical texts, he focused primarily on the reading for the day. Like Origen, he exercises his exegetical talents by staying very close to the text as he attempts to elucidate its meaning. For example, in Homily 4 on Mark 8:1–9 (the second food-multiplication story in Mark), he writes, "we have to know the very flesh and blood of Holy Writ, so that when we understand exactly what is written, we can grasp its import."[47] To elucidate the texts under study, this and others, he applies a threefold method of interpretation (historical, literal, spiritual): "The historical sense is clear enough to those who are listening without any explanation on our part" (Homily 2).[48] In Homily 5, discussing Mark 8:22–26, he further explains his exegetical method: "Reflect upon the text. The historical facts are clear, the literal sense is obvious; we must search into its spiritual message."[49] He also reveals his understanding of the organic connection between the entire work when he writes, "Since there was not enough time last Sunday to go as far as this text, we ought to begin with it today, for all of Holy Writ is animated and held together by one spirit. It is not unlike a necklace held together by the union of its links, so that whichever link you pick up, another suspends from it."[50] In these ten sermons, he shows his careful notation of Markan characteristics, for he chooses, in general, unique Markan pericopes and emphasizes close textual analysis rather than developing an elaborate theology of his own.[51] In Homily 2 on Mark 1:13–31, he notes Mark's unique use of *statim*, "immediately," a characteristic also noted by John Chrysostom. Remarking on the Markan habit of intercalation, he discusses the combined stories of the hemorrhaging woman and Jairus's daughter (Mark 5:30–43). In Homily 3, he again selects a dramatic Markan phrase, "Quis me tetigit?" (Who touched me?), to begin his exegesis, in which he compares the resuscitation of Jairus's daughter, Peter's mother-in-law, and the Resurrection of Jesus. A careful interpretation leads Jerome to a conclusion in which he connects all these events to the historical reality of the resurrection and Christ's role in rescuing humans from moral and physical illness. In Homily 4 on Mark 8:1–9, Jerome deals with the problem of the two food multiplication stories in Mark, noting the differences between the stories and the meaning conveyed by them. He concludes, "Consequently, we must not be careless in reading scripture" (4).[52] In other words, he proposes a philologically based theory of reading in which the "literal" meaning of words rather than their symbolic or allegorical implications claims priority. Because Jerome was a very careful reader who was skilled in languages, he takes up passages in Mark that may also appear in the other synoptics, but he wrests a specifically Markan sense from them because he is less interested in allegories than in the literal level of the text. His skilled exegesis proves it was not by accident that he earned a reputation as the most intelligent commentator on the literal level of the Bible.[53]

John Chrysostom's remarks on Mark are rare like his fellow patristic writers (about one to every seven for Matthew), with the bulk of his references occurring in his *Commentary on Matthew*. Like Jerome, he was sensitive to historical and philological issues in the Gospels, and he had read Mark carefully enough to note his use of *euthus* (Latin, *statim*, English, immediately), which he understands as a "historical" sign of the time when actions take place in the gospel.[54]

On the whole, whether in the second, third, or fourth centuries, among Antiochenes or Alexandrians, Romans or Carthaginians, scant attention was directed to Mark. As this discussion shows, the uses of the gospel indicate the interests of the Fathers. They read Mark carefully enough to select the pericopes unique to him that they then used to support theological or doctrinal positions or liturgical practice. This suggests that they did not read the Gospels as distinct narratives but as a single *evangelium* to bolster Church teachings. Since this work was not merely patronized by powerful bishoprics but was often the writing of the bishops themselves, the Gospel of Mark, along with all other canonical texts, was used to support the primary ecclesiastical goals of the period. Nonetheless, as this discussion has shown, Mark's contribution to this agenda was minor.

Rhetorical Standards and Expectations

Having noted the attention to the Gospel of Mark and the reasons for it, I now turn to an analysis of what rhetorical expectations the Fathers brought to the texts they read. The importance of pagan education, whether rhetoric or philosophy, in this period cannot be underestimated.[55] So widespread was the habit of learning from pagan authors that in 362 the Emperor Julian, attempting to restore the pagan religion of the Roman Empire, prohibited all Christians by edict from teaching and studying pagan literature. Pagan education was so important to the intellectual strength of Christian leaders that Julian believed he could destroy their influence if he could confine their teaching to the Bible, which was written, he believed, in a "lowly" style.[56] The Council of Carthage in 398 prohibited the reading of pagan books by the people and the bishop (Canon 16),[57] a prohibition in response to widespread interest in pagan learning. Whether born Christian or later converted, both the Latin and Greek Fathers were educated in the rhetorical schools. The curriculum in these schools, besides training in Greek and Latin, guaranteed that students who graduated were thoroughly versed in the literary culture of antiquity, knowing the central texts of Latin literature and often of Greek also.

Five of eight Latin church fathers (Tertullian, Cyprian, Arnobius, Lactantius, and Augustine) were professional rhetoricians before they became Christians. In addition, Ambrose, Hilary, and Jerome were thoroughly trained in the rhetorical schools.[58] In the East, from the middle of the fourth century to the beginning of the fifth, besides Anthony and his monks—who had no rhetorical training—Athanasius, Basil, John Chrysostom, Theodore of Mopsuestia, Gregory of Nazianzus, and Gregory of Nyssa were steeped in ancient philosophy and rhetoric.[59] This training could not have been removed from their habits of mind when they altered their intellectual and religious interests and changed professions from rhetoricians to priests. Confronted with a text lacking the very features of "bene latine dicere" in which they were reared, it was almost natural for them to find the biblical texts stylistically deficient, and Mark especially so.[60] Furthermore, their interpretive methods cannot be separated from their rhetorical training, for training in rhetoric was also training in hermeneutics.[61]

Such an education formed the Fathers' convictions about literary style in terms of genre, rhetorical range, and grammar and interpretation, whether philological or philosophical. Therefore, evaluation of the style of the text cannot be ignored in an assessment of the Fathers' responses to the Gospel of Mark. Many of them refer to the simplicity of the language of the Bible,[62] defending its rusticity on the grounds that its veracity is transcendent and arguing that simple diction was necessary so that all could understand it. The story, written in a "low style," intermingles transcendence, simplicity, humility, and sublimity: God's favor toward the humble; Christ humbled in the person of a slave; fishermen as the first converts, and so forth. Such characteristics might have encouraged them to make Mark's gospel their favorite, since its "rusticity" is so evident, but just the opposite occurred. From the perspective of literary taste, one might see the Fathers' stylistic attitudes undergoing a transition from the strict codification of high and low styles characteristic of ancient Greek and Roman culture[63] to the mixture of styles in which the canonical Christian texts were written—a new style that the literary culture of Christianity had nurtured. As a "popular" movement appealing to all social strata, early Christianity adopted a mixed literary style appropriate for its mixed clientele. The Fathers' own writing shows the influence of their education, and though they often wrote in the "low" (humilis) or "intermediate" style, their writing displays a sophisticated knowledge of the art of eloquence and the literary texts from which this style developed.

For example, knowledge of the concepts of genre the Fathers might have brought to their reading of the Gospels is important to understanding how they read them. If they believed the Gospels were a type of popular biography[64]—and their attempts at harmonization suggest that conviction— then specific methods and rules for writing would have directed their composition and later assessment. Hermogenes' *Progymnasmata*, a second-century exercise book, lists the details belonging to a biography, including birth and childhood, personal attributes, friends, possessions, accomplishments, death, and after-death events.[65] Mark lacks most of these details, and when he does provide some, he is less informative than Matthew and Luke or even John. The characteristics for a biography Hermogenes lists appear in many ancient biographies and histories, as for example, Suetonius's *Lives of the Caesars,* Herodotus and Thucydides, Plutarch, *Makers of Rome,* Tacitus, *The Annals of Imperial Rome,* and so on. When the Fathers approached their reading with these genre requirements in mind, their expectations would have been more satisfied by Matthew and Luke, less by John, and not at all by Mark.

Mark's rhetorically low style, suggesting its origins in low culture, did not ingratiate it either. The Fathers' immersion in the pagan literature of the high culture shows itself in their fondness for quoting from the pagan literary canon and in their approval of ancient learning. Clement of Alexandria quotes the *Iliad, Lysistrata, Iphigeneia in Aulis, Phaethon,* and Hesiod frequently, alongside all four Gospels. Clement believed that Christianity and Platonism could be harmonized, and he used ancient Greek texts almost as freely as Holy Scripture. To support his arguments in *Stromata, Paidagogus,* and *Eclogae propheticae,* he appropriated texts from the *Septuagint,* the Greek canon, the four Gospels, and other Christian documents (1 Peter, 1 Timothy, for example) that he used often with parallel authority and emphasis. He sought to accommodate Christianity to the legacy of Greek learning. Basil the Great (330–379), who spent five years at the "University" at Athens, was also immersed in pagan learning. In *Ad Adolescentes,* while referring to Plato throughout, he represents a broad-minded attitude toward the writings of pagan authors, from whom, he argued, much could be learned.[66] Perhaps patronized by Constantine, Iuvencus (c.325) translated/transformed the Gospels into Virgilian Latin hexameters in an effort to show the true God against the false gods of the Romans. Calling his poem "carmen," to link his work with the Roman poetic tradition, and identifying its origin with the divine in the tradition of epic poetry, he announces that the song of the true deeds of Christ, a gift of divine origin, is a work he offers so the world may not snatch it away.[67] Apollinaris of Laodicia responded to the edict of Emperor Julian (362) forbidding the study of Greek poetry and authors by translating "Christian" literature, particularly the First Testament, into Greek forms and making Platonic dialogues from the Gospels.[68]

Christianity in the West also absorbed pagan culture. It synthesized biblical and pagan learning, Christian with pagan culture, and accommodated the Church legally and politically to the society around it. Among the Latin Fathers, Lactantius, Jerome, and Augustine habitually repeat Cicero's habit of quoting from classical poetry, although such quotations do not appear in Tertullian, Cyprian, and Arnobius, and they are rare in Ambrose and Minucius Felix. Lactantius, Jerome, and Augustine together quote 342 full lines of Virgil.[69] In these last three cases, we might note that the Latin classics are quoted far more than the Gospel of Mark, but quotations from Matthew and John surpass all others. Jerome's unreserved admiration for Roman literature and particularly Cicero, whose influence is so evident both in his style and his literary theories, led to the nightmare he recounts in Letter 22, in which he is accused of being a Ciceronian, not a Christian. Nevertheless, though not quite as radically as Tertullian before him, who believed that paganism and Christianity were incompatible, Jerome did believe that reading pagan works for themselves alone would certainly lead to damnation.

Augustine's affection for the Latin classics and particularly Virgil, whom he appropriated to Christianity for polemics against pagans, is well established. He admired Virgil's elegance and correctness of diction as well as his formal facility with language, and he used Virgil's writing to make points about syntax and style, history, religion, and philosophy. But there is a great diversity in his attitudes toward this pagan learning in the various periods of his writing career. Certainly, there appears to be a growing aversion to secular culture, but he vacillated, particularly on Virgil.[70] Thus, he seemed to divorce style from sense, justifying pagan literature *de verbo,* but not *de re,* just as he must also have done with the rusticity of the Gospels. It is hard to imagine that someone with his developed rhetorical sensibility and literary expectation could have found Mark, which he knew from numerous versions of the *Vetus Latina,* other than stylistically barbaric. We know from *Confessions* that in his youth he found the Christian Scripture unworthy of his attention because it lacked the "nobility of Cicero's writings."[71] The early Latin versions of Mark, with their imported Greek terms and Aramaic expressions, neologisms, and coarse and vulgar Latinity (by the standards of the time) must likewise have struck him as uncouth, leading him to his problematic conclusion: Mark has little to add to Matthew and John. Probably even more important to Augustine than Mark's stylistic flaws were all the gaps in its version of the story and its theological ambiguities in contrast to Matthew and John. Without a theory of narrative, even though he himself was a master of it, he was incapable of or refused to consider that Mark's narrative style was a dimension of what constitutes the gospel's understanding of the events it retells.

In terms of interpretive methods—whether influenced by ancient Roman, Greek, or Jewish traditions that produced allegorical, typological, historical, and literal modes as represented by Origen's *De Principiis*—neither Augustine's *De Doctrina Christiana* nor the preserved works of Theodore of Mopsuestia, nor Jerome's many letters on the subject led to an appreciation of the Gospel of Mark in its own right.[72] In essence, these methods of reading supported reading the "fourfold witness" as harmonious, a habit that overcame, or at the very least, ignored the differences in the Gospels. Whether individual Fathers favored allegory, typology, or history, they nevertheless assumed a distinction between form and content. They were propelled by a desire to read "through" the text rather than look "at" its surface features. To look "at" prose is to perceive its stylistic or narrative surface that may convey its ideological or thematic communication, but to "look through" is to concentrate on its central meaning or underlying structure,[73] or focus on a particular "trace" in the work from which to construct meaning.

Mark's arrangement of his material and the rhetorical style of his discourse represent a literary and theological interpretation of Jesus and the events of his life; he attempts to show the moral significance of events and the characters who participated in them, just as is the case in myth, fable, folklore, and historiography. It is in Mark's choice of language, arrangement of events, and selection of genre that the essentially literary nature of his writing is revealed as a religious activity, for his composition is a literary and religious interpretation of temporal events.[74] Augustine, in seeking to uncover the spiritual dimension of the text, separated (literal) meaning and sign, with the idea that scriptural meaning must somehow be discerned.[75] Jerome's conviction, on the other hand, about the *proprietas verborum* as expressed in the Letter to Pammachius (57), led him to a literary theory based on respect for the integrity of signs as philological entities as well as makers of eloquent sense.[76] He did, however, agree with Augustine that the Incarnation had changed all interpretation of the Bible, because its sense must support this absolute reality.[77] The "what" of their reading of Scripture emerged from their experience of their religion combined with their learning. The "how" of their reading and writing combined these two ideologies of the Word, and often these were in conflict.

But no approach to reading or interpreting current in the period, whether in terms of stylistics, genre, or interpretive methods, facilitated the Fathers' appreciation of the Gospel of Mark. Gospel harmonies demonstrate that in contrast to Matthew and John, Mark has little to add. Translations, on the other hand, draw attention to unique stylistic characteristics of Mark, to which Jerome was very attentive. The many commentaries on Matthew, Luke, and John employing the range of patristic methods of interpretation demonstrate the relationship between the interests of the Fathers and the document being interpreted. The absence of commentaries on Mark, on the other hand, suggests that neither the interpretive nor ecclesiastical interests of the Fathers were excited by Mark. If, as I have suggested, ecclesiastical concerns—particularly those connected to sacraments, church consolidation, dogmatic formulations, and a coherent theology—were their primary preoccupations in the period, Mark offers little help in these areas, especially when compared to Matthew and John. Mark's incompleteness of information and lack of articulateness on specific theological and ecclesiastical concerns of the time as well as his "low" Christology (as was clear in Irenaeus's remarks) may have contributed to the gospel's exclusion from attention. The gospel lacks the necessary data found in Matthew and John useful to the Fathers in clarifying liturgical, ecclesiastical, doctrinal, or sacramental practices. Mark's uniqueness is precisely in its parsimony of information, liveliness of reportage, excess of miraculous and extraordinary cases, arrangement of narrative kernels, and intentional ambiguities, but appreciation of these characteristics and their connection to his theological message would have to wait almost a millennium and a half. The Gospel of Matthew, following the conventional requirements for a biography, also reflected current ecclesiastical interests. John, while providing the greatest amount of narrative that did not appear in the other Gospels, also uses a vocabulary that resonates with the Neoplatonic philosophical interests of the rhetorically trained Fathers. The Gospel of Mark, on the other hand, has none of these "redeeming" qualities.

Furthermore, in an era when Church authorities were searching for teachings to bolster an orthodox creedal formulation against the threat of gnosticism, the Gospel of Mark did not proclaim its message directly or dogmatically. Matthew's message was more compatible with the ecclesiastical attitudes and interests of the time (Matt. 16:18–20; 28:19–20). Matthew establishes Peter as the rock on which the Church was built (Matt. 16:18–20), thus providing a text later to be employed in securing the authority of the bishop of Rome as successor to Peter. This was of interest to the Fathers, whereas the Gospel of Mark presents Peter as a disciple, who, despite his assertion of knowledge about who Jesus is (8:29), continually shows his own deficiencies and failure to understand or respond to what Jesus' calling requires (8:32–33; 14:68, 70, 71, for example).[78] Matthew also enjoins his readers or listeners, through the words of Jesus, to preach to the world—that is, to all people; naming baptism, which would later become a "sacrament," he exhorts his audience to baptize in the name of the Father, Son, and Holy Spirit (Matt. 28:19–20), laying the groundwork for the doctrine of the Trinity and establishing a definitive role for Jesus in that Trinity. In fact both Irenaeus and Origen drew attention to specific Markan pericopes that referred to Jesus' relationship to the Father in order to clarify them. These concerns conformed with the ecclesiastical interests and beliefs of the Church (sacraments, trinitarian theology, the divine nature of Jesus, and evangelism, for example) in the four centuries that witnessed the growth and acquisition of power of the Church and its multiethnic constituency. Mark lacks Matthew's clarity of expression and greater specificity in doctrinal issues, but it is precisely his elusiveness, his brevity of expression, his paradoxicality, and his muted Christology that our own era has found so stimulating.[79]

The history of the responses to the Gospel of Mark in the first four centuries shows how attitudes and values, informed by literary training (particularly in rhetoric and hermeneutics) as well as ecclesiastical and theological interests influenced how the Fathers "read" the gospel. Though they commented on pericopes unique to Mark to promote the Church as an institution and the doctrines that were emerging as normative, their primary interest was in a harmonization that would support theological and ecclesiastical purposes. This interest underlay the focus on Matthew and John. The Fathers' reading and writing habits reflect converging traditions (the unifying of their rhetorical training with the Judeo-Christian experience) and divergent ideologies of the word (the literary word and the Word of God), but in this effort to harmonize their education with their religious convictions, it appears Mark had little to contribute.

CHAPTER 3

Medieval Reception:
Commentaries,
Glossing, and Popular Genres

Unus igitur omnia, et unus in omnibus
(Therefore all is one, and one is in all.)
> Ambrose, *Expositio Evangelii secundum Lucam*, Prol. 8

. . . ye woot that every Evaungelist
That telleth us the peyne of Jhesu Crist
Ne seith nat alle thyng as his felawe dooth;
But netheles hir sentence is al sooth,
And alle acorden as in hire sentence,
Al be ther in hir tellyng difference.
> Chaucer, *The Canterbury Tales*, VII, 942–48.

A ugustine and the early Church's goal of overcoming "gaps" in their unified view of Judeo-Christian history and in the text that would uphold that vision was so successful that together they handed over to the Middle Ages a fourfold witness that had become one witness. Naturally Mark was lost in this narrative because, aside from a few exceptional sequences, his gospel overlaps with the others. The reception of the Gospel of Mark in the patristic period laid out the twin sides of its future: presence through canonicity—assuring that it would continue to appear in the Bible and harmonies—and virtual absence from a commentary tradition. Two dominant kinds of reception in the Middle Ages reflect the power of patronage in the period, for the high culture up until the fourteenth-century plague was dominated by the monasteries and the bishoprics, where highly articulated scholarly traditions and intellectual inquiry directed the reception of the Bible.

As collectors, copiers, commentators, exegetes, and systematicians, medieval scholars had encyclopedic interests.[1] They sought to produce complete and total compendia to the universe of knowledge, embracing history, geography, science, astronomy, literature, philosophy, and theology combined with numerous methods for interpreting texts,[2] all as parts that could be made to fit within the whole of one universal history. The scholarly reception of the Bible reflects these encompassing interests. On the other hand, the medieval imagination assured that the Bible's stories would reappear in the various genres that grew in the Christian West. The rewriting of the canonical Gospels in popular forms in the Middle Ages demonstrates Augustine's success in making them a single *evangelium,* for these new genres elide all the distinctions among the Gospels, as one in four and four in one.

An increasingly vibrant vernacular culture from the eleventh century on supported a very different reception of the Bible. The numerous biblical scene windows at Chartres, for example, patronized by carpenters, joiners, barrel makers, wine-makers, butchers, fishmongers, and so on, testify to an avid interest both in art and in the narratives of the Bible sponsored by the emerging mercantile classes.[3] As a consequence, two cultures of the Bible coexisted, the highly articulated commentary tradition and the more popular forms of biblical reception. Indeed, in contrast to the general opinion, shared by many Reformation scholars, that the Bible was ignored in the Middle Ages, it was, in fact, incorporated into every facet of culture. Whether in the liturgy, as ornamentation of churches, cathedrals, and houses, in illuminated manuscripts and glossed secular and sacred texts, in popular oral and written narratives, meditative genres, late medieval pageant drama, or in commentaries, the Bible, with its store of narrative and teaching, penetrated every aspect of medieval high and low cultural activity.[4] But this was a Bible with a single story from Creation to the end of time.

This chapter reflects the medieval division between the scholarly work of authorities, whether monastic or clerical, and other popularizing efforts. The first section of this chapter will discuss reading the New Testament as a single story, which led to the medieval literary re-creations of the Bible in Latin and vernacular harmonies, biographies, liturgy and drama, and romances. These more inclusive literary forms convey the medieval desire to make the "truths" of the religion and the stories conveying them accessible to larger numbers of people. While these forms dismissed the uniqueness of the Gospels when read by themselves, they supported the ideology of a unified narrative without the differences the fourfold witness creates.

The second section discusses the high culture, authoritative reception of Mark's gospel. The commentaries of the medieval period are ruled by a "glossing" rhetorical strategy, that is, they interpret the text by the smallest units, sometimes word by word or verse by verse. These glosses expand and elaborate on the text's implications and, while often deferring to authoritative traditions, they emphasize the particular interests of the commentator, for the glosses are always far more extensive than the original words. Heirs to the interpretive mode epitomized in the verse, "Littera gesta docet, quid credas allegoria, / Moralis quid agas, quid speres anagogia," from the time of Gregory the Great medieval interpreters made use of many interpretive strategies, including allegory, typology, history, and philology. Despite the range of interpretive approaches, however, the strategy of the commentary worked to bring the original text from its past into a present that conformed to an unbroken and complete vision of salvation history. The dominant authoritative tradition of writers, commentators, and artists, above all, served to incorporate all learning and biblical expression into an all-encompassing book of the universe. Both the high culture commentary tradition and the popular attention reveal that Mark was read carefully enough to note what was in the text, in terms of words, that was not elsewhere in the Gospels, but both learned and popular reading strategies sought to overcome these differences and accommodate them to the single story.

During the Middle Ages, a number of works on Mark were produced, including those of the Irish monk Cummeanus(?) (c.650)—listed in Migne as *S. Hieronymi Operum Mantissa* and *Scripta Supposita*[5]—Sedulius Scotus (c.858),[6] and Pseudo-Jerome.[7] Besides these, Venerable Bede (672–735), whose wide-ranging interests led him to write complete commentaries on as much of the Bible as he found time for, left a full work on Mark,[8] as did Albertus Magnus (b.1193–1206–d.1280).[9] The *Catena Aurea* of Thomas Aquinas (1225–6–1274) summarizes the church fathers' comments on all the gospels.[10] In the eastern church, Euthymius (late eleventh–early twelfth century), wrote commentaries on all four Gospels,[11] and Theophylactus, Archbishop of Ochrida (c.1050–c.1108) also wrote on the four Gospels.[12] Repeating the tradition that Mark was converted by Peter at Rome, these Greek commentaries are complex, expansive, verse by verse treatments of the gospel, incorporating orthodox theology and the other Gospels to gloss the Markan text. In the tradition of the Antiochene Church, Theophylactus's interpretation is primarily a literal (philological) and historical exegesis. All these medieval commentaries, Greek and Latin, together with medieval glosses and *postillae*, became sources for Erasmus (1466–1536), who produced his *Paraphrase on Mark*, a new genre for biblical commentary, in 1523.[13]

Popular Genres: Harmonies, Biographies, Drama, and Poems

Though the church fathers worked to establish a normative sacred text to undergird Church teaching and exclude all challenges to its universal teaching, the popular medieval response to the Bible unraveled the weaving it inherited. Medieval popular responses to the Bible realigned the boundaries between apocryphal and orthodox and between high and low culture, and in doing so they returned the Bible to its social roots. The Bible, originally written in the vernaculars of the day (Hebrew, Aramaic, *koine* Greek), once again was rendered in vernacular translations in the medieval period. Medieval versions of the New Testament story circumvented the decisions of councils that had eliminated the non-canonical gospels, for medieval writers in the vernacular languages ignored distinctions between canonical and extra-canonical gospels in their verse and prose revisions of the Bible. Distinctly medieval political, social, and religious developments characterize these biblical versions, in which the contemporary social structure, whether as court culture, the emerging mercantile culture, or subversive elements identified as heresies, colored the biblical scene. The popular versions of the Gospels reveal the medieval conviction about the timelessness of the Christian message, a conviction that underlay the kinds of reading practiced in the period. One of the most profound examples of this effort to make the story relevant to the present is late medieval Crucifixion depictions that show the soldiers at Golgotha dressed as medieval armored knights and Mary Magdalen as a well-dressed, late medieval courtesan. Using these reading strategies (and of course here I am expanding the meaning of reading to include the reception of the ancient text via any semiotic media), writers and artists deliberately accommodated the story to their own socio-political situations.

In the Middle Ages, the Bible appeared in the vernacular languages and became central to popular cults and religious custom, while its stories appeared in many new genres. In this respect, the Bible, rather than being restricted to an elite clerical caste, became the major source for new cultural forms in the period. Writers and artists who used the Bible as their primary source thus re-created the sacred text to suit the emerging needs of medieval believers. The popular medieval reception of the Bible contrasts with the dominant interests of the patristic era that sought to accommodate the "low" style of the texts to the high cultural demands of orthodoxy.

"Matter" is the word used to describe sources of medieval narratives, as "The Matter of Britain" (Arthur, and so on), "The Matter of France" (Charlemagne, and so on), "The Matter of Thebes" (based on Statius's *Thebaid*), or "The Matter of Rome" (Aeneas, and so on). One example of how closely the Bible was associated with other story-sources in the period is that of Jehan de Malkaraume's Bible, whose very faithful translation of Genesis and Exodus is followed by Benoît de Saint Maure's *Roman de Troie*, which is then followed by the rest of the *Old Testament*.[14] Another example is the *General Estoria* of Alfonso X el Sabio, which tells a universal history that incorporates harmonized biblical events.[15] In the history writing tradition of Orosius's *History against the Pagans*,[16] the Bible was brought into the sequence of events retold in these universal histories, from the division of the world into three continents, each peopled by one of Noah's sons, to

Ninus's and Semiramis's empire, and then through all the great empires, and so on.

The Bible provided another major source for stories and therefore can be classified as one of the many, and in this case the most important, "matter" offering a store of material for writers, whether historians or literary writers, and artists. The medieval interest in making all human experience reflect an unbroken sacred narrative with a beginning and an end is reflected in the popular versions of the gospel "matter" of the period. Like erudite commentaries, medieval harmonies, biographies, drama, and poetic versions of the New Testament share one important characteristic: they all tell the story of Jesus as a single timeless story (*evangelium*) and as the central event in history. Harmonies, as the original form of these genres, also set the pattern for "writing" the story of the Gospels as a single story that would form the Christian imagination for all time, a story, as I have argued, that still prevails to this day.

Tatian's harmony, known as the *Diatessaron* (c.170), is probably the origin of all the medieval European harmonies in Latin, which became the fount for vernacular versions. Along with Peter Comestor's *Historia Scholastica*,[17] it is the likely source for many vernacular prose and poetic versions of Jesus' life in the Middle Ages. The *Diatessaron* appeared in Armenian, Arabic, Persian, Latin, Georgian, Anglo-Saxon, Dutch, German, and Italian in the Middle Ages, in turn becoming the primary source for many of the lives of Jesus.[18] In the nineteenth and twentieth centuries, scholars have continued to produce harmonies, although the adoption of the eighteenth-century style synopsis to replace the harmonies as a support for exegetical studies of the New Testament signified an important change in approaches to scholarly reading of the Gospels. Mediated through harmonies, the Gospels inspired both poetic and prose versions of the Bible in the Middle Ages. But Mark had the most to lose in any harmony because its ending at 16:8, its beginning *in medias res,* and the dramatically structured trebling that characterizes its narrative style disappear.[19] Furthermore, Mark's paratactic style generally depends far more on brevity than on elaboration, whereas the central point of harmonies is to compensate for absence or contradiction by overcoming the discrepancies among the Gospels. The *Diatessaron* version of the Gospels had a most profound effect on the Christian imagination, for it formed traditional narratives of the Jesus story, creating a kind of biography. To move from harmonies to "lives of Jesus" was a step into biographical writing, which became a vital form of religious writing in the Middle Ages.

The biographical form has always been a more popular genre.[20] Like biographies, harmonies satisfied an apparent need for a complete biographical-type story, with inconsistencies erased. Ironically, Augustine's agreement among the Gospels produced the single *evangelium,* which in turn would produce a fascination with the "life of Jesus" as a historical quest in the nineteenth century. But while the unique stylistic qualities and specific cultural ambience of individual Gospels in their first-century setting were overlooked by popular interests in the Middle Ages—as they had been in the patristic period—creative revisions of the gospel story in vernacular languages turned out to be exegetical undertakings that retell the gospel stories according to the social and cultural needs of the receiving culture. In other words, they are another variety of commentary on the Gospels. However, like the commentaries of the period, which fill in Mark's gaps with the other Gospels, these versions lose Mark in their wholesale rewriting of the Gospels.

Reintroducing verse into the rendition of the biblical story characterizes many of these medieval rewritings of the New Testament. Two verse settings of the New Testament—Otfrid's ninth-century, south-Rhine, Frankish *Liber Evangeliorum*[21] and the Old Saxon *Heliand* (c.830)[22] (meaning savior)—show how the fourfold witness became a single gospel as all the distinctions among the Gospels became the resources for a harmonious rewriting, whether in verse or prose. Both products of monastic communities concerned with spiritual and pastoral needs, these two poems are especially interesting because they show how the biblical texts and the religion to which they are attached were adapted to totally new cultural circumstances. The Palestinian origins of the story are effaced as the essentially Jewish story is given an Old Saxon ambience in a moment of cultural crisis. The Saxons had been converted by force as a consequence of their defeat in Charlemagne's war of conversion against them (772). In a pattern of intolerance familiar to us from 1492 on, the successful army attacked the religious customs of the Saxons, treated the Saxons brutally, and undermined their code of warrior honor and their native cultic practice. The opening lines of the *Heliand* demonstrate how the author both overcame the differences among the Gospels and indigenized the story. Invoking "secret runes" as the Word of God, Christ becomes the "Might-Wielding," and all the gospel writers— who he names as Matthew and Mark, Luke and John—become the recorders of the single "holy Word," the *evangelium*, or "holy heavenly word," with John replacing all other gospel openings. In the *Heliand* version of the passion, the story of Jesus' betrayal and the conflict between the militarily powerful and the oppressed powerless took on a special poignancy for the conquered Saxons. The story thus became a ninth-century version of liberation theology, intertwining religious and political concerns. The *Heliand* author brought the New Testament story into the Saxon ambience. Most remnants of its Palestinian culture disappear, as the story becomes the narrative of a Saxon warrior, who passionately supports the poor, the enslaved, and the conquered.[23] But in this story, Mark loses all uniqueness. Even the story of the blind man of Bethsaida (8:22–26), one of the few pericopes unique to Mark, becomes an allegorized story of the healing of many blind people along the road, people who had been tricked into sin and thus had lost the light.

Otfrid's *Evangelienbuch*, a harmony in rhyming octosyllabic couplets and divided into five parts, does not have the political interests of the *Heliand*, but a respiritualization of the biblical story does emerge, as was the case with a number of these medieval biblical revisions. Each of the five parts also includes spiritual commentaries on the symbolic significance of moments of the life of Jesus. Like the harmonies, it uses Matthew, Luke, and John, but it is most dependent on John, with many Latin phrases translated directly into German. Mark does not make a major contribution to this poetic rendition of the life of Jesus, although once again the Easter morning scene is Mark's (16:3).

In the prologue to all four evangelists of Peter Riga's *Aurora*, the author distinguishes Mark's traditional traits: the iconographical association with a lion and the gospel's style as "merum" or bare. The *Aurora* version of the evangelists, like other medieval poetic versions of the Bible, pays special attention to Mary, beginning the *Evangelium* proper with Luke and the beauty of the "blessed Virgin Mary" (1. 31). Indeed, Luke takes on greater prominence in Peter Riga than he had in patristic writings on the Gospels. In Peter Riga's first edition, the *Evangelium* was only one-third finished, but the second edition of *Aurora*, completed between 1283 and 1312, includes a verse commentary on the Bible covering the Old Testament (the first five books, Joshua, Judges, Ruth, Kings, and Maccabees; Song of Songs, Job, Tobias, Daniel, Judith, Esther), and, in the New Testament, Acts, and the evangelists.[24] Considered a Christian classic, a counterbalance to Ovid and Virgil, in Latin hexameters and distichs, it is also written as a single *evangelium*.

Peter Riga, perhaps because of the few references to Mary in Mark, shows scant interest in the gospel, but he includes Mark's story of the blind man at Bethsaida (Mark 8:22–26; *Aurora*, II, *Evangelium*, 1767–76), which he allegorizes to make blindness human cupidity, God as the light mediated through the sputum placed on the blind man's eyes. Significantly, this is a pericope singled out earlier by Origen (in the Commentary on Matthew) and Jerome (Homily 79, on Mark 8:22–26), as unique to Mark. Apologizing for appearing to "force the Scriptures," Jerome allegorizes the "spittle" as Christ's means of wiping away the errors of blindness. Aegidius of Paris, who added to the *Aurora* in his *Evangelium Aegedii*—making it twice as long on the grounds that Peter had omitted much material—nonetheless is not particularly attentive to Mark.

Peter Riga's *Aurora* became the source for at least one of the thirteenth- and fourteenth-century translations into vernacular languages. This period witnessed an explosion in translating the Bible into romance languages,[25] which will be discussed in the next chapter. In addition to these direct translations, France also produced a number of verse translations of the Bible.[26] Because the Virgin Mary rose in devotional prominence beginning in the twelfth century, particularly in France, where so many cathedrals in her honor were erected, Luke, because of his many references to Mary, acquired a new prominence as did the *Protevangelium of James*[27]—the apocryphal gospel of Mary's birth and later proof of her virginity—the *Gospel of Nicodemus*,[28] and the *Infancy Gospel of Pseudo-Matthew.*[29] Further demonstrating her importance, the cathedrals dedicated to Mary incorporated sculpture and stained glass windows, recalling the apocryphal events in Mary's life alongside those dramatized in the Gospels of Luke and John.

In the French verse translations of the New Testament, all four Gospels, enriched by this apocryphal material, became the source for new poems, which integrated the tone of the romance.[30] Three names are associated with these creative rewritings of the New Testament woven together with revisions of apocryphal texts: Herman de Valenciennes (thirteenth century), Geufroi de Paris (1243?)[31]—both of whom name themselves in their manuscripts—and Mace de la Charite.[32] Another verse Bible is an anonymous fourteenth-century text (ms. Paris B.N.f. fr. 763), mostly Matthew and John, and no Mark at all.[33] Herman de Valenciennes recounts how the Virgin commanded him to translate the Bible from Latin to "romanc":

> Dame, a toi voil parler qui ai fait cest sermon:
> Je ai a non Hermans, pas n'oblie mon non!
> Je voil, ma doce dame, q'entendes ma raison:
> Prestres sui ordenez et tes sers et tes hom,
> Je ai fait ton commant: fine ai mon sermon.
> (*Li Romanze de Dieu et de Sa Mere,* 545–49, p. 357)

The romance's ten line rhymed laisses produce a mixture of the *chanson de geste,* romance, and saint's life genres, beginning with the Creation and Fall, including events from the canonical and apocryphal writings about Mary's life, death, and Assumption, and ending with her burial. Like the *Heliand,* it localizes the story, in this case making it French. For example, the writer calls Caiphas a bishop (Kafas, l'evesque) (l. 6127, p. 327), the three kings with courtly manners talk to Herod like medieval knights, "Tout a vostre commant" (l. 3559, p. 263), and Herod consults "Les clers de la cite" (the clerks of the city) (l. 3592, p. 264). Herman's romance also mixes apocryphal and canonical in order to praise the Virgin Mary, who, as mother of Christ, is the inspiration for the writer's work. With Luke, the apocryphal gospels, and other apocryphal material about Mary's life taking such prominent roles in Herman's Bible, Mark was naturally neglected, for Mary's role in that gospel is negligible. There is no Annunciation, Visitation, Nativity, wedding at Cana, and no mother at the Crucifixion—or at the tomb), which are found in either John or Luke. In Mark there is only the memory of Mary coming with Jesus' brothers to interrupt his teaching, which is the occasion for him to define family as those who listen to him (3:31–35). For the Crucifixion, John's gospel takes precedence, "Issi com nostre sire commenda sa mere a mon seignor saint Jehan" (p. 343) (John 19:26–27), and for earlier events, Luke is Herman's primary source.

However, he does use Mark for two events, one his extended narrative of the death of John the Baptist, which is most elaborated in Mark (Mark 6:17–29) (ll. 3947–84; ll. 4019–101, pp. 273–75), brief in Matthew, and passed over by Luke and John. He also uses the Markan version of the preparation for the Passover (Mark 14:12–16), suggesting that Herman used the readings from the lectionary, since both of these are sections that were read on specific liturgical occasions.[34] His version of the John the Baptist novella is fully as developed as Mark's, with attention drawn to John's polemic against Herod, Herodias's malice, Herod's blind promise on the occasion of his birthday banquet, the role of "the young girl," and John's eventual beheading. Herman's version is the act of a very self-conscious writer who saw in Mark's novella an inspiration for an extended dramatic interlude in the story of Jesus and his mother. Introjecting himself by name into the Bible he claims as his own, his revision of the canonical Bible, which he says was undertaken at the request of the Virgin, incorporates her role in salvation history, as understood theologically in the twelfth–thirteenth century and as represented in apocryphal writings.

The many extant manuscripts of Geufroi's *La Passion des Jongleurs,* a section of his *La Bible des sept estaz du monde,* affirm its popularity. Geufroi himself attests to his having undertaken to rewrite the Bible: "Ci define, ce m'est avis, La bible Geffroi de Paris."[35] A harmonized version of the Gospels, the Gospel of Nicodemus, apocryphal versions of the descent into hell, and details from the apocryphal life of Mary are the central resources for Geufroi's version of the passion. He has no unique references to Mark, remembering that Jesus uttered "Eli, Elo" (l. 2306) (Mark 15:34; Matt. 27:46) but also that he uttered "Consummatum est" (l. 2367) (John 19:30). This is not surprising, since the versions of the passion are so close in the New Testament. Both Geufroi's and Herman's "bibles" are examples of a popular theology that revised the high culture authoritative *Vulgata,* replacing the fourfold witness with a single version that folds apocryphal material into the canonical.

Mace de la Charite produced a French octosyllabic, rhymed couplet, verse Bible based primarily on the *Aurora.*[36] Like the other French poetic versions, its New Testament, written like a *chanson de geste* and called "Les granz fez de la loy novelle" (The great deeds of the new law), shows renewed interest in Luke, although as in the patristic period Matthew still holds pride of place, with Mark barely discernable. Though less elaborated than in Herman, Mace's version briefly recalls Mark's John the Baptist story (ll. 27454–60).[37] These medieval efforts to rewrite the Bible are both commentary on the canonical texts and efforts, like all the religious plastic art of the period and stained glass windows, to render the story vivid and contemporary, and at the same time to respond to national interests connected to newly empowered language media. These vernacular verse bibles, however, are above all indicative of the resurgence of the *ordo laicorum*, which began to aspire to participation in religious life in a way prohibited by the clerical hierarchy in earlier times. Of necessity, because of the new interest in Mary, these translations effaced the unique character of Mark's version, for Mary is a minor presence in Mark. However, the emphasis on Mary in these French versions suggests the primarily vernacular origin of these bibles. Although Bernard of Clairveaux (1091–1153) endorsed the cult of the Virgin, it was first and foremost, as to this day, a popular cult.

Another popular harmonized version of the Gospels in the Middle Ages, preserved in numerous extant manuscripts, is Ludolf of Saxony's Latin biography, *Vita Christi*, which was translated into numerous vernacular languages (Dutch, 1400, 1487; extracts in German, 1470; 1570 into Italian; Portuguese, 1495; Catalan, 1495–1496; Castilian, 1502–1503; French, 1483–1498).[38] Ludolphus was a Carthusian. He entered the Order of St. Bruno in Strasbourg in 1340 and died in 1348. His *Vita Christi* combines meditation with biography, so for each event in Jesus' life, like the Stations of the Cross for the passion, he provides a meditation framed as an "oratio." He tells the story of Jesus, inviting his readers to see Jesus' life as a model for meditation and imitation (Proemium). Like many harmonies, his begins with John. Then he moves to apocryphal material recounting the birth of the Virgin Mary, using the *Protevangelium of James* for Mary's birth and John for the Incarnation of the Word. Luke is the main source for the beginnings of Jesus' life—including the Annunciation, the Mary and Elizabeth story, Joseph's reluctance, Jesus teaching at the temple—but John supplies the wedding at Cana story. Mark is notably absent in the first portion of Ludolphus, for Matthew provides Jesus' baptism. Prior to recounting the last events in Jesus' life, he offers a general meditation on the passion. He continues the gospel story with material from Acts (Pentecost) and apocryphal stories, including the Assumption of Mary, the Final Judgment, the pain of hell, and the glory of the heavens. Though Ludolphus blurs distinctions among the Gospels, he makes specific references to the gospel he is using as he recounts events. In fact, Matthew, John, and Luke by themselves are the sole sources for many of the events in the *Vita*, and only once does Mark serve alone as the source for a meditation (Mark 7:31–37—the curing of the deaf-mute possessed by a devil, a miracle told in Matthew [15:29–31], but Mark's version is more elaborate). Showing the medieval tendency to use allegory to rationalize the miracles—with the help of Jerome, Augustine, Chrysostom, and Theophilus—Ludolphus uses Mark's more detailed account of the curing of the deaf and dumb man to emphasize that all "Christ's" actions are meant to educate us. Unlike the vernacular "gospels," the *Vita Christi* ignores local cultural and religious practice, which perhaps explains its pan-European popularity, for it was translated into numerous vernacular languages.

As a new genre, a meditative-biography, the *Vita Cristi* quotes from all four Gospels, elides distinctions between canonical and extra-canonical by including material from apocryphal gospels like Pseudo-Matthew, the *Evangelium de Nativate Mariae,* and other infancy gospels, and makes full use of commentaries by the Fathers and the scholastics. Though written in Latin, the *Vita Christi* is an effort to remake the *Vulgata,* which by the twelfth century was associated with high culture or "grammatica," in a more accessible genre. While clearly making use of the harmonies, the *Vita* strikes out on a new path of biblical re-creation, with its combination of history, biography, meditation, and erudite commentary.

In terms of habits of reading and the reception of the Gospel of Mark, the *Vita* testifies to an ongoing popular interest in a historical biography of Jesus, the same kind of interest that would inform the search for the historical Jesus in the nineteenth century, where Mark took precedence over the other Gospels because it came to be regarded as the earliest. At the same time, Ludolphus' version of Jesus' life weaves high and low culture together. He brings the Gospels, apocryphal and canonical, the Fathers' and the scholastics' commentaries, and his own mystical program into a new biographical-historical genre whose story and purpose successfully substituted for these earlier works in the popular imagination.

In addition to harmonies, biographies, and verse rewritings of the New Testament, the Gospels contributed to liturgical innovations in the period. When Mark 16 was added to the Easter vigil of the Roman rite beginning in the second century, its future role in the Easter liturgy was set in motion. Its use in this liturgy proves to have been one of the most significant literary events, for the Easter morning or nocturnal liturgy underlies the *quem quaeritis* trope, from which scholars have argued the medieval drama developed, an event that reinvigorated liturgical practice and gave birth to lay participation in a biblical culture.[39] This authoritative decision eventually provided the occasion to turn the Scriptures into a popular entertainment that would dramatize all of salvation history from Genesis to the Resurrection. The liturgy was the perfect medium for this transference from the authorities to the laity to take place, because the liturgy mediates between all cultural layers and brings all social classes together in common worship.[40]

A trope is a phrase, sentence, verse, or strophe inserted into the liturgy. Sometime in the ninth century, the Gospel of Mark's startling ending, with the three women seeking the dead Jesus and finding only an empty tomb, formed the kernel for the trope added to the Easter morning ritual. By the early tenth century this trope had become the following dramatic representation:

> Questioner: "Whom do you seek at the tomb, o followers of Christ?
>
> Reply: "Jesus of Nazareth who was crucified, o heaven-dwellers."
>
> Angel: "He is not here; he has risen, just as he predicted. Go and announce that he has risen from the tomb."[41]

Slightly expanded versions of resurrection plays based on the *quem quaeritis* trope appear as early as the tenth century, and this trope continues to appear in medieval liturgical and pageant drama,[42] as typified in the following example:

> (Angelle): "Whom seke ye, women sanctifiede?"
> Three Maryes: "Jhesus of Nazareth crucified,
> The redemer of mankind."
> Angelle: "He is resyne! He is not here!;
> To his disciples he shalle apere—
> In Galilee thay shalle hym fynd!" (ll. 134–39)[43]

Although Mark was used in the liturgy of the Roman rite—only sixty-five times to Matthew's 130 times, to Luke's and John's one hundred times—Mark 16:1–7 was consistently used at Easter.[44] Further proof for this trope having its source in Mark 16 is found in Amalarius, who as Bishop of Metz (780?–850) produced the *Liber Officialis*. While detailing the medieval order of the mass, this work provides a sustained allegorical interpretation of the events of the mass.[45] His work was immensely popular, seeing three editions between 821 and 835. In his description and interpretation of the action of the Easter night mass, he refers specifically to Mark 16:1–8 as the reading, with the core of the *quem quaeritis* trope supplied by quotes from Mark (Mark 16:6). He supports his discussion of the Markan reading with single references to Matthew, Luke, and John, focusing especially on 16:8, "Et illae exeuntes, fugerunt de monumento, invaserat enim eas tremor et pavor; et nemini quicquam dixerunt; timebant enim" (And they went out and fled from the tomb; for trembling and astonishment seized them; and they said nothing to anyone, for they were afraid), which he explains away with Luke's, Matthew's, and John's versions.[46] The action of the mass described by Amalarius reveals the seed for the *quem quaeritis* trope. Medieval pageant drama, which developed from the liturgy, is yet another popular version of the entire Bible. The existence of the earliest trope and of intermediary versions of it up to the more developed cycle drama versions is convincing evidence of the role played by the Markan reading in the Easter liturgy in the development of medieval English drama in particular.

This liturgical contribution to Mark's reception history demonstrates the link between high and popular culture and connects contemporary cultural interests to established ecclesiastical practice. It is also an example of how the sacred text could in fact be revitalized in response to contemporary needs. The fact that the Roman rite remained fairly stable from the patristic era through the Middle Ages likewise assured unchanging continuity with the past. Mark's presence in the Easter liturgy proved to be the legacy of the early Church to specifically medieval interests and needs. More particularly, Mark's more mysterious conclusion served as the prompt for this early morning, central liturgical feast day.

In many instances, functioning as commentary in themselves, the medieval versions of the original biblical stories, whether in drama, stained glass windows, romances, or popular stories, became substitutes for the sacred text, whose meaning was never patently evident. The liturgy is one of the means to bring all social levels of the Christian community together (whether literate or illiterate, male or female, rich or poor, and so on), although unfortunately this has not always been the practice. By the late Middle Ages, reading Scriptures in Latin could hardly contribute to the general public's coming to know the actual words of the Bible. However, the monastic liturgical experimentation with the mass in the ninth century contributed to developing popular vernacular versions of the Bible through liturgical drama in the ensuing centuries, which assured that the stories, sentiments, and meaning of Scripture if not the actual words would inform the spiritual and imaginative lives of the laity. We know for certain that the *Aurora*, distributed in some 250 manuscripts, was used as a schoolbook and recommended to Louis, King of France, by Vincent of Beauvais as a suitable book for instructing the young.[47] Its translation in Mace de la Charite's Bible made it even more available to a non-Latin reading public.

Commentaries

Continuing the patristic concern with harmony, the medieval traditions of interpretation tended to treat the biblical narratives as a single *evangelium*. During the early Middle Ages, commentators also had their favorites, just as in the patristic period, and Matthew still came first in terms of the number of commentaries produced (thirteen); Luke and Mark had four each, and John seven. Paul received the most attention, with sixty-six commentaries on the letters (including Hebrews, which in the Middle Ages was ascribed to Paul).[48] Other books of the Bible were of immense interest, especially Genesis, the Song of Songs, and Psalms.

What strikes a contemporary reader immediately is that the medieval writers approached their text as if it were a series of pericopes to be systematically glossed. Writers proceeded verse by verse rather than advancing a "total" interpretation of the biblical text they commented on. In contrast to modern commentaries, particularly since the development of redaction criticism, which take up the overall strategy of the Gospels or the structure of the narratives as units in themselves, medieval commentaries attend to the text section by section, producing glosses rather than full interpretations. The idea of developing an extended argument like Pesch's *Das Markus-evangelium* is a comparatively recent development.

Glossa were used to comment on secular as well as sacred literature in the Middle Ages. They were usually associated with *verba* or philological issues as opposed to "sense" or "rhetorical-hermeneutical" issues,[49] although in the case of biblical *glossa*, all conventional criteria for responding to texts—including literal, historical, moral, allegorical, and anagogical—may apply. Medieval glossing, both Latin and interlanguage, is nonetheless primarily a philological activity. Defining "gloss" as "Glossa Graeca interpretatione linguae sortitur nomen" (the Greek term gloss really means "language"),[50] Isidore of Seville (570–636) emphasized this focus on philology, for "interpretatione" is closer in meaning to translation than interpretation. Many glosses use the word "interpretatione" to give a translation. These "running" commentaries had many advantages, for they allowed the reader, without having to refer to other books, to have a word translated, a reference to earlier commentaries summarized, or a difficult passage explained according to some earlier authority (see fig. 2, p. 23).[51] Mark does not differ from other evangelists in being singled out for marginal comments, although the few Aramaicisms unique to him in the gospels, "Abba" (14:36) and "talitha cumi" (5:41), were often noted.

During the twelfth and thirteenth centuries, to retain philological knowledge and enforce the continuing education of the clergy, a group of scholars brought together the *Glossa Ordinaria*, an attempt to replace all the glosses that had appeared on biblical texts since the Carolingian revival with one uniform version.[52] From the twelfth century on, working with a distinction between "glossa interlinearis" (interlinear glosses), which were usually philological, and "glossa marginalis" (marginal glosses), glosses included both erudite comments based on authoritative positions (*per usum*) as well as speculative and personal interpretations (*per ingenium*).[53] In an encyclopedic effort, the *Glossa* collected together all the brief comments on particular biblical passages made by the revered authorities of the Church, from the Fathers to the twelfth century.

A work epitomizing medieval approaches to gospel reading, the final section of Peter Comestor's *Historia Scholastica* (twelfth century), "Historia Evangelica," is a combination harmony, commentary, and collection of authoritative glosses on the entire Bible.[54] Petrus harmonizes the gospels, ending with the Ascension, so no specific Markan references appear in his work, but like other universal encyclopedic medieval histories (Hrabanus Maurus's *De Universo*, Alfonso X el Sabio's *General Estoria*, for example), he made use of all authorities available, whether canonical or non-canonical; besides the conventional patristic authorities, he even uses Josephus to explain the three "sectae" of ancient Judaism (Sadducee, Pharisee, and Essene). As he tells his harmonized gospel story, the "Historia Evangelica," he concludes each section with an *additio* that offers analysis and explanation of the gospel event he has just told, often with an emphasis on history. As with other popular texts in the Middle Ages, Peter also includes apocryphal material.

Peter Comestor is a critical source and milestone in the history of the reception of the Bible in the Middle Ages. One of the first books to be printed, the *Historia* is extant in innumerable manuscripts. In addition to being copied in Latin, it was widely dispersed in the vernacular languages. It was translated into Saxon, Old French, Portuguese, Castilian, Catalan, Czech, Old Norse, and Middle English, for example. Like everyone from Augustine on, Peter followed tradition, writing of Mark that he was Matthew's abbreviator.

Because Peter was used as a reference tool and a resource, the fact that he repeated Augustine's ancient refrain further cemented Mark's reputation as abbreviator and follower of Matthew. However, rather than representing a poverty of ideas, such references to the authorities attest to the medieval respect for earlier work to be preserved and repeated rather than dismissed as no longer useful—a kind of respect that the post-Enlightenment spirit, with its emphasis on originality at the expense of tradition, has condemned. This medieval habit reflects scholars' commitment to a continuing culture with a past and a future affirmed in an ongoing textual history. They were members of a long-standing community of interpreters working with what Brian Stock has called "communities of texts" in continuity with each other.[55] These commentaries and glosses testify to the gospel's ongoing canonical presence, a fact that was not in the least compromised, as commentators repeated Mark's connection to Peter, his sojourn in Alexandria as bishop, or that he had abbreviated Matthew.

The commentaries produced in the period, though dominated by the glossing technique, do, however, use a range of interpretive methods, the major ones of which show very careful reading. Cummeanus's, Bede's, and Albertus Magnus's commentaries, and Nicholas of Lyra's *Postillae* are most carefully produced and provide detailed interpretations of the gospel, adopting a variety of approaches depending on the passage under discussion. They are the works of outstanding scholars, using the most developed academic tools available to them. The Irish monk Cummeanus, for example, singled out all the pericopes unique to Mark and examined them according to their historical, allegorical, and moral implications. Albertus Magnus, a Dominican, both an innovator and scholar of the new interest in historical and scientific studies that emerged in the twelfth century, adapted the new approaches to his biblical work.

The earliest medieval commentary on Mark, "Commentarium in Evangelium Secundum Marcum" (c.650), though collected with Jerome's supposed writings by Migne, was probably authored by Cummeanus during the Irish textual renaissance of the first millenium.[56] The association with Jerome is not surprising, because stylistically the commentary is very well written, and the author is attentive to philological issues. Furthermore, except for Venerable Bede's commentary, it is the most carefully developed work on the Markan gospel from the patristic period to the commentary of Albertus Magnus.

After giving a conventional history of Mark, his association with Peter and Rome, and the tradition that he was bishop of Alexandria—which serves to explain why he is writing the commentary—Cummeanus interprets the gospel chapter by chapter, providing a literal, moral, or allegorical interpretation depending on the text. But his philological knowledge is expansive enough to include explanations for words, "parabole" (Ch. iv, col. 605), for example, for which he gives the Greek word, also defining it as the discrepancy between what constitutes an apparent and real meaning. To expand from the definition of "parable," he uses the stories of the bleeding woman and Jairus's daughter's resurrection as examples. He makes many references to Greek, including "kata markon," "Xristos," "hagiou," "pneumatos," "soter," and "evangelion" (Ch. I, col. 591). Also, showing his historical knowledge, he points out that "Messias" is Hebrew and so is "Jesua." He also makes use of other biblical texts, without providing the citation, as he develops his interpretations. (For example, to explain Mark's opening, he refers to the Apocalypse of John's promise, "Vincenti dabo ei edere de ligno, quod est in paradiso mei" [To him who is victorious I will give to eat from the tree that is in my paradise] [2:7]). He allegorizes a number of episodes in the gospel, including the food multiplications, Gerasene demoniac, and Peter's denial. He overcomes Peter's dramatic failure through a universal application of the story about the failure of faith, with "the cock" calling us all to reform. Less a word-for-word gloss and more attentive to narrative units, Cummeanus's commentary demonstrates the highly developed biblical scholarly activity in Ireland in the early Middle Ages. It also proves the originality of its scholars, for clearly Cummeanus did not share Augustine's notion that Mark has nothing to add. His commentary shows he believed that Mark makes a significant contribution.

The brief "Expositio in Argumentum Evangelii Marci" of Sedulius Scotus (c.858) is not a commentary, but a standard preface to the gospel that provides conventional information about it. Pseudo-Jerome's equally slight allegorical commentary offers one-to-one explanations for words, using "id est" (that is) to explain, for example, " 'serpentes,' id est, 'propter doctrinam hereticorum' " (col. 562) (serpents, that is, heretical teachings). But these two nondescript early works are followed by Bede's, a carefully argued and developed verse by verse gloss of the gospel, using the earlier work of the church fathers and bringing Matthew, Luke, and John into the discussion to "fill in" Mark's absences.

This habit that Bede shared with Albertus Magnus has the effect of eliding the differences among the Gospels. A good example is the opening to the gospel. Perhaps suggesting the influence of the harmonies, or at the very least Augustine's *De Consensu*, to compensate for Mark's abrupt opening, Bede glosses "Initium evangelii" (1:1), and so on, by introducing the openings of Matthew and Luke to give Matthew's genealogy: "Beginning the gospel of Jesus Christ, son of God. As it is written in the prophet Isaiah. We must collate this beginning of the Gospel of Mark with the beginning of Matthew which says, 'Book of the generation of Jesus Christ, son of David, son of Abraham.' "[57] He follows this with Matthew's, Luke's and John's openings, for contrast as well as completeness. For "Vox clamantis in deserto" (voice crying in the wilderness)(1:3), he uses John's "In principio erat verbum," and so on (In the beginning was the Word) (John 1:1) to explain that the "vox" (voice) of John the Baptist is so called because it precedes the "verbum" (Word). This variety of intertextual commentary, in which the other Gospels provide the explanations for the gospel under discussion, is one important feature of Bede's interpretive method, an effort to make the four one and the one four. When he makes use of earlier glosses or patristic authorities, he often identifies the author and the work by name, a trait he had in common with the medieval encyclopedists (Isidore, Hrabanus Maurus, and Vincent of Beauvais, for example). The effect of this elaboration of Mark is to efface the gospel's uniqueness and bring all current and former knowledge of the Bible into the circle of universal knowledge, in essence continuing the work of Augustine's *De Consensu Evangelistarum* to make all the Bible conform to a harmonious single version.

In addition to these features, Bede combines Augustinian allegory with a literal (philological) and moral exegesis. For example, showing that this highly educated medieval commentator seeks to transcend the literal meaning for the miracle narratives, Bede allegorizes the story of the curing of Peter's mother-in-law (as Jesus cures fornication, impurity, lust, evil desires, and cupidity, which are idolatrous enslavements, all "figured" in the fever of the body); similarly, he allegorizes the food multiplication stories; for Peter's denial (denying not only that he knew Christ but that he was a Christian)[58] and Judas's betrayal ("infelix Iudas") (unhappy Judas),[59] he offers moral judgments. His interest in expounding the literal level shows his concern with philological issues, for he is quick to discuss specific language questions. About Levi, he writes, "And passing by, he saw Levi, son of Alpheus, seated in the custom-house, and said to him, 'Follow me' "(Et cum praeteriret vidit Levi Alphei sedentem ad teloneum at ait illi: Sequere me) (2:14). Using Matthew and Luke for support, he links the word "teloneum" to the Greek "telos," saying it means the place where taxes are paid.[60] The word "abba" (father) (14:35) he glosses as the Hebrew word for Greek and Latin "pater."[61] When the servant girl reminds Peter that he is a Galilean, Bede explains that although Galilee and Jerusalem had essentially the same language, Hebrew, the provinces had slightly different dialects.[62] Bede's analysis of these philological features shows his interest in the literal level of the text. His application of an allegorical interpretation actually works to extract a literal meaning. Finally, his commentary continues to Mark 16:20 with no reference to any doubts about this ending for the gospel. On the contrary, he specifically uses the post-Resurrection scenes of the other Gospels to support the longer ending and show how its events are corroborated by Matthew, Luke, and John. This ending emphasizes that Augustine's "agreement" still prevailed. It also affirms that medieval Christian learned understanding continued this tradition of a single *evangelium*.

Reproducing the gospel in its entirety—surrounded by the other Gospels, patristic comments, and his own work as additional commentary—Bede's is the first major commentary on Mark. It is the product of careful scholarship and shows the best skills of medieval commentary; it is balanced in its interest in allegorical, philological, and moral commentary. It takes the original text as its starting point to produce a compendious glossing of Mark's text. When Erasmus wrote his *Paraphrase,* he used Bede's commentary as well as Nicholas of Lyra's, Euthymius's, and Theophylactus's.

The second major medieval commentary is the work of Albertus Magnus, whose vast biblical exegetical work covers all the Gospels and a good portion of the First Testament. It reflects the new interest in the literal sense of the Scriptures in the thirteenth century as well as Albertus's doctrinal and philosophical exegetical style, in which he makes use of the natural sciences and provides moral applications.[63] Like Bede's, Albertus's commentary is comprehensive; in fact it is even more detailed than the earlier work. He proceeds as follows: First he cites an entire chapter of Mark, beginning at 1:1; this is succeeded by a complete verse and a general statement about it, which is followed by a word by word or phrase by phrase gloss on every phrase in the chapter. Adopting allegorical, moral, literal, and anagogical approaches to interpretation, he uses earlier Church writers like John Chrysostom, Dionysius, and Gregory to help explain figural and literal meanings in the Markan text. He is interested in philological issues, like the meaning of words in certain contexts, "parabolis" (4:2), for example. He explains that Jesus' entrance into a "synagogue," a Jewish institution that his audience may not have understood, has a historical meaning, but that it also refers to his entrance into a solemn place (3:1). He allegorizes textual details to show

how the Bible supports contemporary monastic practice, making John's "vestitus pili cameli" (dressed in a camel skin) represent *asperitas, humilitas,* and
paupertas (austerity, humility, and poverty). John's "zona pellicea" (girdle of
hide) (Mark 1:6) represents chastity, monastic continence, castigation of the
flesh of concupiscence, and the memory of death. "Talitha cumi" (5:41),
Mark's use of Aramaic, he explains as Hebrew words calling the girl to life,
referring to Ephesians 5:14 and Romans 4:17 to connect this resurrection to
all risings.

A good example of Albertus's allegorizing technique is his interpretation of the food multiplication story at Mark 8:1–3: here the seven loaves
become the seven virtues.[64] But he doesn't stop with one possible allegorical
meaning. He also includes the possibility that the seven loaves represent the
seven sacraments (baptism, confirmation, penance, eucharist, matrimony,
extreme unction, and holy orders) or the seven effects of the Word of God,
for those who partake. In Albertus's particular case, these allegorizations
reflect his effort to rationalize the problems posed by the literal level of the
text (e.g., miraculous stories that are not consonant with natural science and
philosophy.)[65] As in Bede, Albertus brings Mark's puzzling ending into the
context of all the gospel endings and of Acts, to emphasize their common
sense. His interpretation, besides being completely achronistic as well as
anachronistic, demonstrates his interest in bringing the gospel into line with
the central teachings of the Church (the established seven sacraments, for
example) and the monastic lifestyle as they stood in the thirteenth century.
It is clear that Albertus Magnus makes use of a variety of techniques to
interpret the text, including those ruled by philology, history, and allegory.
Like Bede, he does not read the gospel as a narrative; rather he comments on
each part according to his chosen criteria, remaking the text to contemporary
ecclesiastical interests and to established Church teachings, while introducing his own monastic convictions in his allegorical and moral interpretations.

A student of Albertus, Thomas Aquinas, followed in the footsteps of
the church fathers. He produced a commentary on Matthew and one on
John, and chose a less original path than his teacher for the remainder of the
Bible. Typical of the medieval encyclopedic mentality, he collated all the
church fathers' extant remarks on the four Gospels in his *Catena Aurea,*
which became a standard scholarly reference work. Erasmus, for example,
used this work in his *paraphrases.*[66]

Erasmus's work is akin to earlier medieval encyclopedic activity, for his
approach to his subject was compendious, including paraphrases of all the
Gospels, an edition of the New Testament in Greek, an *annotation* of the
text, and his own Latin translation. Likewise, in the tradition of medieval
exegetes, he made use of all the intellectual and scholarly resources available
to him to offer a fully authoritative interpretation of the Gospels, supported

by his own reforming theology. But he enriched his *paraphrases* with the newly recovered Greek and Latin pagan and patristic texts.

The last of his *paraphrases* is the one on Mark (1523). "Paraphrase" is really a far-fetched description for what Erasmus does in this work, for he moves far from the Markan text. Rather than commenting on each verse, as in the earlier commentary style, Erasmus writes an extended critique of each chapter of the gospel. He develops a complicated statement of his own, using the Markan text to express his humanist and spiritual interests. He applies his vast knowledge of many earlier commentaries and sermons (his work is a good source for identifying the commentaries on Mark from the end of the patristic period to his own work, showing he knew the work of Petrus Chrysologus [d.450], Fulgentius [d.533], Hrabanus Maurus [d.856], Bernard of Clairvaux [c.1090–1155], Hugh of St. Cher, Nicholas of Lyra, and Euthymius), the other Gospels, and classical references from Plato to Seneca, Horace, and Ovid to develop his rewriting of the gospel.

Commenting on Mark's opening, Erasmus begins, "It is natural for all mortals to seek happiness," an Augustinian echo defining true happiness as the love of God. This is expanded into several paragraphs leading to the discussion of John the Baptist and the meaning of his ministry: "John taught that the teacher must acquire authority, not by the splendour of his garment or the pomp of his life, but by the integrity of his character."[67] In contrast to Albertus Magnus, who treated John the Baptist as a model for monastic asceticism, Erasmus's analysis and emphasis show that he aligned himself with the reforming spirit of his times. He confronted the opulent living standards of those who held ecclesiastical authority and focused on a spiritual interpretation, recommending a simple and austere life that would benefit his readers. Though he notes that Jerome's text and other codices end at 16:8 in the *Annotations* and in his edition of the Greek New Testament, Erasmus concludes his *Paraphrase on Mark* by making use of the other Gospels and the longer ending of Mark. Essentially, like Augustine before him, Erasmus demonstrates Mark's agreement with the other Gospels. Also like Augustine, he uses the Markan text as the basis of his own theological agenda, addressed to "Christian soldiers" who are encouraged to reform.

Erasmus left the *Paraphrase on Mark* to the last because he shared the common prejudice that it was an abbreviation of Matthew.[68] He dedicated it to a ruling prince—Francis I—just as he had done with the earlier *paraphrases* on the other Gospels. This dedication testifies to a dramatic patronage shift. As the recipient of the commentary, the sovereign became not only the inspiration for the author, but the preserver of the "sacred" work for the public good, an action that demonstrates the "absolute power of the prince."[69]

Erasmus identifies his *Paraphrase on Mark* as "a saleable object,"[70] testifying to the technological and economic revolution under way. Patronage had moved from the monasteries and ecclesiastical control to powerful monarchs, but Erasmus's comment suggests a future buyer's patronage. Such a change—the simultaneous consequence of technological developments and early capitalism resulting in cheaper publication and distribution of books, the circulation of money, and the expansion of a reading public—was about to alter radically the consumption of biblical texts.

Apart from Erasmus's study of Mark, Reformation scholars did not reverse Mark's neglect. Indeed, theological interests in this period turned attention further from Mark. Among the reformers, Wyclif (1329–1384)—who belongs to an earlier period and who completed a lost *postilla* on the entire Bible—Luther (1483–1546), Colet (1466?–1519), Calvin (1509–1564), and Melanchthon (1497–1560), for example, there is no shift in attitudes toward Mark. Zwingli (1484–1531) did write a commentary on Mark, using the tradition that Mark abbreviated Matthew to emphasize that "humans," not God, wrote the Gospels.[71] For Wyclif, John emerges as the favorite gospel,[72] as it was for Calvin. Calvin writes, "When we want to read in Matthew and the rest that Christ was given to us by the Father, we should first learn from John to what end He was manifested."[73] Following the pattern of the patristic era, in Calvin's harmony he quotes Mark four times, in contrast to thirty-seven for John, thirty-two for Matthew, and sixteen for Luke. Philip Melanchthon produced work on John, Paul, and the other Gospels, but he ignored Mark.[74] Luther produced volumes of biblical commentary, covering the Old and Second Testament, and wrote three volumes on John alone, but of the synoptics, he wrote only on the Sermon on the Mount and the Magnificat, ignoring Mark completely.[75] Even his large collection of sermons shows no evidence of interest in Mark, other than the conventional remark that he was the abbreviator of Matthew and had been Peter's amanuensis. In fact, as part of his attack on the Roman Church, which he contrasts with the superior churches of Alexandria and Antioch, Luther cites the tradition that "St. Mark" became bishop of Alexandria.[76] Paul, always a strong presence in the canon, especially occupied the interests of the reformers. Colet,[77] Calvin, Luther, and Zwingli all wrote copiously on Paul. John, however, overtook Matthew among the reformers. Considering the reverence the reformers awarded to the patristic period over the scholastics, as part of their interest in the recovery of the early Christian experience and learning, it should not surprise us that the reformers adopted patristic opinions of Mark.

In contrast to the patristic period, where the literary culture of the Bible remained primarily in the control of authoritative readers of the Church, the Bible in the Middle Ages, while maintaining its priority among the intellectual elite, also crossed into popular culture, particularly as the vernacular languages emerged as viable literary media and Latin became associated only with high culture. Vernacular versions of the Bible, whether as romances, chansons de geste, or pageant dramas, represent a crossing over of the high and vernacular cultures, for popular interests inform them and they are written in the popular languages, although monks and clergy may have written many of them. While some Church intellectuals were attentive to Mark in the Middle Ages, probably because of the lack of earlier commentaries, popular versions of the Bible further undermined Mark's presence in the canon. The fourfold witness, transformed for general consumption by Peter Comestor or the harmonies, existed as a single *evangelium*. In contrast, the apocryphal gospels, systematically excluded by the official Church but powerful presences in medieval popular culture, infiltrated the emerging vernacular literary cultures. Differences between high and low and canonical and non-canonical disappeared in these medieval re-creations of the Bible as the distinctions the Fathers had striven so ardently to establish faded. But Mark had no significant role in these popularizing efforts. Even though in the case of the drama his gospel formed the basis of the imaginative developments, and the concept of a "life of Jesus" forecasts later historical inquiries when Mark would become the focus of interest, the medieval popular versions of the Bible eliminated distinctions among the gospels. The sophisticated reading strategies of learned medieval writers worked to make the biblical stories fit into an unbroken pattern of salvation history, in which the Bible was the medium of God's word. But Mark's fragmented version of the Jesus story disappeared into this circumscribed, complete vision. Not until the eighteenth century, when this imagined mirror image of an orderly cosmos was cracked, would Mark begin to be read on its own.

CHAPTER 4

"Taking the Text Captive": Philology and Presence

> . . . he captured the ideas and transposed them into his own language, by right of conquest.
>
> Jerome, Letter 57, 6[1]

> Thus it happened that even the Sacred Scripture . . . was set forth in one language, but so that it could be spread conveniently through all the world it was scattered far and wide in the various languages of translators.
>
> Augustine, *De Doctrina Christiana* II.V.6[2]

I n exploring the monumental cultural effort to make the Gospel of Mark available to all readers through translations and editions from the patristic era to the Renaissance, this chapter examines the emergence of philology as a reading strategy in the reception of Mark. Like the work of the church fathers in the patristic period, particularly as seen in the contrast between Augustine and Jerome, these translating and transforming acts launched directly from the words in the text expose the difference between doctrinal and philological interests, often referred to as the critical/creative dichotomy in biblical scholarship, an ongoing binary opposition in hermeneutical and translating activities. Doctrinalists, interpreting the text to support current or established teachings or convictions choose the creative path, whereas philologists, attempting to make the text speak for itself, adopt the critical method. Long before the concept of "sociology" as a discipline emerged, biblical translators were aware of a "sociosemantic" approach to translating meaning,[3] in which the social sense of words had to be transferred into another linguistic society.

Though Mark, as part of the fourfold witness, was not the specific interest of translations or editions, the record of these reflects Mark's canonical history, for although some Gospels were translated separately, Mark was never excluded from translations of the New Testament. Furthermore, Mark's specifically philological characteristics (frequent Aramaicisms, ungrammatical Greek, Latinisms, paratactic sentences, and *vulgar* vocabulary) posed particular challenges for translators, who, in reacting to the gospel's style, often felt compelled to correct it. "Humanism" reintroduced philology and refocused attention on it as it was practiced by Jerome, continued by Alcuin, and regenerated by Nicholas of Lyra. In fact, philology became the soul of the act of interpretation in the early modern period, leading to new editions of the Latin Bible based on the original Hebrew and Greek and to vernacular translations directly from the original languages. This shift in interpretive focus, though not directly affecting the reception of the Gospel of Mark, shows the emergence of "historical" interests, a significant first step toward the eventual discovery of the Gospel of Mark as a central witness to the early strata of the New Testament.

In contrast to harmonies, verse translations, and Peter Comestor's *Historia Scholastica*, translations and commentaries do not elide differences between the Gospels to create a single *evangelium*, for they remain decidedly Matthew, Mark, Luke, and John, the canonical Gospels. Translation and editing are dominated by philological interests in which *verbum* (word) and *sensum* (sense) must reach a tentative agreement, though most translators have had to compromise one or the other in an effort to achieve this truce. Thus while ecclesiastical, hermeneutical, and rhetorical interests dominated patristic reading habits, often at the expense of philology, philological "prejudices" ruled the activities of translators and editors from the patristic to the Reformation periods, although these too were guided by rhetoric and hermeneutics.

Philology

The widespread loss of Hebrew and Greek in the western Middle Ages made philological studies difficult if not impossible, and the period struggled with the literary problems that naturally emerged with the decline of philological tools. Latin commentators were puzzled by Aramaicisms in Mark's gospel particularly, but this was just one of the textual problems that arose. Bibles like the Lindisfarne and Rushworth, with their interlingual, interlinear glossing, testify to the difficulties even with the Latin text that perplexed the Anglo-Saxon Christian community. Inspired by Jerome's earlier activity, those who were interested in philology maintained the literal and historical studies that supported efforts both to establish a reliable text and to reconstruct the chronological events in the life of Jesus. From the sixth century onward, a vigorous monastic philological effort thrived in Ireland;[4] in the ninth century Alcuin attempted to restore Jerome's edition of the Bible, which became the dominant version until Erasmus[5] and the Spanish Theodulf, bishop of Orleans, privately undertook editing the Latin text.[6] Nicholas of Lyra's *Postilla* refocused attention on philological aspects of the Bible.[7] All these efforts eventually led to Lorenzo Valla's *Collatio Novi Testamenti* (1449–1450)[8] and to Erasmus's *Novum Instrumentum Omne* (1516).[9] The reasons for these philological activities are diverse. Like Pope Damasus's earlier request of Jerome, Charlemagne had political reasons to order Alcuin's new edition of the Bible, for his political ambitions were aligned with his cultural program, through which he sought to guarantee textual uniformity for his entire realm.[10] Theodulf was engaged in a private undertaking. Nicholas of Lyra (1270–1334), a French Franciscan, was acting independently as a serious scholar of biblical philology, intent on appealing to Jews to convert to Christianity by adopting common interpretive habits. Valla, like Erasmus, was inspired by a sincere scholarly interest to restore the "original" text. Nonetheless, a desire for philological accuracy inspired all of their work. The advent of the printing press in 1456 heightened the need for an accurate text that could be readily reprinted as it escalated the desire to finally settle ongoing textual problems.

From the thirteenth century onward, renewed interest in the original languages of the Bible contributed to further expansion of philological approaches to reading it. In the Middle Ages, the Latin Bible was authoritative throughout the West. Yet in 1311 the Council of Vienne, under the pressure of Ramon Lull, had decreed endowed chairs of oriental languages (Hebrew, Greek, Arabic, and Chaldean) in the central studia of western Christendom[11] and ordered Hebrew exegesis when possible. The Council of Vienne laid the groundwork for the later philological revival of the Renaissance, when the Bible would be reestablished with greater textual accuracy, based on knowledge of the original Greek and Hebrew texts.

Paving the way for the humanist, philologically dominated approach to exegesis, Nicholas of Lyra's *Postilla* rejected the traditional medieval style of glossing. Nicholas knew Hebrew, and his *Postillae perpetuae in universa Biblia* (1322–1330), a commentary on the entire Bible, gives priority to the literal meaning of words, a radical shift from the usual interests in symbolic and moral aspects of the text, although for him the "literal" equaled the spiritual sense[12] (see fig. 6). Though the *Postilla* on Mark begins with the conventional prologue, explaining Mark's relationship to Peter and why Mark is associated with a lion, Nicholas's philological interests break ground for medieval glossing, for he is primarily interested in the historical and philological meaning of the texts. Noting the corruptions in the Latin text before him, he complains in the second prologue, "The literal sense has been obscured because of the mode of exposition others have left us." This may have been because of copying errors, the inexperience of the correctors, the nature of the translation itself, or lack of knowledge of the original lan-

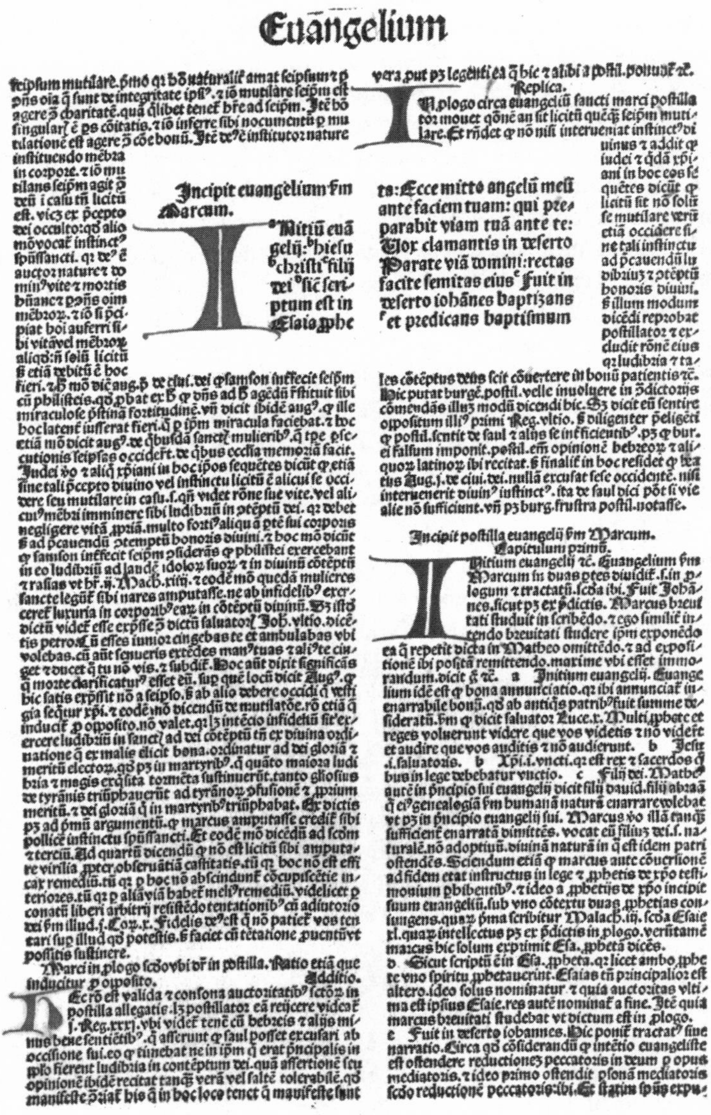
Euangelium

Incipit euangelium s̄m Marcum.

Initiū euā gelij: ihesu christi filij dei sicut scriptum est in Esaia p̄phe ta: Ecce mitto angelū meū ante faciem tuam: qui preparabit viam tuā ante te: Vox clamantis in deserto Parate viā domini: rectas facite semitas eius. Fuit in deserto iohānes baptizans et predicans baptismum

Fig. 6. Nicholas of Lyra's postilla style in the opening to the Gospel of Mark.

guages.[13] This "other" mode multiplied the mystical senses and ignored the literal. Nicholas recommended consulting Hebrew scholars in particular for enriched literal readings. His own knowledge of Hebrew made him able to distinguish, for example, between Hebrew and Chaldean (Aramaic) in his explanation of the word "Abba," "father," a word that occurs only in Mark (of the Gospels) and that Jerome had carried over to the Latin. Nicholas offered a running commentary on the literal level of the narrative, writing, for example, on 16:1–8, precisely who the three women were who arrived at the tomb, that they wondered how they would move the stone, and pointing out which day of the week it was since the Jewish setting changed the day of the sabbath. He avoided all allegories. Valued by humanists and reformers alike because of their philological interests, Nicholas's *Postilla* was the first medieval biblical commentary to be printed, showing how closely aligned the changing technology of print was with the resurgence of philological studies.[14] Establishing the value of the literal level of the text, Nicholas's work led to the saying, "Si Lyra non lyrasset / Lutherus non delirasset."[15] In fact, Nicholas's explanation of his interpretive convictions often sound similar to the reformers' notion of "sola scriptura."

During the early Renaissance, with widespread academic access to Hebrew and Greek, philological interests took control of biblical studies. The commentary style of the early humanists transformed medieval textual methodologies. In contrast to the medieval multifold exegesis, the radical change introduced by the early humanist Lorenzo Valla's *Collatio* divorced philology from other kinds of interpretation and commentary. This text was attentive *only* to philological questions. Erasmus, following Valla's lead, divided his philological work from his commentary work, the former focused on textual accuracy and meaning, while the latter broke with the rhetoric of "glossing" of the medieval period to advance a new rhetorical strategy for commentary.

Jerome became the hero of the philologists of the period, though his work came under the closest scrutiny it had experienced for a thousand years.[16] This was partly because his letters were retrieved—and edited by no less a scholar than Erasmus—and partly because scholars had greater access to vast numbers of biblical manuscripts. The first major assaults on the authority of Jerome's Bible came from an orthodox Italian humanist, Lorenzo Valla (1407–1457), whose philological studies led him to recognize that there were serious errors in Jerome's translation. These philological studies, with their emphasis on the literal level of the words in the text, provided the foundations for wholly new approaches to reading the Bible. And the Gospel of Mark was the most important beneficiary of this new focus.

Scholars have argued that it was indeed the printing press that forced this radical new attention to the letter, one of the invention's primary consequences. Even more importantly, the technological revolution made mass production possible, and less expensive books made the Bible available to more and more readers. From the twelfth century to the fourteenth, parchment was gradually replaced by paper, a material introduced by the Arabs, who had acquired the technology of making it from the Chinese. The widespread use of paper and the emergence of the technology of the printing press opened up the possibility of mass-produced, cheap books, as bookmaking moved from monastic control to a lay commercial enterprise. The Bible was, of course, the most printed book in the period, which we can mark as initiating the Age of the Reader, although the age was dominated by the text itself.[17]

With its focus on philological issues, Valla's *Collatio Novi Testamenti* represents a striking breakthrough in biblical studies. As discussed above, medieval commentators had not been oblivious to these concerns, but *sensum* generally took precedence over *verbum*. The *Collatio* assembles all the Gospels, in their New Testament order, as well as the Acts of the Apostles, Paul's letters, and the canonical letters. Valla compared Jerome's New Testament with the Greek, noting all the word-for-word deviations. Matthew received the most extensive editorial overhaul and Mark, because of its abbreviated size, the most restricted. Valla's purpose, as he announced it in his first preface ("Praefationis Forma Antiquior"),[18] was to examine the philological accuracy of Jerome's text, on the same grounds that Jerome himself used a thousand years earlier. Alluding to Jerome's and Augustine's concerns about the numerous versions of the Bible in the fourth century, Valla emphatically writes, "If it is true after four hundred years, a stream of confusion flowed, how extraordinary, on the other hand, if after a thousand years—indeed there are so many from Jerome to this age—that this stream, never cleaned from the slime in any direction, has collected squalor?"[19]

And degeneration he did indeed find, although he failed to recognize that the Greek text was just as subject to degradation as Jerome's had been over the thousand years of its copying history. Although Valla followed the established order of the texts in each gospel, he did not necessarily cover every line. His collation of Mark, for example, begins at 1:12 ("Et statim Spiritus eum expulit in desertum") (And immediately the Spirit drove him into the desert). This is a particularly interesting verse because Valla's comments radically contrast with those of Bede and Albertus Magnus. In the tradition of earlier commentators, Bede expanded his discussion of Mark, using Luke and Matthew to discuss the temptation of Jesus in the desert for forty days; Albertus Magnus, on the other hand, using the text to support his own monastic ideology and convictions about the interrelationships of all biblical texts and the Judeo-Christian tradition, scrutinized the passage linked to quotes from Ezekiel, John Chrysostom, Psalms, Romans, and Jerome among others, to talk about forty days of fasting, Moses' sojourn in the desert that prefigured Jesus' later perfection, and the desert as a quiet place where the mind is not troubled. Both writers made full use of numerous textual interpretive approaches, including allegory, typology, anagogy, and history. But Valla was concerned with the accuracy of word choices and tenses in Jerome's text.[20] His comments show that he chose to collate codices, probing accuracy of word choice and grammar and analyzing lexical and syntactic anomalies in the text. Valla has no comments on typology, allegory, or history. Rather, he concentrated steadfastly on the literal level of the text, which from Origen, Jerome, and Augustine forward had been the philological.

In the *Collatio*, Valla isn't even necessarily interested in the literal meaning. He focuses primarily on discovering what the accurate text would read, providing the Greek equivalent to expose every problem he finds in Jerome's text. One example is at Mark 4:38, "Master, does it not perturb you that we are perishing?" Valla writes, "Accurately in the Greek, it is not 'is it not a concern to you,' but rather, 'do you not care that we perish?' "[21] Although Valla set out to systematically expose the textual problems in the *Vulgate*, he nonetheless agreed with Jerome on the ending to Mark. In contrast to all the harmonies, commentaries, and translations from the fourth through the fourteenth centuries, Valla returned to Jerome's conclusion for Mark at 16:8. Thus with the new resource (the Greek text) for textual analysis available to him, Valla abandoned the traditional approach to commentary by adopting the single philological interest that would form the basis of an accurate text (see fig. 7). Jerome's conviction about taking the text captive certainly characterizes Valla's valiant new approach to biblical studies. In shedding a thousand-year tradition of considering numerous levels of texts when commenting on them, he seized the "book" itself, systematically showing that the very foundation for all these many "significations" was insubstantial.

Like Lessing later, who would see in Reimarus's *Apology* that a new path had been opened in biblical studies, Erasmus recognized a radical development in biblical studies when he came across Valla's *Collatio*. Like Jerome earlier, Erasmus had ostensibly abandoned secular literary interests in favor of theological scholarship, but philology offered him the opportunity to use his secular literary skills in his religious scholarship, and to bring Jerusalem and Athens together in his professional and private life. In 1500 he began to study Greek, so that he could dedicate himself more accurately to his biblical scholarship. He produced a new translation of the Latin Bible, and his *Novum Instrumentum*, a Greek New Testament, became the most used text of the Greek New Testament until the nineteenth century. The *Annotations*, the Latin Bible, and the Greek New Testament were published together in 1516 as *Novum Instrumentum Omne*.

Both Erasmus's *Annotations* and the paraphrases on the four Gospels were new genres for biblical commentary. The *Annotations* make use of Nicholas of Lyra's *postilla* style, even though Erasmus was often harsh on

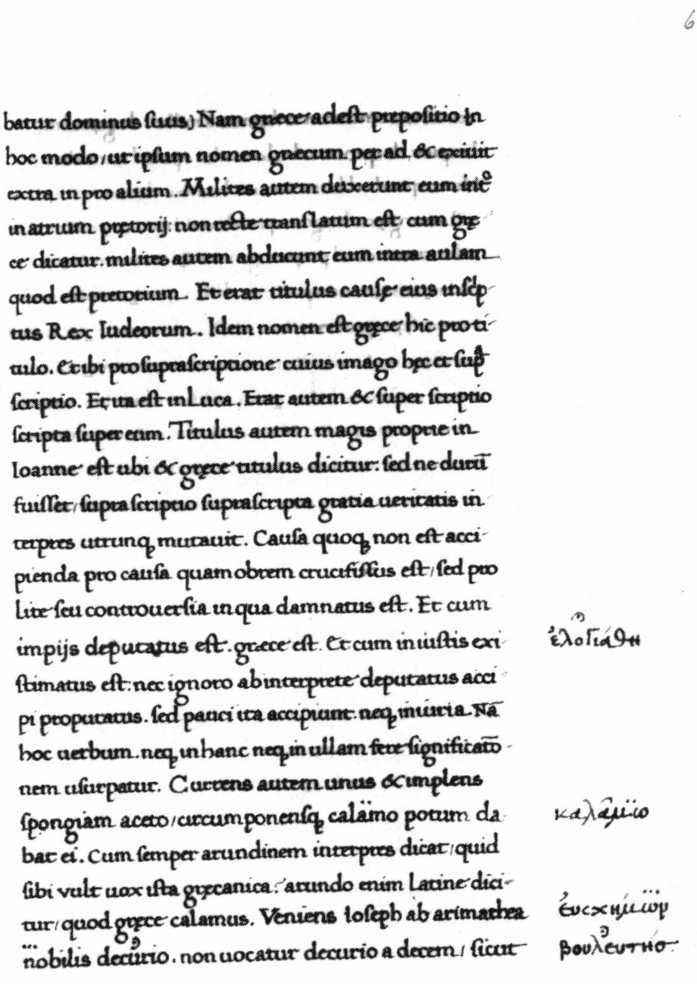

batur dominus suus) Nam grece adest prepositio in
hoc modo, ut ipsum nomen grecum per ad, & exiuit
extra in pro alium. Milites autem duxerunt eum inté
in atrium pretorij: non recte translatum est cum grece dicatur. milites autem abducunt eum intra aulam
quod est pretorium. Et erat titulus cause eius insép-
tus Rex Iudeorum. Idem nomen est grece hic pro titulo. Et ibi pro suprascriptione cuius imago hec et sup
scriptio. Et ita est in Luca. Erat autem & super scriptio
scripta super eum. Titulus autem magis proprie in
Ioanne est ubi & grece titulus dicitur: sed ne durú
fuisset, supra scriptio suprascripta gratia ueritatis in
terpres utrunq, mutauit. Causa quoq, non est acci-
pienda pro causa quam obrem crucifixus est, sed pro
lite seu controuersia in qua damnatus est. Et cum
impijs deputatus est. grece est. Et cum iniustis exi-
stimatus est. nec ignoro ab interprete deputatus acci
pi pro putatus. sed pauci ita accipiunt. neq, iniuria. Na
hoc uerbum. neq, in hanc neq, in ullam fere significatio
nem usurpatur. Currens autem unus & implens
spongiam aceto, circumponensq, calamo potum da
bat ei. Cum semper arundinem interpres dicat, quid
sibi uult uox ista grecanica, arundo enim Latine dicitur, quod grece calamus. Veniens Ioseph ab arimathea
nobilis decurio. non uocatur decurio a decem, sicut

ἐλογιάθη

καλάμῳ

εὐσχήμων

βουλευτής

Fig. 7. Valla, *Collatio*. The last verses of the Gospel of Mark, showing Valla's focus on
philological issues and the conclusion of the gospel at 16:8.

centurio a centum et tribunus a mille, de græca lingua
loquor. de quo uocabulo in alio opere latius diximus.
Nunc quod ad hunc attinet locum, decurio est ipsa &
testante græca lingua, qui ad consilium rei publicę suę
admittitur & id propter generis splendorem, siquidem
plebeij admitti non possunt. Illud quoq nobilis non
minus sepe pro honestus, idest honoratus, q̄ per nobilis
transfertur. Et accessito centurione interrogauit eum
si iam mortuus esset. græce est si dudum siue iam du
dum mortuus esset. Nam & dudum & iamdudum
huic conueniet loco. Inuaserat enim eas pauor, &
tremor. grece est ceperat siue habebat eas tremor &
ecstasis.

Laurentij Vallensis uiri clarissimi Collatio euan
gelij Marci cum græca ueritate finit. Eiusdem col
latio euangelij Lucę incipit.

Lyra's work; likewise the paraphrases show some deference to the glossing style of the commentary tradition, but Erasmus broke away from the conventions followed in these earlier works. He looked to the patristic era for hermeneutical guidance and more or less ignored scholasticism, though he used Thomas's *Catena Aurea*. Yet in contrast to Augustine, his interpretive methodology was ruled by a grammatical theology rather than a desire to prove the accuracy of traditional views. This does not mean that he abandoned allegory; drawing attention to the fact that according to the Gospels, allegory is Christ's pedagogical technique, Erasmus argued that "allegoria" is a single-layered metaphorical vehicle as well as a sustained figurative interpretation.[22] Nonetheless, though he, in a sense, finessed allegory as an interpretive method as it was practiced in medieval commentaries, he found in the church fathers, particularly Augustine and Jerome, a justification for the value of "profane" knowledge and ancient philosophy for which Augustine proved a most worthwhile source.[23] In contrast to all medieval commentators, Erasmus followed Valla's path by dividing the theological study of the Bible into philological interpretation (editing, translations, and annotations) and hermeneutics (spiritual and moral meaning). But he sought to overcome traditional biblical interpretation by theologizing philology. This was not a "theological grammar" as adopted by Hugh of St. Cher (1200–1263), who was one of his sources[24] and whose *Postilla* continued to be printed into the Reformation period[25]—for Erasmus avoided fanciful, medieval etymologies in favor of literal accuracy. Committed to a simplified version of Christianity, Erasmus shows in the *Annotations* that his goal was to establish a text unencumbered by doctrinal convictions, but ruled by a philological theology that could revive the Christianity of the early Church.

His deference to establishment voices (medieval authorities that went back to Augustine and Jerome) obscured the novelty and challenges of his approaches.[26] Like Origen and Jerome, Erasmus possessed exceptional language talents and an acerbic tendency, which are reflected in his *Annotations*—a systematic analysis of the textual condition of the Latin New Testament collated against Greek and Latin manuscripts.[27] Naming earlier Greek and Latin commentators in his marginal comments on Mark, he makes references to their work, but not necessarily to cite them as authorities, as in medieval glosses. For example, though he repeats Augustine's remark that Mark is the epitomizer of Matthew,[28] he also writes, "Hieronymus memoria lapsus" (Jerome's memory slipping),[29] though he accepts Jerome's authority for the shorter ending of Mark, "Saint Jerome . . . indicates that Mark ends here."[30] He also makes his own marginal observations based on his philological studies, such as "Christus raro dictus deus" (Christ rarely called God).[31]

Erasmus's *Annotations* created a furor, for in insisting on recovering the purity of the letter, he launched a frontal attack on medieval exegetical habits. Putting grammar at the center of the hermeneutical process, making the "Word" *sermo* rather than *logos,* Christ became for him the "grammar of many meanings," in an ever shifting interpretation of the relationship of God to man and man to God.[32] Though, as I have pointed out, philology was never ignored among patristic and medieval scholars, these earlier writers tended to "interpret" (that is, make decisions about textual transcription and translation, glossing, and explanation) the Bible from the perspective of Christian dogma or current Christian practices. By contrast, in a major hermeneutical paradigm shift, Erasmus laid out a system for reading the Bible that put the "objective" text before tradition, dogma, and common practice.[33]

Valla had set the trend toward philological approaches to the Gospels, Erasmus followed his lead, and these philological approaches reached their climax with another project of humanism: the Spanish Complutensian polyglot Bible (1520), with Latin in the middle, and Hebrew and Greek on either side for the First Testament, and Greek and Latin for the New Testament. The *Vulgate*'s position shows that it still held authority with editors, although the appearance of the Bible points to the *Vulgate*'s future demise and to the emerging reign of philological approaches to the Bible. From Erasmus on, biblical scholars became obsessed with the annotation style as well as with philological problems, so much so that in England, for example, supported by the new print technology, they produced editions of the Bible that attempted to reestablish the Gothic and Anglo- Saxon texts or that contrasted the Roman Catholic with the Anglican translations to highlight doctrinal disputes between the two strands of Christianity (see figs. 8, 9, and 10). Such philological commitments in the form of close reading of the texts and interest in original sources, once aligned with a scientific approach to history, could not fail to relegate the *Vulgate* to the status of anachronism and lead to greater attention to individual works within the Bible as separate texts with their own rhetorical strategies. Mark, of course, would be the beneficiary of these efforts.

However, this philological work on the part of the humanists did not overturn official Church positions. The Council of Trent (1546) confirmed the *Vulgate* as the only official Church Bible, on the grounds that Jerome's text, once revised, was still the closest to the original Bible.[34] Though the Council did not draw any conclusions about the Greek or Hebrew texts of the Bible, it did reaffirm the authority of the *Vulgate,* and Pope Sixtus V and Clement VIII commissioned a revision based on a collation against the Greek and Hebrew texts. A new edition was published in 1590, with further corrections under Clement VIII in 1592, and even more in 1593. With specific reference to the Gospel of Mark, the Council of Trent ignored the scholarly opinions of earlier authorities—including Origen, Jerome, and Eusebius—as well as the textual work of Valla and Erasmus. In keeping with the Lutheran and King James versions of the Bible, the council concluded

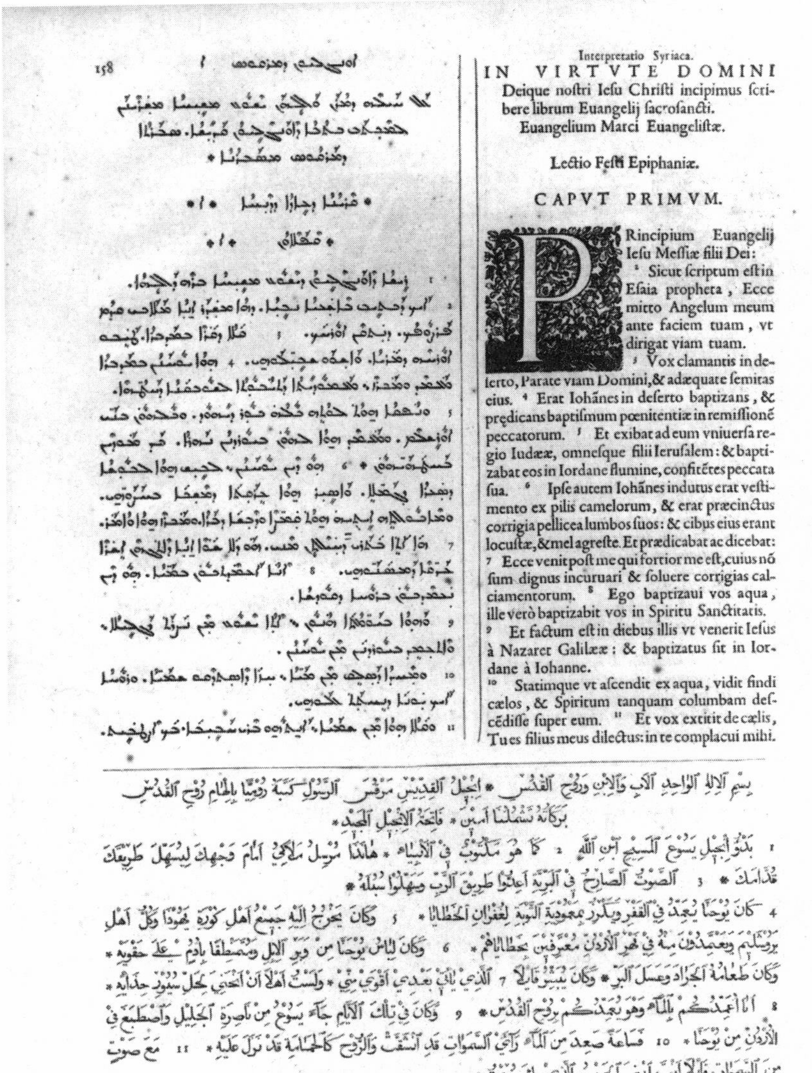

Interpretatio Syriaca.

IN VIRTVTE DOMINI

Deique noſtri Ieſu Chriſti incipimus ſcribere librum Euangelij ſacroſancti.
Euangelium Marci Euangeliſtæ.

Lectio Feſti Epiphaniæ.

CAPVT PRIMVM.

Rincipium Euangelij Ieſu Meſſiæ filii Dei: [2] Sicut ſcriptum eſt in Eſaia propheta, Ecce mitto Angelum meum ante faciem tuam, vt dirigat viam tuam. [3] Vox clamantis in deſerto, Parate viam Domini, & adæquate ſemitas eius. [4] Erat Iohânes in deſerto baptizans, & prædicans baptiſmum pœnitentiæ in remiſſionê peccatorum. [5] Et exibat ad eum vniuerſa regio Iudææ, omneſque filii Ieruſalem: & baptizabat eos in Iordane flumine, confitêtes peccata ſua. [6] Ipſe autem Iohânes indutus erat veſtimento ex pilis camelorum, & erat præcinctus corrigia pellicea lumbos ſuos: & cibus eius erant locuſtæ, & mel agreſte. Et prædicabat ac dicebat: [7] Ecce venit poſt me qui fortior me eſt, cuius nô ſum dignus incuruari & ſoluere corrigias calciamentorum. [8] Ego baptizaui vos aqua, ille verò baptizabit vos in Spiritu Sanctitatis. [9] Et factum eſt in diebus illis vt venerit Ieſus à Nazaret Galilææ: & baptizatus ſit in Iordane à Iohanne. [10] Statimque vt aſcendit ex aqua, vidit findi cælos, & Spiritum tanquam columbam deſcêdiſſe ſuper eum. [11] Et vox extitit de cælis, Tu es filius meus dilectus: in te complacui mihi.

Fig. 8. *Novum Testamentum Jesu Christi,* Syriac, Vulgate, Latin translation of the Syriac, and Greek polyglot bible.

SANCTVM EVANGELIVM SECVNDVM MARCVM.

CAPVT PRIMVM.

Nitium Euangelij Iesu Christi filij Dei, ¹ sicut scriptum est in Isaia propheta: Ecce ego mitto angelum meum ante faciem tuam, qui praparabit viam tuam ante te. ³ Vox clamantis in deserto, Parate viam Domini, rectas facite semitas eius.

⁴ Fuit Iohannes in deserto baptizans, & pradicans Baptismum pœnitentia in remissionem peccatorum.

⁵ Et egrediebatur ad eum omnis Iudaa regio, & Ierosolymita vniuersi: & baptizabantur ab illo in Iordanis flumine, confitentes peccata sua.

⁶ Et erat Iohannes vestitus pilis cameli, & zona pellicea circa lumbos eius : & locustas & mel syluestre edebat.

⁷ Et pradicabat, dicens : Venit fortior me post me, cuius non sum dignus procumbens soluere corrigiam calciamentorum eius.

⁸ Ego baptizaui vos aqua, ille verò baptizabit vos Spiritu sancto.

⁹ Et factum est in diebus illis, venit Jesus à Nazareth Galilaa: & baptizatus est à Iohanne in Iordane.

¹⁰ Et statim ascendens de aqua, vidit calos apertos, & Spiritum tanquam columbam descendentem, & manentem in ipso.

¹¹ Et vox facta est de calis, Tu es filius meus dilectus, in te complacui.

ΤΟ ΚΑΤΑ ΜΑΡΚΟΝ ἅγιον Εὐαγγέλιον.

ΚΕΦΑΛΑΙΟΝ ΠΡΩΤΟΝ.

Ρχὴ τῦ εὐαγγελίου ἰησῦ χριστῦ υἱοῦ τῦ θεοῦ, ² ὡς γέγραπται ἐν τοῖς προφήταις, ἰδοὺ ἐγὼ ἀποστέλλω ⟨τὸν⟩ ἄγγελόν μου πρὸ προσώπου σου, ὃς κατασκευάσει τὴν ὁδόν σου ἔμπροσθέν σου. ³ φωνὴ βοῶντος ἐν τῇ ἐρήμῳ, ἑτοιμάσατε τὴν ὁδὸν κυρίου, εὐθείας ποιεῖτε τὰς τρίβους αὐτοῦ.

⁴ ἐγένετο ἰωάννης βαπτίζων ἐν τῇ ἐρήμῳ, καὶ κηρύσσων βάπτισμα μετανοίας εἰς ἄφεσιν ἁμαρτιῶν.

⁵ καὶ ἐξεπορεύετο πρὸς αὐτὸν πᾶσα ἡ ἰουδαία χώρα, καὶ οἱ ἱεροσολυμῖται, καὶ ἐβαπτίζοντο πάντες ἐν τῷ ἰορδάνῃ ποταμῷ ὑπ' αὐτοῦ, ἐξομολογούμενοι τὰς ἁμαρτίας αὐτῶν.

⁶ ἦν δὲ ὁ ἰωάννης ἐνδεδυμένος τρίχας καμήλου, καὶ ζώνην δερματίνην περὶ τὴν ὀσφὺν αὐτοῦ, καὶ ἐσθίων ἀκρίδας καὶ μέλι ἄγριον. ⁷ καὶ ἐκήρυσσεν, λέγων· ἔρχεται ὁ ἰσχυρότερός μου ὀπίσω μου, οὗ οὐκ εἰμὶ ἱκανὸς κύψας λῦσαι τὸν ἱμάντα τῶν ὑποδημάτων αὐτοῦ.

⁸ ἐγὼ μὲν ἐβάπτισα ὑμᾶς ἐν ὕδατι, αὐτὸς δὲ βαπτίσει ὑμᾶς ἐν πνεύματι ἁγίῳ.

⁹ καὶ ἐγένετο ἐν ἐκείναις ταῖς ἡμέραις, ἦλθεν ὁ ἰησοῦς ἀπὸ ναζαρὲτ τῆς γαλιλαίας, καὶ ἐβαπτίσθη ὑπὸ ἰωάννου εἰς τὸν ἰορδάνην.

¹⁰ καὶ εὐθέως ἀναβαίνων ἀπὸ τῦ ὕδατος, εἶδε σχιζομένους τοὺς οὐρανοὺς, καὶ τὸ πνεῦμα ὡσεὶ περιστερὰν καταβαῖνον ἐπ' αὐτόν.

¹¹ καὶ φωνὴ ἐγένετο ἐκ τῶν οὐρανῶν, σὺ εἶ ὁ υἱός μου ὁ ἀγαπητός, ἐν ᾧ εὐδόκησα.

TRANSLATIO ARABICA.

In nomine Dei vnius, Patris, & Filij, & Spiritus sanctitatis. Euangelium sancti Marci Apostoli, quod scripsit lingua Romanâ per inspirationem Spiritus sanctitatis. Benedictiones eius ambiant nos. Amen. Initium Euangelij gloriosi.

CAPVT PRIMVM.

Initium Euangelij Iesu Christi filii Dei, ² prout est scriptum in prophetis. Ecce mitto angelum meum ante faciem tuam, vt explanet viam tuam ante te. ³ Vox clamans in deserto, Parate viam Domini, & complanate semitas eius. ⁴ Erat Iohannes baptizans in deserto, & pradicabat baptismum pœnitentia in remissionem peccatorum. ⁵ Et egrediebantur ad eum omnès incola regionis Iuda, & omnes incola Ierosolymaæ,& baptizabantur ab illo in flumine Iordane, confitentes peccata sua.

⁶ Et erat vestimentum Iohannis ex pilis camelorum, & erat cinctus pelle super lumbos suos: eratque cibus eius locusta, & mel syluestre. ⁷ Et euangelizabat, dicens: Qui venit post me, fortior est me : & non sum dignus qui incuruer ad soluendas corrigias calciamentorum eius.

⁸ Ego baptizo vos aqua, ille verò baptizabit vos Spiritu sancto. ⁹ Et factum est in illis diebus, venit Iesus à Nazaret Galilaæ,& baptizatus est in Iordane à Iohanne. ¹⁰ Et qua hora ascendit ex aqua, vidit calos scissos esse, & Spiritum tanquam columbam descendisse super eum, ¹¹ cum voce de calis, dicente : Tu es filius meus dilectus, in quo acquieui.

ΛΙΥΛΓΓΕΛΟ℞ ΨΛΙℛҺ ΜΛℛℛҺ
ΛΝΛ𝖲𝖳℞Λ𝖦ΕΙΨ·

C A P. I.

1. 𝕬𝕬𝕬𝕬ΝΛ𝖲𝖳℞Λ𝖦ΙΝ𝖲 ΛΙ-
ΥΛΓΓΕΛΟ℞Ν𝖲 ϊΛΙ-
𝖲Νϊ𝖲 ΧℛΙ𝖲𝖳ΛΝ𝖲
𝖲ΝΝΛΝ𝖲 Γ℞Ψ𝖲·
2. 𝖲Υ𝖦 ΓΛΜ𝖦ΛΙΨ
ϊ𝖲𝖳 ϊΝ Ε𝖲ΛϊϊΝ ΠℛΛΝϜΕ𝖳ΛΝ. 𝖲ΛΙ
ϊℛ ϊΝ𝖲ΛΝΔ𝖦Λ ΛΓΓΙΛΝ ΜΕΙΝΛΝΛ
ϜΛΝℛΛ ΨΝ𝖲. 𝖲Λ𝖦Ι ΓΛΜΛΝΥ𝖦ΙΨ
ΥΙΓ ΨΕΙΝΛΝΛ ϜΛΝℛΛ ΨΝ𝖲·
3. 𝖲𝖳Ιℛ ΝΛ Υℛ𝖓𝖦ΛΝΔΙΝ𝖲 ϊΝ ΛΝ-
ΨΙΔΛΙ· ΜΛΝΥ𝖦ΙΨ ΥΙΓ ϜΛΝΙΝ𝖲.
ℛΛΙҺ𝖳℞𝖲 ΥΛΝℛℛΕΙΨ 𝖲𝖳ΛΙΓ℞𝖲
Γ℞Ψ𝖲 ΝΝ𝖲ΛℛΙ𝖲:
4. ΥΛ𝖲 ϊℛҺΛΝΝΕ𝖲 ΔΛΝΝ𝖦ΛΝΔ𝖲
ϊΝ ΛΝΨΙΔΛΙ· 𝖦ΛҺ ΜΕℛ𝖦ΛΝΔ𝖲
ΔΛΝΝΕΙΝ ϊΔℛΕΙΓ℞𝖲· ΔΝ ΛϜΛΛ-
𝖳ΕΙΝΛΙ ϜℛΛΥΛΝℛҺ𝖳𝖦:
5. 𝖦ΛҺ Ν𝖲ΙΔΛ𝖦ΕΔΝΝ ΔΝ ϊΜ-
ΜΛ ΛΛΛ ϊΝΔΛΙΛ ΛΛΝΔ 𝖦ΛҺ
ϊΛΙℛΝ𝖲ΛΝΛΥΜ𝖦Ι𝖲· 𝖦ΛҺ ΔΛΝΝΙ-
ΔΛΙ ΥΕ𝖲ΝΝ ΛΛΛΛΙ ϊΝ ϊΛΝℛΛΛΝ𝖦
ΛΟΛΙ ϜℛΛΜ ϊΜΜΛ· ΛΝΔҺΛΙ𝖳ΛΝ-
ΔΛΝ𝖲 ϜℛΛΥΛΝℛҺ𝖳ΙΜ 𝖲ΕΙΝΛΙΜ:
6. ΥΛ𝖲 ΝΨΨΛΝ ϊℛҺΛΝΝΕ𝖲 ΓΛ-
ΥΛ𝖲ΙΨ𝖲 𝖳ΛΓΛΛΜ ΝΛΒΛΝΔΛΝ𝖲·
𝖦ΛҺ ΓΛΙℛΔΛ ϜΙΛΛ𝖦ΙΝΛ ΒΙ ҺΝΠ
𝖲ΕΙΝΛΝΛ· 𝖦ΛҺ ΜΛ𝖳ΙΔΛ ΨℛΛΜ-
𝖲𝖳ΕΙΝ𝖲 𝖦ΛҺ ΜΙΛΙΨ ҺΛΙΨΙΥΙ𝖲ℛ:
7. 𝖦ΛҺ ΜΕℛΙΔΛ ΥΙΨΛΝΔ𝖲· ΥΙ-
ΜΙΨ 𝖲ΥΙΝΨℛℤΛ ΜΙ𝖲 𝖲Λ ΛϜΛℛ
ΜΙ𝖲·

I N C I P I T
E V A N G E L I U M
secundùm
M A R C U M.

C A P. I.

1. En yr goðrpel-
lyr angyn hæ-
lendeſ Lpiſteſ
Goðeſ ſuna.

2. Spa appiten iſ on þæſ
pitegan bec Iſaiam. Nu ic aſen-
de minne engel beſoran þinne
anſyne. ſe gegeappa𝖉 þinne
pes beſoran 𝖉e.

3. Llypigende ſteſen on
þam peſtene. Liegeappia𝖉
Dpihtneſ pes. ðo𝖉 ſihte
hyſ ſiðaſ:·

4. Iohanneſ pæſ on peſte-
ne. ſulligende and boðigende
bæðbote ſulpiht. on ſynna
ſongyſeneſſe:·

5. And to him ſende eall
Iudeiſc ſuce and ealle Hiero-
ſolima-paſre. and þænon ſram
hym geſullode on Ionðaneſ
ſlode. hyſa ſynna andbæt-
tende:·

6. And Iohanneſ pæſ ge-
ſcpyðð mið oluendeſ hæſum.
and ſellen gynðel pæſ ymbe
hiſ lenðenu. ⁊ gæpſtapan ⁊
puðu hunig he æt.

7. ⁊ he boðude and cpæ𝖉.
𝖲tpengpa cym𝖉 æſteſ me.
þæſ

Fig. 9. A 1665 example of Gothic and Anglo-Saxon scholarship, reconstructing and
contrasting these earlier translations of the New Testament.

the next townes and cities, that I may preach there also: for to this purpose am I come.

39 And he was preaching in their Synagogues, and in all Galilee: and casting out deuils.

Mt.8,2.
Luc.5,12.

40 And a * leper commeth to him beseeching him: and kneeling downe saith to him, If thou wilt, thou canst make me cleane.

41 And IESVS hauing compassion on him, stretched forth his hand: and touching him, he saith vnto him, I will, be thou made cleane.

42 And when he had spoken, immediatly the leprosie departed from him, & he was made cleane.

43 And he threatned him, and forthwith cast him forth.

‡ Our Sauiour euen when he healed the leper by extraordinary miraculous power, would not yet breake order, but sent the partie to the Priest. Leui.14,3.

44 And he saith to him, See thou tell no bodie: but goe, shew thy selfe ‡ to the high priest, and offer for thy cleansing the things that * Moyses commanded, for a testimonie to them.

45 But he being gone foorth, began to publish, and to blase abrode the worde: so that now hee could not openly goe into the citie, but was abrode in desert places, and they came together vnto him from all sides.

next townes, that I may preach there also: for therefore am I come.

39 And he preached in their Synagogues in all Galilee, and cast the deuils out.

Matth.8,2.
luke 5.12.

40 * And there came a leper to him, beseeching him, and kneeling downe to him, and saying vnto him, If thou wilt, thou canst make mee cleane.

41 And Iesus hauing compassion on him, whē he had put forth his hand, touched him, and saith vnto him, I will, be thou cleane.

42 And as soone as he had spoken, immediatly the leprosie departed from him, & he was made cleane.

43 And after hee had giuen him a straight commandement, he sent him away forthwith:

44 And saith vnto him, See thou say nothing to any man: but get thee hence, shewe thy selfe to the Priest, * & offer for thy clensing those things which Moyses commanded, for a witnes vnto them.

Leui.14,4.
luke 5,12.

45 But he, as soone as he was departed, began openly to declare many things, and to publish this rumor: insomuch, that Iesus could no more openly enter into the citie, but was without in desert places: and they came to him from euery quarter.

MARGINALL NOTES. CHAP. 1.

RHEM. 1   4. Vnto remission.) *Iohn baptised not them in hope onely of remission of sinnes as a preparatiue to Christs Sacrament by which sinnes were in deede to be remitted. Aug.lib.5 de bapt. c. 10.*

FVLKE. 1   Forgiuenesse of sinnes is onely in Christ: yet was the baptisme of Iohn, a true seale of forgiuenesse of sinnes by Christ, as the baptisme of Christs disciples was. As for the *preparation to Christes Sacrament, by which sinnes were indeede to be remitted,* be your owne words and none of S. Augustines: who was indeede deceiued, because he supposed, that some were baptised againe by Paul, which had receiued Iohns baptisme, which the text rightly translated, doth not say: yet he concludeth the matter in these wordes: *Tamen ne quisquam, &c. Yet lest any man should contend, that euen in the baptisme of Iohn, sinne: were forgiuen, after some larger sanctification to be giuen by the baptisme of Christ, vnto those whom Paul commanded to be baptised againe, I doe not greatly striue.*   *Iohn baptisme.* *Acts 19.*

RHEM. 2   15 Be penitent.) *He doeth not preach beleefe or faith onely, but penance also.*

FVLKE. 2   No Christian man doeth preach faith onely without repentance, or voyde of good workes, though they preach, that faith without workes doth iustifie.   *Faith onely.*

ANNOTATIONS. CHAP. 1.

RHEM. 3   5. Confessing their sinnes.) *A certaine confession of sinnes there was euen in that penance which Iohn preached, and which was made before men were baptized. Whereby it is cleare that Iohn made a preparation to the Sacramentes of Penance which afterward was instituted by Christ, as well as he did by baptizing prepare the way to Christes baptisme.*   *Confession.*

FVLKE. 3   You are neuer able to prooue, that Christ did institute any Sacrament of penance. Iohn by his doctrine and baptisme, which was the seale thereof, prepared a way to Christ, but not to the baptisme of Christ, for he preached not his owne baptisme, but the washing away of our sinnes by Christ: therefore he also was a minister of the baptisme of Christ.   *The popish Sacrament of penance.*

RHEM. 4   5 Their sinnes.) *He doth not say that they confessed themselues to be sinners, which may be done by a generall confession: but that they confessed their sinnes, which is a particular confession.*   *Particular confession.*

FVLKE. 4   If he heard a particular confession of sinnes, of so many thousands as he baptized, he needed to haue exercised his office more yeeres, then he did moneths.   *Confession of Christ.*

RHEM.   6 Clothed.) *The holy Ghost thought he is worthy of speciall reporting how straitly this Prophet liued, and how he abstained from delicate meates and apparell.* See Mat.c.3.   *Iohns example of penance.*

RHEM. 5   8 With water.) *Iohn with water only, Christ with the holy Ghost, not only, as the Heretikes hold, that say water is not necessary, but with water and the holy Ghost, as it is plaine Io.3. vnlesse a man be borne againe of water and the holy Ghost, he shall not enter into the kingdome of heauen.*   *Baptisme in the water. Cal.c.4.*

FVLKE. 5   Christ baptised none with water, Ioan.4.2. Notwithstanding, the baptisme with water by his ministers, is necessary, if it may be had according to Christs institution, neither doth *Caluine* teach otherwise. But if it cannot be had in them that are preuented by death, the lacke of water shall not depriue Gods children of their inheritance. *Ambrose de obitu Valentin. Imper.* doubteth not of the saluation of the Emperour, which was slaine before he was baptized. *Sed audiui vos dolere. &c.* But I haue heard (faith he) *that you are grieued, because he receiued not the Sacrament of baptisme, Tell me what other thing is there in you but a will, but a request?* Further he citeth the saying of the wise man, *The iust by what death so euer he is preuented his soule shalbe in rest.* And the example of Martyrs which were slaine before they were baptized, *who if they be washed in their owne bloud* (faith he) *this water will hath washed him.* And the text of Iohn 3, maketh no more for the necessitie of water, then the like Iohn 6, for giuing the communion to infants, Except ye eate the flesh of the Sonne of man, &c.   *Insist.c.16. The necessitie of baptisme. Slander.*

        9 Baptised

Fig. 10. The 1601 Rheims Bible published in London with comments to contrast the Catholic and Protestant English bibles and to draw attention to doctrinal deficiencies in the Catholic bible.

that Mark 16:9–20 should be included in the authoritative Bible, thus effectively eliminating the unique Markan conclusion.[35] These bibles held authority in the Roman Catholic, Lutheran, and Anglican churches until the translating activity of the twentieth century. A new Latin Bible was published under the supervision of Vatican II, and though the notes inform readers that 16:9–20 "desunt in aliq. codd.,"[36] it still held to the longer ending of Mark—even though modern scholars from Lorenzo Valla to Desiderius Erasmus and Johann Jakob Griesbach[37] to the edition of Kurt Aland had concluded the longer ending was dubious.

Translations and Editions

The reception of the Gospels through translation and editions is a history of the equally demanding purposes of philologists and theological interpreters or doctrinalists, and their goals are often contradictory. When it comes to establishing the authority of the text, the philologists have won out. Today we have, comparatively speaking, accurate texts, but the translations manage nonetheless to subvert these efforts, both because of their own necessary cultural subjectivity and because they have inspired writers and artists who have used the Bible in their own languages as the foundation for new literary and creative forms.

Ostensibly efforts "to close the text" with some kind of definitive philological and theological integrity, translations and editions often become associated with names: Ulfilas's Gothic version, Jerome's Latin Bible, Wyclif's Bible, Tyndale's Bible, Luther's Bible, the Douay Bible, the King James Bible, or the Clementine *Vulgate*. In a sense, rather than "closing," the translator(s) or editor(s) replaces an earlier version of the text, as the New English Bible or the New American Bible, as opposed to an "old" Bible. The new editions and translations testify to the impossibility of finishing or completing the Bible's communication with any kind of definitive closure, for its status makes it endlessly open to new eras and new communities.[38]

In the case of the Bible, translation becomes more complicated than with a "secular" text because of the value assigned to the text. This value may include, for example, doctrinal convictions associated with words in the text (e.g., baptism, Resurrection, Father-Son-Holy Spirit, and so forth) that have been used to support a teaching or practice of Christianity; the idea that the words are holy in themselves because they are magical or intimate some mystery; foreign words carried over because they are given special status, such as *abba, hosannah,* or *amen;* or convictions about the essential integrity and authority of the original communication, in other words, that it is the Word of God.[39]

Raised by Cicero in his *De Optimo Genere Oratorum,*[40] the problems of translation were further expanded on by Jerome, when he confronted the interpretive puzzles uncovered by his translations of the Bible. Though engaged in translating a holy text of a religion that biblical translators believed was the unveiling of God's Word, the "universal truth," translators had to confront the alien status not only of God's Word, but of the medium through which God's Word comes to humans. All translators of the Bible have wrestled with this problem of reading. They have engaged in a passionate labor to overcome "otherness" only to be thwarted by the words that could not become other words without becoming another sense; nevertheless, to undermine the literal word is indeed to change the text. Thus translation is both a philological as well as a hermeneutical exercise. Literal meaning versus the sense and eloquence of the text are the competing matrices dividing the goals of the translator between *verbum* and *sensum*. This also holds for editors of biblical texts who must make decisions based on their own informed understanding of the intended meaning of the texts before them.

In upholding *verbum* over *sensum*, Jerome deferred to traditional "readings" of earlier interpreters and philologists like Origen even when they put current practices and beliefs into doubt. In his prologue to the Old Testament, Jerome distinguishes between translation and prophecy: God's word, he argues, is mediated through human language, and thus it is not a direct communication, as in the case of prophecy.[41] Compare this with Augustine's argument in the *De Doctrina* that all interpretation must lead back to the fundamental Christian teaching, "istam geminam caritatem dei et proximi" (the double love of God and neighbor), and with his advice to readers to construct this meaning if the text does not clearly unveil it (*De Doctrina*, I, XXXVI, 40).[42] Given the widespread dispersion of the *De Doctrina*, it is not hard to see how Augustine's preconception influenced the kinds of textual decisions and emendations with his tacit approval that emerged in copied texts of the Bible during the long period from the collapse of the Roman Empire (476) to the reemergence of philological interests in the High Middle Ages.[43]

Jerome's and Augustine's differences typify the conflicts between philological and theological interpretation characterizing the history of the translation of the Bible. Translators themselves are caught in this controversy as they unravel the words that are both *verbum* and *sensum*, "signe" and "signifiant."[44] At the time that Pope Damasus asked Jerome in essence, "to straighten out the problem of the Bible," there were, according to Jerome, almost as many different Latin versions of the Scriptures as there were manuscript copies: "For if we rest our faith on the Latin texts, our opponents can tell us which; for there are almost as many versions of the texts as copies. If, on the other hand, we must find the truth from a comparison of many, why not return to the original Greek and correct the mistakes made by inaccurate translators, and the blundering changes of confident but ignorant critics?"[45] Augustine, agreeing with Jerome, also noted, "We can enumerate those who have translated the Scriptures from Hebrew into Greek, but those who have translated them into Latin are innumerable. In the early times of the faith when anyone found a Greek codex, and he thought that he had some facility in both languages, he attempted to translate it."[46] In the *De Doctrina Christiana*, in fact, Augustine advises his readers that if they find it difficult to understand a passage or word as they read the Bible, they should consult any one of the numerous translations available, for certainly, having referred to all these possible renderings, they would find the approximate meaning. According to Bonifatius Fischer, founder of the Vetus Latina Institute in Beuron and editor of the *Vetus Latina* version of the New Testament, there are traces of the *Africana*, a Carthaginian translation that predates Cyprian, in all the extant Latin fragments and translations.[47] Thus, as already noted, Jerome and his translators were not only working from Greek and Hebrew to Latin as they translated, they were also assessing the qualities and efficacy of the existing translations.

In his Letter to Pammachius (395), Jerome elaborates on his method for translating Scriptures, following the Ciceronian style of rendering *sensum de sensu* rather than *verbum e verbo:* "I myself not only do proclaim freely that in translating from the Greek (with the exception of the Holy Scriptures where the order of the words is a mystery) I render sense for sense and not word for word. For this course I have the authority of Cicero who has translated. . . ."[48] Defending himself against those who accused him of not respecting the literal level of the text in his translation, Jerome makes a superb argument in this letter for translating sense from sense. Using the Latin tradition, he quotes from Cicero's *De optimo genere oratorum* and Horace's *Art of Poetry*,[49] advising "Do not render word for word like a faithful interpreter."[50] Emphasizing the close connection between locution and meaning, and using Hilary the Confessor as his authority, he states with characteristic vehemence that the sense of the text must be taken captive.[51]

Jerome's convictions about translations allowed him to make the kinds of changes to Mark's gospel we can observe when comparing his version with the Greek. First, while he maintains Mark's paratactic style and does not deviate from the order of the narrative, he does correct the syntactical anomalies. (See, for obvious examples, 1:1, Initium evangelii Jesu Christi for Arche tou euangeliou Iesou Christou; or 16:8, et nemini quicquam dixerunt, timebant enim for kai oudeni ouden eipan, ephobounto gar.) He varies the vocabulary when Mark repeats the same words: for example, *statim* and *protinus*, two time words for *euthus*, immediately; *fuit* and *factum est* for *egeneto*, it happened; *solitudine* and *deserto*, depending on the context, for *eremos*, lonely place/desert; *fide* and *credere* to convey the loaded word *pisteuo* (believe); *surrexit, ressurexit*, or *resurgit* for the equally loaded word *egerthe* (rose). When Jerome took up the task of translating the Bible, he inherited a Latin Bible with many neologisms that were rejected by the standards of high

Latinity.[52] Using Cicero's rhetorical defense, he brought neologisms into his Latin text on the grounds that to describe new realities required a new vocabulary.[53] Following the earlier Latin translations, Jerome adopted Hebrew/Aramaic and Greek words like *talitha cumi* (5:41), *abba* (14:36), *synagogam* (1:21), *pascha* (14:12, passim), *amen* (14:25), and *baptismus* (*baptizatus*, 1:9), which he took directly from Mark.

When Erasmus took up the task of reediting the Bible in the sixteenth century, he drew attention to the changes Jerome had introduced in his translation.[54] In contrast to the Old Latin translations, which tended toward literalism, Jerome's changes show he had set out to take philological and rhetorical charge of the Bible. As I pointed out in chapter 2, of all the writers of the patristic period, Jerome was undoubtedly the one most familiar with the Markan text, and though he was more attentive to Matthew (as the number of citations and his commentary reveal), he noted the unique pericopes and stylistic traits of Mark. His translation and his ten extant sermons on the gospel demonstrate his commitment to philological and rhetorical integrity, as he renders interpretations, when possible, to favor literal and stylistic preferences over symbolic suggestions—in contrast to Augustine, who clearly favored allegorical interpretations that would bolster current teachings.

Jerome's, of course, was not the first translation. Tatian's Syriac *Diatessaron*, for example, circulated as early as 170 c.e. In fact, one of the most fascinating aspects of Christianity is its habit of translating its sacred Scriptures into new languages as part of its evangelical mission.[55] In the history of Christianity, harmonies and translations court and overcome Babel simultaneously. On the one hand, they attempt to overcome differences by moving from one language-cultural arena to another with the same "message," but on the other, the transference automatically highlights the differences among languages and people and the rupture that prevents the easy conjuring of the presence of the Word.[56] The Peshitta Syriac version of twenty-two books of the New Testament, like Jerome's Bible—both projects of the late fourth-early fifth centuries—was most likely an edited recension of earlier Syriac versions of various New Testament books. In the first millennium, the Christian Bible was translated from Greek, Hebrew, and Aramaic into numerous languages, including Old Syriac, Gothic, Latin, Coptic, Armenian, Georgian, Ethiopic, Arabic, Persian, Sogdian, Old Slavic, and Anglo-Saxon.[57] In the second millennium, during another innovative period for biblical translations, the High Middle Ages, the Bible also appeared in Old French,[58] Old Spanish,[59] Portuguese,[60] Tuscan and Venetian,[61] Old Norse,[62] Dutch,[63] Old High German,[64] and Middle English, all long before the focus on the Bible during the Reformation.

The fact that the corpus of sacred Hebrew texts had been translated into Greek in Alexandria in the third century b.c.e. and into Aramaic around the same time set the precedent for later biblical translations, a fact recorded by Jerome in the prefaces to his edition. (Such prefaces were commonplace in medieval bibles.) During the patristic era, the three languages of the script on the cross were considered the media for sacred Scriptures—Hebrew, Greek (*koine*), and Latin. Nonetheless, as I mentioned above, even in the patristic period the Bible had already been translated into a number of other languages.

Many assume that the authoritative Latin Bible commissioned by Damasus was the sole version of the Bible from the fourth century to the Council of Trent (1546). This bias shows up in numerous books dealing with Reformation translations of the Bible, which often assume that the Catholic Church suppressed the reading of Scriptures.[65] But Jerome's Bible did not sustain itself as an inviolable version. His efforts were undermined almost as soon as the official Bible appeared, and within a century serious copying errors violated it as parts of the *Vetus Latina* also reentered versions.[66] Though the goals of biblical scholars interested in philology—with some notable exceptions—were eroded during the Middle Ages because of the loss of Greek and Hebrew, Venerable Bede (672–735) is one of the exceptions to the general loss of philological skills in the period.[67] As discussed in the last chapter, Bede wrote a commentary on the Gospel of Mark in which he is attentive to philological questions. The Carolingian scholar Alcuin (735–804), a defender of the literal sense of the text, also used his philological work on the Bible to reestablish the *Vulgata* according to correct standards of grammar, punctuation, and spelling. Alcuin's recension became the standard Latin version of the Bible for the following seven centuries, until the Clementine Bible.[68]

Germanic Language Translations

The earliest Germanic language translations demonstrate an interest in the "literalism" of words, almost as though the words themselves have magic power. This is true of both the Gothic and Anglo-Saxon attempts at translating the Bible. It has been argued, indeed, that in a culture where writing is uncommon, the process may have appeared magical. For example, Bede recalls that a man, believing his brother was dead, had prayers said for him, and the prayers set him free. Those who had captured him asked to see if he had magical writing on him because "magic was bound up with writing." There are numerous examples of particular Christian prayers that in Anglo-Saxon practice were believed to have magical power.[69] *The Heliand,* in which Christ becomes "the Lord of the Runes, [70] integrates the Christian gospel with Northern-European magic. Whether this habit is due to a belief in linguistic magic formulae, harking back to runic incantations,[71] or to some other explanation, the fact remains that early German and Anglo-Saxon translations stick as closely as possible to the literal original, suggesting that to the translator the "words" have mystical power. The first translation of the Bible into a European language outside of Latin, Ulfilas' Gothic Bible, demonstrates this commitment to the very substance of the words themselves.[72]

Ulfilas (b.318–d.381–383), whose mother was Cappadocian and father Gothic, was consecrated as bishop of the Goths in 348. A scholar of Greek and Latin, and clearly a brilliant philologist, he made an alphabet for Gothic, based on the Greek and Latin alphabet, and translated the Bible into the language of the Goths by 360,[73] twenty-five years before Jerome's Latin bible. This Gothic translation is not an anomalous curiosity confined to Dacia, for the Goths moved westward, Visigoths into Spain and Ostrogoths into Lombardy, and Ulfilas's New Testament traveled with them. In fact, Bruce Metzger argues that Ulfilas's version was found among the Goths in both Spain and Italy, so it may have been the vernacular Bible of a large section of Europe in the fifth and sixth centuries.[74]

The Gothic translator unflinchingly followed the principle of *verbum de verbo*. G. W. S. Friedrichsen's 1926 study of the Gothic Bible's style noted "the systematic correspondence of the Gothic text with the Greek, word for word, and in precisely the same order."[75] Georges Cuendet concludes that the Gothic translator was so keen on preserving the form of the original Greek that he even kept to the order of words in the Greek when they made no sense in Gothic. But this order of words was only saved at the expense of Gothic syntax showing little respect for the receiving language.[76] This focus on literalism suggests that Ulfilas never came under the influence of Roman rhetoric, which would have given him a theory for translation to overcome his pedantic approach to the text. First of the European language translators, he followed Mark's Greek and brought Jesus' Aramaic words into his Gothic text. Ulfilas elected literalism over sense or eloquence, one must surmise, because for him the "true" sense was somehow conveyed even in the order of the words in the original. One can't help suspecting that he believed that some unique "presence" or magic was conveyed by words as entities in themselves.

The Anglo-Saxons also produced a rendition of the Gospels. This translation, dated the second half of the tenth century, must be distinguished from the well-known Lindisfarne and Rushworth Anglo-Saxon glosses of the Latin Bible, dated before 970.[77] Classic examples of philological glossing, the Anglo-Saxon *glossa* to the Lindisfarne (c.698) and Rushworth bibles, dated at the close of the tenth century and inscribed as the work of Aldred, Provost of Chester-le-Street (970), are especially interesting because they are again literal renderings, word-for-word, of the Latin, which follows line by line (see fig. 1, p. 22). As David Fowler points out, these were the first attempts to translate the Bible into Old English.[78] There was absolutely no effort on the part of the glossator to interpret the text, except philologically, and even that is at the expense of Anglo-Saxon syntax. On the other hand, as with the subsequent translations of the Bible into Anglo-Saxon, the vocabulary of these interlingual glosses turns the Latin source, which contains hints of its Aramaic history, into a culturally Anglo-Saxon work. Anglo-Saxon words and compounds are favored over Jerome's Latinate neologisms, as for example, *geherdon* for *ministrabant* (Mark 1:12). And the traces of Hebrew-Aramaic disappear from the gospel as *reste dagas* replaces *sabbatis* (1:21) in the Rushworth Bible, *synagogam* becomes *somnung* (1:21), and *aldormenn* substitutes for *archesynanogo* (5:35). *Fader* replaces *abba* (14:36) and *talitha cumi* is simply dropped (5:41), although the glossator remarks that "he" spoke in Hebrew words. Significantly, since it is a word Mark uses, *godspell* replaces *evangelium* (1:1). These glosses appear in expensive editions of the Bible, so it is assumed they must have served a major monastery, cathedral, or royal house. In fact, the text of the Lindisfarne Gospels is believed to be one that Pope Gregory sent to England.[79] Whether for the less educated clergy who needed a very concrete trot to help them understand the Latin or for members of a royal family whose Latin was weak but who could read Anglo-Saxon, the glosses resemble the kinds of linear notes made by students studying a foreign language.

In contrast to the Old Gothic translation, which, like the Jerome Bible, adopted Hebrew and Greek words as neologisms—*Taleitha cumei* and *sabbato,* for example—the Anglo-Saxons domesticated the Bible to their own cultural and linguistic needs. The most obvious example of this is *euangelion* (Greek), *evangelium* (Latin), *aiwaggelyo* (Gothic), and *godspell* (Anglo-Saxon). As with the glosses, special words—Latin neologisms brought over from Greek and Hebrew into the *Vulgata*—are dropped in favor of Anglo-Saxon compounds, with the exception of *abba,* which, as with Jerome, is translated. For example, *parabolis* (Mark 4:2) is rendered *bigspellum* (roundabout story), *baptismum* (1:4) by *fulluht/fulwiht* (full/complete person), and *pascha* (passover) (14:1) by *eastron*. Disciple is rendered *leorning-cnihtas* (learning-servants) (2:23), *sabbatis* is *restedagum* (rest-day) (1:21), *synagogam* (1:21) is *gesamnunge* (assembly), and *doctrina* is *lare* (teaching, learning)(1:22).[80] Whether compounds or simple Anglo-Saxon words, they were used to adapt to local cultural conditions and to replace a remote Latin, Greek, and Hebrew vocabulary with all its tacit cultural and, in some cases, doctrinal or sacramental assumptions (baptism, for example). Here philological accuracy was replaced by Anglo-Saxon cultural interests that had abandoned the special status of Latin words in favor of Anglo-Saxon compounds and understanding, thus asserting local cultural needs over universal standards.

In contrast to the Anglo-Saxon versions, and reflecting the impact of French and Latin culture on late medieval English society, many of the

Anglo-Saxon compounds or equivalents to the Hebrew, Greek, or Latin words return to the *Vulgata* forms in the Wycliffite Bible. As in the Anglo-Saxon and Gothic versions, the questionable ending to Mark (16:9–20) reappears, as do Jerome's Latin neologisms like "sabbath" and "synagogue," taken from Hebrew. *Parabolis* (Mark 4:2) is *parablis, baptismum* (1:4) is *baptym, pascha* (passover) (14:1) is *pask,* disciples is rendered *disciplis* (8:10), *sabbatis* is *sabotis* (1:21), and *synagogam* (1:21) is *synagoge. Doctrina* becomes *techynge* (1:22), but *evangelium* (13:10) remains *gospel.* Once again, these brief examples are meant to suggest ecclesiastical and cultural developments affected hermeneutical and philological understanding and decisions about translations. This vernacularization program was in itself a radical development, for it was a direct assault on the primacy of the *Vulgate,* reflecting an insistence on local national needs over pan-Latin, that is, Roman Church unity. Although the Wycliffite Bible was eventually condemned (1409), numerous manuscripts are still extant, testifying to its importance in the late fourteenth century.[81] Wyclif's translation influenced those of Hus and Luther as well as Tyndale.

Romance Language Translations

When the English set about translating the Bible in the fourteenth century and a flurry of polemical response to this perceived attack on the Latin Bible broke out, defenders of an English Bible used the existence of the French versions, which had been circulating for well over a century, to support their position.[82] The thirteenth and fourteenth centuries witnessed an outburst of biblical translating activity in the Romance languages. These bibles, many still in manuscript form, were inventoried in the nineteenth century. In fact, Samuel Berger's work, reprinted in the twentieth century, still provides highly respected surveys of these Romance vernacular bibles.[83] For the purposes of this study, what is important about them is first of all, contrary to Reformation biases about medieval biblical scholarship, they existed, and they were not condemned or proscribed until the Counter-Reformation. Secondly, Mark, like the other evangelists, was always represented, but these versions do not show any distinctive appreciation of Mark's specific traits. These translations, like the English ones, were due less to a decline in clerical knowledge of Latin than to a resurgence of lay interest in religious issues or to monastic commitment to lay biblical education.[84]

The Romance bibles comprise several French translations, several Florentine bibles, probably translated from the Provençal version along with the *Vulgate*— a Venetian version, and several Iberian translations, including Portuguese, Catalan, and Castillian. Often the product of work patronized by monarchs or their queens,[85] many show that the translators were aware that their "vulgarizing" efforts were radical accommodations to popular interests. For example, in the Jean de Sy manuscript, the translator refers to Robert Grosse Teste, who had translated Genesis from Greek into Latin, and he adds, testifying to his distinction between French and spoken romance Latin, "Je mettrai en françois tout son livre."[86] The most widespread Bible in French before the sixteenth century was the "Bible de Saint Louis," a thirteenth-century Bible, which Samuel Berger argued was translated from the best Latin text available into the best Parisian French between 1226–1250. The French vernacular Bible was widely dispersed on the continent and in England. Dante, in his *De Vulgari Eloquentia* (1304)—an eloquent defense of the vernacular as the maternal language—alludes to it, praising French as a language suited to prose writing. On the other hand, he makes no reference to an Italian Bible, even though a Tuscan one did exist.[87]

The spread of private reading in the late Middle Ages and the greater availability of books due to the introduction of paper in the twelfth century must also have played roles in the translation of the Bible, which, when put into "the mother tongue," became accessible to a larger audience and to more readers. As with the verse translations discussed in the last chapter, these bibles responded to an increased lay interest in the sacred Scriptures themselves. Naturally, because of the cost, they tended to be restricted to court circles. These translations have been associated with movements deemed heretical in this period (Catharism and Waldensianism) that appealed to popular religious interests, particularly among the emerging bourgeois class. But although it is evident that these movements would turn to biblical translating as a way of serving particular religious yearnings, the bibles actually reflect orthodox rather than heterodox theologies.[88]

Numerous medieval manuscripts of the Castillian Bible are extant—many translated directly from Hebrew and often the work of Spanish Jews—and of the New Testament translated from Latin.[89] Alfonso X el Sabio's *General Estoria* contains a translation of the Bible as part of its compendious approach to the universal history of the world, in which Hebraic, Greco-Roman, and Christian myth and history are woven together. Partly because the Romance languages are so closely aligned with Latin linguistically and culturally, significant distinctions in word choice do not emerge, as in the case of the Germanic languages. In contrast to the northern bibles, the 1260 Castillian New Testament is interesting precisely because it shows no need to explain away the Hebraic/Aramaic residue left in the Greek and Latin versions of the Gospels. For example, especially interesting is Mark 1:21, "E entraron en Capharnaum Jhesus en los sabados preigava en la sinoa" (And they came into Capharneum on the sabbath and Jesus prayed in the synagogue), where there is no effort to explain that Jesus is practicing Jewish customs, showing that at least in Castille, Jesus' Jewish history had not been covered over. However, despite the closeness of Latin, it proved to be remote enough for the thirteenth- and fourteenth-century intellectual and cultural elite to set up a program for making ancient and modern texts available in the vulgar languages. In the case of the Bible, its dissemination in these emerging spoken languages paved the way for the final demise of the Latin text as the only authoritative version. The polyglossic explosion served to undermine the authority of the single text that the patristic period had struggled so hard to establish, but as the many clerical disputes over the translations show, it also threatened to create Babel out of the universal Church that the Latin translation had been produced to support.

Focus on editions and translations brings to the surface how doctrinalists and philologists approach the text: the former strives to make the text match current ideological passions whereas the latter endeavors to bring the text to light, according, of course, to the particular prejudices of the translator or editor. In the tradition of Jerome, philologists like Nicholas of Lyra and the humanists Valla and Erasmus continued many patristic and medieval traditions and interests, particularly those that would fulfill encyclopedic intellectual goals, but they unsettled the balanced interpretive habits of the medieval period, dividing philological interpretation of the text from hermeneutical interests. Following a more "scientific" approach to textual analysis, made possible by the full recovery of Greek and Hebrew and the technology to publish texts that could be safely replicated, their contribution established a new interest in historical philology in biblical scholarship that would eventually lead to the Gospel of Mark becoming the central focus of gospel study. The reformers who followed them adopted similar philological and hermeneutical approaches but ignored the Gospel of Mark.

The Council of Trent brought to an end the great philological experimentation of the High Middle Ages when the Bible first appeared in the modern vernacular languages. The French Bible was looked on with suspicion and fear, the Index of the Spanish Inquisition banned the Bible in Castillian romance, and the Index of 1559, repeated in 1564, put an end to unofficial biblical translations in Italy or any other Catholic country. These acts were, of course, in reaction to the explosive consequences of the Reformation and the translations of the Bible directly from Greek and Hebrew by reformers who produced Bibles in German, Italian, French, Czech and Polish, Dutch, Spanish, Danish, and, of course, English.

Though no major arguments can be made about the particular reception of the Gospel of Mark on the basis of the medieval translations, nevertheless, as the explosive reactions of the Reformation and the Counter-Reformation show, the *Vulgate* no longer held absolute power over Bible reading. These translations into the vulgar languages draw attention to some interesting aspects of the reception history of the Bible and of Mark in particular. First, as already pointed out, they show that the *Vulgate*, though still authoritative, was already under siege as a normative text during the Middle Ages. To undermine the *Vulgate*'s central position was to challenge the authority of the tradition that secured its place. Normally associated with the Reformation or even more with Descartes and the Enlightenment, this was the first step to calling into question the authority of tradition. Second, the translations show that once the vernacular languages began to assert themselves into literary culture, these local cultural interests, with language as the critical feature of any culture, went on the offensive against the Latin text—which was becoming a foreign text. The Latin text could not by itself support or speak to the linguistically diversified Christian community. Clearly the translations responded to this enlarged community, in which there may have been some who were trained in Latin. But this new audience for the Bible also included a larger range of social classes, whether nobility or the new middle classes, people outside the clerical orders, or women. The translations reveal that the authority of the *Vulgate* and the authority of the Roman Church that supported it could not overcome these local cultural and individualistic interests for much longer. Furthermore, while translation was attentive to the original text, it nonetheless revealed the degree to which the text could come unraveled as it responded to the polyglossic stimulation of these newly emerging cultural media. Rather than being a static revelation that could undergird absolute teachings, the *Vulgate,* when translated, ultimately proved to be an unstable foundation, as Augustine himself recognized in the *De Doctrina* when he referred to the innumerable Latin versions of the Bible then in circulation. Finally, in contrast to the return to the original language of Greek and a restored classical Latin, which would preoccupy the late Medieval and Reformation periods, these vernacular bibles responded to popular religious needs. Though these efforts appear contradictory, each in its way laid the groundwork for a major shift in interpretive focus. The first established history and origins as objects to be discovered. The second supported individuals and their unique interests in this effort. Together these efforts would discover Mark as the first gospel.

CHAPTER 5

Mark in the Age of Doubt: Recovering the Text

"One has to read the books of ancient authors in order to find out what was correctly discovered in those days . . . But now and then there is a great danger that the stains of error may adhere to us in our all-too attentive readings, however cautious we may be."

René Descartes, *Regulae ad directionem ingenii,* Rule 4

I n an attempt to demythologize, demystify, and question the theology of their ancestors, eighteenth-century thinkers brought doubt to the biblical texts, applied reason, and asked questions of texts based on reason and doubt. Scholars became absorbed by historical questions. History moved to the forefront of biblical studies, constituting a radical break with past practices. An effort to apply Cartesian doubt and "rational" questioning to the Bible first emerged in the eighteenth century. Hermann Samuel Reimarus's (1694–1768) scintillating and probing *Apology for Rational Worshippers of God,* published posthumously by G. E. Lessing (1729–1781) as *Fragments,* introduced assertions about the Gospels that threatened to undermine previous theological convictions and interpretive methods. On reading Reimarus, Lessing recognized that all earlier methods of interpreting and understanding the body of writings called the New Testament were irrevocably challenged by Reimarus's assertions. It is an ironic fact of cultural history that these eighteenth-century deists in search of a rational Christianity without the ideological and theological accretions upheld by doctrine and theological method (that is, hermeneutics, homiletics, and dogma) should be the foundation stones for a revision of the assessment of the Gospel of Mark. Beginning with this endeavor to question and unravel the theological and intellectual structure on which beliefs about Jesus and the Bible were built, a scholarly-literary and historical-cultural enterprise was set in motion that

---

led in 1901 to Albert Schweitzer's *The Secret of the Messiahship and the Passion*[1] and Wilhelm Wrede's *The Messianic Secret in the Gospels*[2] and which continues in our own century.

In a patronage shift not experienced since the rise of autocratic monarchies in the early modern period, scholarly patronage in the eighteenth century began to move from the control of the aristocracy to the universities and independent scholars. Such a change in patronage naturally affected the shape of scholars' goals and interests. The Copernican revolution and an age of mathematics had succeeded in moving science to the forefront of humanistic inquiry, and, as a consequence of all these developments, new methods of scholarly research replaced those which had formerly prevailed.

Eighteenth-century educated men and women began to trust their own rational capacities in a way that had not previously been apparent in Western intellectual activity. Many believed they had left behind the material crises (disease, war, famine, and so on) of earlier times, and they approached the "new" world with courage and self-confidence. Pursuits of knowledge and freedom, unhampered by "tradition" and "prejudice," were the beacons of the age, and these inevitably had an impact on the practices and beliefs of Christians everywhere. With the emergence of science, belief in miracles and divine forces was overpowered by more logical and provable notions of knowledge. For the first time, the Augustinian theology that had ruled religious belief and practice for a millennium and a half came under critical investigation by clergy and scholars of all denominations.[3]

It was in this climate that modern biblical scholarship, as we now know it, grew. Building on the scientific and humanistic developments that began in the twelfth century and escalated in the fifteenth and sixteenth, the intellectual rationale for the modern historical-critical method first took shape in the seventeenth century. While Augustinianism and patristic theology in general were revived during the Reformation, both came under intense scrutiny from the eighteenth century on, with many of their ideological and doctrinal convictions and theological boundaries not only called into question, but, in some cases, repudiated. Rene Descartes' "cogito," his principle of doubt, and such academic disciplines as geography, genealogy, paleography, textual criticism, numismatics, and epigraphy, which support an objective approach to learning, combined to advance the science of humanistic research.

The aim of modern scientific history developed in this period was the creation of a systematic knowledge of the past,[4] dealing with actual events and the everyday lives of women and men. Modern historians, dominated by the desire for empirical information, and armed with newly developed investigative tools, asked the critical questions, "When, where, how, who, and why?" They believed that the answers to these questions would give them access to a provable truth, an objective reality. History would emerge as a science divorced from the rhetorical practices that had always colored its stories. Rhetoric, with its satisfaction with probability rather than provability, was on its way to being relegated to the periphery as a method and standard for understanding and interpreting human activities. Rhetoric's understanding of the subjectivity of knowing was replaced by a quest for objectivity. In search of an abstract notion of "truth," scholars acceded to an objective, single-method, scientific "way" to stable, demonstrable knowledge.

In addition to Descartes, the work of John Locke, particularly *An Essay Concerning Human Understanding* (1690), contributed to the reassessment of traditionally held notions or convictions about the acquisition of knowledge and understanding. For Locke, knowledge is the product of experience, both of the mind and of society. Locke rejected the idea that there are innate principles in the human intellectual makeup. He also rejected Christian dogmatism and its practice in forming human consciousness. While he did not deny the existence of God, he questioned the Christian ideas of original sin and innate flaws in human cognitive capacity.

In the intellectual environment of eighteenth-century Europe, scholars raised questions about the probity, efficacy, and validity of long-held convictions. This interrogative scholarly enterprise led to the possibility of asking historical questions about Jesus' life and establishing the historical reliability of sources. Nineteenth-century biblical studies focused on three related scientific enquiries: the search for the historical Jesus, the relationship among the biblical texts, and establishing a reliable Greek text of the New Testament. C. H. Weisse's two-source theory (1838)[5] attempted to prove that Mark was the oldest gospel; J. E. Renan's *Life of Jesus* (1863) presented a version of the Jesus story deprived of all the legendary and miraculous details so problematic for the nineteenth-century skeptical imagination; and in 1881 a "scientifically" based *New Testament in the Original Greek* appeared.

At the end of the nineteenth century, Albert Schweitzer (1875–1965) traced the history of the search for the historical Jesus, posing questions like "What was the nature of the contemporary Jewish world of thought?"[6] Interest in such issues emerged as a consequence of the rational convictions and attitudes as well as the interpretive methods that had appeared in force in the previous century. Also, independent scholars and researchers like Reimarus, Lessing, and Johann Jakob Griesbach (1745–1812) in the eighteenth century and Schweitzer and Wrede in the nineteenth possessed a freedom of intellectual inquiry not enjoyed by scholars since the independence of the great schools of the twelfth and thirteenth centuries—Chartres, Paris, St. Victor, and Bologna, for example. Advances in science and mathematics as well as shifts in interpretive and scholarly methods partially explain these changes in intellectual inquiry, but the shift in patronage also contributed to the transformation of biblical scholarship in these centuries. And the Enlighten-ment ideology of "private judgment" spurred the shift in interpretive focus.

Three eighteenth-century scholars epitomize the changing attitudes in the intellectual milieu of theological studies in the eighteenth century: Reimarus, Lessing, and Griesbach. Reimarus was the first modern scholar interested in the historical life of Jesus. A German and professor of Oriental languages at the Hamburg gymnasium, Reimarus advanced the "claims of rational religion as against the faith of the Church."[7] Reimarus is considered the father of modern gospel criticism and of its recent emphasis on redaction studies, the attempt to identify the specific strategies and ideological/theo-logical emphases of each gospel writer. Despite his importance—Schweitzer called him the first scholar to suspect what eschatology was[8]—Reimarus's "On the Goal of Jesus and His Disciples" was out of print, even in German, until 1972, and it wasn't translated into English until 1970.[9]

Lessing immediately recognized that Reimarus's work would have a revolutionary impact on religious convictions and that the traditional manner of conducting theological inquiry was irrevocably altered. Gone were the allegories of the past; so too the philological spirituality of the Reformers. When Lessing responded to it, Reimarus's work prompted new historical interests in the origins of Christianity and the Jesus movement, the origins of the texts, and a re-hypothesized relationship among the Gospels.[10] Les-sing, the epitome of the eighteenth century *homme de lettres*, repeatedly re-turned to the questions posed by religion. He was a passionate advocate of tolerance, and his thinking and writing about religion reflected this convic-tion. He vehemently opposed creeds that had woven believers together for fifteen hundred years, for what mattered to Lessing was the freedom to search beyond normative boundaries.[11]

At the same time a scientific approach to history was developing, scholars began to approach established texts with a "scientific" and philologi-cal integrity that was rare in previous eras. With the exceptions of Origen, Jerome, Alcuin, Nicholas of Lyra, Valla, and Erasmus, few previous scholars possessed either the resources or the interest for textual matters. Griesbach's *Synopsis* (1774–1776) and his *Commentatio qua Marci Evangelium totum e Matthaei et Lucae commentariis decerptum esse monstratur* (1789–1790)[12] were major contributions to undermining conventional attitudes about the rela-tionships among the synoptic Gospels and the occasions for their composi-tion.

By placing gospel passages side by side, Griesbach's *Synopsis* drew at-tention to textual gaps among them that the harmonizers from Tatian's *Dia-tessaron* onward had filled in. Johannes Clericus's *Harmonia evangelica, cui subjecta est historia Christi ex quatuor evangeliis concinnata* (1699) was the first real attempt to create a synopsis. It placed the gospels side by side, with the Greek on the left side and the *Vulgate* on the right. Below both, a paraphrase takes up the individual passages on each page. But this first effort at a synopsis still deferred to the single unified story.[13] In a successful effort to overcome the differences and create a universal story from the Gospels, the harmonizers had ignored their unique textual characteristics. By the time Griesbach was working on his *Synopsis*, Johann Fabricius, Reimarus's father-in-law, could identify one hundred and fifty harmonies and concordances.[14] The format and objectives of the synopses were in direct contradiction with the harmonies that had regulated biblical reading since the patristic era. Like the harmonies, Griesbach's *Synopsis* drew attention to overlaps among the Gospels, but, more importantly, they dramatically feature their differences, and in doing so they opened the possibility of reevaluating and revising all the traditional ideological, textual, and theological convictions surrounding the reading of the Gospels. Although Griesbach continued to hold to Augustine's position regarding Mark, he helped shape an intellectual and academic environment in which the Gospel of Mark began to be reassessed by its scholarly readers. Indeed, it was the development of new interpretive principles and methods and new prejudices that spurred the re-reading of the gospel.

Besides the fact that Reimarus, Lessing, and Griesbach all lived in Germany and were both makers of and participants in the intellectual crosscurrents of the period, they also shared similar habits of mind. Although they exercised their academic interests in different arenas, they brought to their studies a uniformity of interpretive presuppositions that reflected the dispositions of their times. Only Griesbach was specifically attentive to the Gospel of Mark, but the methods of inquiry adhered to by all three led to the reassessments of the gospel that began in the following century. Thus Reimarus, with his convictions about historical veracity, could assert in "The Goal of Jesus and His Disciples" that his examination of the Gospels would

> separate completely that which the apostles set forth in their own writing from that which Jesus himself really spoke and taught in the course of his own life. For the apostles were themselves teachers and had therefore set forth their own teachings and never claimed that Jesus, their Master, had himself said and taught everything they had written. The four evangelists, in contrast, present themselves only as historians reporting that which was most important of Jesus' sayings and actions.[15]

Likewise Lessing, who rejected Reimarus's polemicism while adopting his historical method, applied a system of rational analysis in an effort to provide critical proof for the religious questions he posed: "First the hypothesis will be set forth in plain, straightforward prose. Then the critical proof of it will be given, and all that follows on from it. After this will be shown the advantage which this hypothesis could have in making intelligible various difficulties and in providing a more exact explanation of disputed passages, and the conclusion will subject it to a closer scrutiny."[16] In the introduction to the *Synopsis,* Griesbach advanced the evaluative and scientific method by which he would proceed in his academic enterprise: "It is above all important to know the sources from which historical writers have drawn things which they have put into their own commentaries, in order to interpret correctly their books, to evaluate justly the trustworthiness of the authors, and to perceive and judge skillfully the true nature of the events that they have recorded."[17]

Reimarus authored numerous works, but his major one, *Apology for Rational Worshippers of God,*[18] was not published during his lifetime. He circulated it among his closest friends during his last years but feared the uproar that would follow its publication. Before he died in 1769, he left the manuscript in the hands of his daughter Elise, who gave it to Lessing, whose acquaintance Reimarus had made during the last year of his life. Claiming to have found the manuscript in the ducal library at Wolfenbuttel, where he was the librarian, Lessing published it as anonymous fragments between 1774 and 1778 in *Contributions to Literature and History.*[19] Though the first fragment attracted little attention, immediately after the publication of the next five (1777), a furor arose from orthodox sectors. When he published the last of the fragments—by far the most controversial—*On the Aims of Jesus and His Disciples* (1778), the censor came down on him, and he was asked by the Duke of Brunswick to desist from further distribution of these highly inflammatory studies.[20] The reaction to Lessing's publication was so controversial that Reimarus's "Defense of the Reasonable Worshipper of God," of which "The Goal of Jesus and His Disciples" forms a part, did not appear in its entirety until 1814, when J. A. H. Reimarus, Reimarus's son, published it and, at the same time, identified his father as the true author. In Lessing's version of this work, Reimarus asserts that the story of Jesus did not have dogmatic significance, that the Jews were expecting a "worldly deliverer of Israel" and "Jesus then must have been well aware that by such a plain announcement of the Kingdom of Heaven, he would only awaken the Jews to the hope of a worldly Messiah."[21] Reimarus attempts to show that Jesus had only human ambitions and that when he died the disciples created the redeemer Jesus because "they had hitherto been constantly looking forward to worldly grandeur and advantages in the kingdom of Jesus, which were put an end to by his death, and that upon this failure they brought out a new creed of Jesus as suffering Saviour, which until some time afterwards had never entered their heads."[22]

Reimarus did not read the Gospels as separate documents; rather he applied his deconstructive method to the "story of Jesus," as if it were a single rendition, although he did scrutinize individual Gospels to advance his interpretation. In his reading he dismisses the idea that Jesus "intended to teach complicated dogmatic theology, the Trinity, the divine Sonship, the sacraments and the rest."[23] Impelled by his own doubting and liberating intellectual environment, he used the texts, deprived of all the theological assumptions with which they had been previously approached, to explore historical questions. His break from conventional readings, which had ruled how the texts would be studied for centuries, shows the creative and critical interpreter confronting "assumed meanings" with new questions or methodologies. His revision and rewriting are examples of using the text as a "trace," a concept he himself adopted, which, rather than prompting a supplement to its established or traditional rendering, attempts to undermine or replace earlier readings. Although he was not specifically attentive to the Gospel of Mark, Reimarus's interest in historical documents with their ideological veneer removed set the course for further studies of the historical Jesus in which the Gospel of Mark would play a central role.[24] Although inattentive to the surface narrative characteristics of the Gospels, Reimarus created a new version of the harmonized Gospels constructed by his interpretive method, which reduced the texts and the theological and spiritual traditions attached to them to what could be comprehended within the framework of eighteenth-century doubt and intellectual freedom.

Lessing, who throughout his life remained a believer within the boundaries of his own rational system, presented his religious arguments in the form of religious studies, the result of the debate fomented by his publication of Reimarus's fragments and their challenge to orthodoxy. Like Reimarus before him, Lessing's biblical discussions—apart from his essay, "New Hypothesis Concerning the Evangelists regarded as Human Historians" (1778)[25]—refer to a theological text in which distinctions between the Gospels are not important. What is important is the application of reason and the assault on the concept of "inspiration" addressed to the problems posed by the texts. Thus in "On the Proof of the Spirit and of Power" (1777), he denies that it was the historical reality of Jesus' miracles that bound him to a faith in the teaching of Jesus.[26] In "New Hypothesis Concerning the Evangelists Regarded as Merely Human Historians," Lessing set out to demonstrate his own historical-critical methodology. Insistent on emphasizing the Jewish origins of Jesus and his first followers, he hypothesizes a Nazarene original text to which the gospel writers turned as source. To prove his hypothesis, he analyzes all former convictions about the relationship of Matthew, Mark, and Luke to their sources. Attempting to examine and expose authoritative positions, he cites the church fathers, raising the arguments they had presented, asking critical questions of them, and casting doubt on earlier assumptions.[27] Though he accords little attention to Mark, repeating Augustine's opinion, he does use the gospel to prove his idea that there was a Hebrew source for the Gospels: "It is still more obvious that Mark, who is commonly held to be only an abbreviator of Matthew, appears to be so only because he drew upon the same Hebrew document, but probably had before him a less complete copy."[28] Through his interest in different versions of the story, he revealed his tentativeness about the notion of an "inspired text."[29]

Lessing was able to justify in his own mind the historical development of the different versions, each with its unique intention, audience, and community. He continued to hold the traditional view that the canon was a fourfold witness, with two Gospels, Matthew and John, the "gospel of the flesh" and the "gospel of the spirit," as Augustine had asserted in *De Consensu*. Nevertheless, he rejected Augustine's theory about Luke and Mark as "scarcely satisfactory." He argued that "Mark and Luke were preserved by the Church in addition to Matthew because in many respects they filled so to speak the gap between Matthew and John; and the one was a pupil of Peter and the other a pupil of Paul."[30] Lessing uses Mark, as well as Luke, Matthew, and John, to assert its unique contributions to the gospel collection, based on rational argumentation. Thus Lessing expressly confronted the "ideology of tradition," that is, the domination of convictions about the Gospels that had been upheld since the patristic era. In an effort to be free of Augustinian prejudices that were accepted as "true" for centuries, he scrutinized the Gospels with the coldness of eighteenth-century rationalism and a fiery demand for freedom in interpretive methodology.

An essential aspect of the exercise of interpretive methodology in the eighteenth century was, as Kant had expressed it, the "courage to make use of your own understanding." The application of personal understanding, however, was a direct assault on dogmatic readings, and this biblical criticism directly challenged ancient and established traditions about biblical texts. As Hans-Georg Gadamer suggests, "the critique of the enlightenment is directed primarily against the religious tradition of Christianity, i.e., the Bible. By treating the latter as an historical document, biblical criticism endanger[ed] its own dogmatic claims."[31] While eighteenth-century writers and thinkers respected the integrity of the individual and rejected extrinsic authorities, they elevated reason as the arbiter of all inquiries and conclusions. Therefore they focused on logical propositions prompted by the texts (which they approached as a single text), and logic and argumentation directed their rhetorical inquiry. These interests overshadowed concerns for style or narrative features that permitted fluidity in interpretive conclusions in the evaluation and scrutiny of texts. Nevertheless, these authors were attentive to the idea that the texts themselves had rhetorical intentions. In fact, Reimarus's *On the Goal of Jesus and His Disciples* is an effort to discover the motives underlying all four Gospels' presentation of historical events.

Reimarus and Lessing brought the scientific critical perspective to theological traditions about the story of Jesus, and Griesbach exercised his critical acumen on the texts themselves. Griesbach tackled the synoptic theory upheld since Augustine's *De Consensu*, that Mark was Matthew's abbreviator and epitomizer, systematically undermining the Augustinian premise in the development of his *Synopsis*. Although he concluded with Augustine that Matthew had priority, he claimed that Mark was written after Matthew and Luke, from whom the gospel was extracted.[32] Griesbach successfully reintroduced the question of sources of the Gospels and hypothesized a different relationship to the one upheld as authoritative from the patristic period. Eusebius's canons, like Augustine's *De Consensu*, were designed to show uniformity, conformity, and comparability among the Gospels, but Griesbach wanted to examine the precise textual relationship among what became known as the "synoptic Gospels" as a consequence of his work. When Griesbach compiled his *Synopsis*, he had the opposite intention to the harmonizers of the past. In fact, his synopsis is a direct challenge to the harmonized Gospels. Rather than erase differences and create a harmonious version of the Jesus story, he strove to feature cacophony or silence. He confessed to the "heresy" that he believed the extant harmonies were not accurate historical accounts, and, in fact, they made it impossible to construct a uniform story without distorting history:

> The authors of the harmonies have principally tried to determine the time and sequence in which the events written down by the Evangelists happened; but this lies far outside my purpose. For I freely admit—and I wish to draw the readers' attention to this—that a "harmonia" in the literal sense of the word is not the aim of this book. For although I am not unaware of how much trouble very learned men have taken to build up a well-ordered harmony according to self-imposed rules, yet I still think not only out of this minute care small advantage may be obtained, or even practically none at all that my synopsis would not also offer; but further I have serious doubts that a harmonious narrative can be put together from the books of the Evangelists, one that adequately agrees with the truth in respect of the chronological arrangements of the pericopes and which stands on a solid basis. For what is to be done, if none of the Evangelists followed chronological order exactly everywhere and if there are not enough indications from which could be deduced which one departed from the chronological order and in what places? Well, I confess to this heresy.[33]

In his effort to evaluate the relationship between Matthew, Mark, and Luke, Griesbach was very attentive to the textual surface, and he recognized that the differences constituted different rhetorical purposes on the part of the evangelists.[34] Herein lies the central contribution of Griesbach to gospel studies: a direct challenge of the harmonious readings of the Gospels that had created an *evangelium*. From this time forward, Griesbach's approach would foster the reading of individual Gospels as single and singular redactions.

Griesbach developed the *Synopsis* as an aid in teaching, but he wanted to draw attention to the "individuality of each Evangelist, his style and vocabulary, his basic idea and structure, his method and sources."[35] Although Augustine had been attentive to individual gospel theologies in the *De Consensu*, and individual commentators in the patristic period were also attentive to the unique characteristics of the evangelists, Griesbach's revolutionary insight was to understand the differences divorced from all previous convictions. His effort to separate traditional understanding from his own understanding, freed from all the superstitious affection for conventional readings, led him to a position that confronted all the beliefs about the Gospels which the Fathers had successfully established.

In an effort to reevaluate the issue of the relationship of the Gospels historically, Griesbach also examined the numerous theories that were currently in circulation. Among these were the theories of G. C. Storr and J. G. Eichhorn. Storr proposed (1786) that Mark was the source for Luke and Matthew,[36] while Eichhorn, developing his idea from Lessing's notion of an original Hebrew source, hypothesized "that Matthew did not use either Mark or Luke; that Mark did not use either Matthew or Luke; and that Luke did not use either Matthew or Mark. The reason for their agreement is therefore to be sought from some other source."[37] Griesbach's theory, which he attempted to demonstrate in the remainder of his introduction, was that "Mark when writing his book had in front of his eyes not only Matthew but Luke as well, and that he extracted from them whatever he committed to writing of the deeds, speeches, and sayings of the Saviour."[38] He presents three arguments for Mark's dependence on Luke and Matthew: an argument from order; an argument that Mark is contained in Matthew and Luke; and the argument that Mark alternately agrees with Luke or Matthew.[39]

In the next section of his demonstration, Griesbach, typifying the eighteenth-century rejection of established beliefs and adherence to an interrogative mode, raises all the objections to his hypothesis arguing against the prejudice of tradition. He first challenges the tradition that Peter dictated his memoirs to Mark. Examining the original statements of Papias, Tertullian, Justin Martyr, Clement of Alexandria, and Origen, Griesbach remarks that he believes it to be a fabrication typical of those "found among ancient writers, and which are today rejected by most scholars."[40] Using rhetorical questions to counter the arguments against his thesis, Griesbach asserts that total dependence on Matthew and Luke would not have made Mark unnecessary or unworthy of gospel status. Furthermore, he deals with the shortness of the gospel as well as Storr's opinion that Mark was the original by insisting that "Mark surpasses Matthew in the clear and definite exposition of events; indeed he is sometimes more accurate . . . and comes closer to the truth of the events."[41] Citing all of Mark's omissions and arguing for their purposeful absence, Griesbach endorses the simplicity of the Markan version of the story—which was compatible with his own questioning spirit. Although he argues that Matthew was Luke's source and Matthew and Luke Mark's sources, he also insists that some of Mark's unique renditions (i.e., those not in the same form in the other synoptic Gospels) were more correct and careful than Matthew's and that Mark's order of events was the accurate sequence because he had access to an earlier source.[42]

On the other hand, despite his attack on long-held beliefs about the texts and their authors, Griesbach stuck doggedly to Matthean priority on the traditional assumption that Matthew was an eyewitness, upholding the tradition yet at the same time asserting in his hypothesis that historical testimonies are not reliable.[43] Though Griesbach's hypothesis is based on a close reading of the texts, it is still a creative reconstruction, with his own imagination taking precedence over what he deems dubious historical references. And he was held captive by the belief that gave Matthew first place in the tradition.

Thus, as with Lessing and Reimarus, Griesbach was concerned with issues of historical accuracy and scientific probity and with questioning long-held assumptions. On the basis of his careful textual argumentation throughout the *Demonstration,* Griesbach discounts in his conclusion most of the consistently held traditions about the origins of the Gospel of Mark. Among other assertions, he concludes that the Fathers' positions were generally false and that Mark's divine inspiration was questionable.

Griesbach's conclusions demonstrate his attempts to scrutinize the positions taken by the church fathers, the intentions of the harmonizers, and the role of divine inspiration in the genesis of the Gospel of Mark. While he sought to exclude prejudice in his scholarly endeavors, he still held to the Augustinian prejudice that Matthew was the first gospel. The eighteenth-century "science of freedom" placed the subjective individual researcher, with his doubts and reasonable questioning, at the center of hermeneutical inquiry, replacing the old prejudice in favor of tradition with the new prejudice of doubt. Because tradition was seen as an impediment to the free exercise of reason, it had to be questioned, and, if necessary, its authority had to be revoked. Thus interpretive exercise became absorbed by the free exercise of rational inquiry, and it was not until the nineteenth century, with the development of the historical-critical method, that the idea of contextual historical readings would modify the assault on tradition mounted by the eighteenth-century rationalists.

In terms of rhetoric and rhetorical standards, eighteenth-century commentators on the Bible lost the idea of "literary depiction" in biblical narratives. In their place, they substituted their conception of the literal sense, a philological or "grammatical-historical" understanding of the texts rather than a literary one. It was through this underlying notion that a "critical reconstruction of reported events" came to replace all other rhetorical aspects of the texts.[44] As the texts were scrutinized according to new methodologies and a restrictive rhetoric, their logical and historical "fallacies" were exposed. As a consequence, the question of what constituted faithful knowledge emerged as the central issue of the Christian religion. The traditional interpretation of the Bible was naturally one of the cornerstones to be set aside under the new methods. These novel methods were adopted consciously, but the exercise of rhetorical standards was tacit. The latter were adjusted according to the directives of the new methodologies and interests of the period, without self-reflection or historical reflection about their roles in the formation of the Gospels and their reception throughout a seventeen-hundred-year history. Thus Lessing could write, "The letter is not the spirit; and the Bible is not religion. Consequently objections against the letter and against the Bible are not objections against the spirit and the religion."[45] For Lessing the "inner truth" of religion or the subject matter of the biblical texts existed separately from the literary communication that had transmitted its message. At the root of this distinction is another radical fracture of "content" from the complex rhetorical and literary machinery of the Bible.

Augustine's harmony, his rejection of Mark as an epitomizer, his attribution of divine inspiration in the creation and interpretation of religious texts: to eighteenth-century thinkers these were all the empty vagaries of the ideology of tradition. For eighteenth-century thinkers, tradition—that is, interpretations, beliefs, customs, and methodologies as practiced by the church fathers—inhibited the freedom of the rational faculties and had to be dismissed as a coercive power leading to false conclusions. It was as though, anxious about influence, these thinkers placed themselves in a contest with the past, elevating their newly established principles of intellectual activity above all previous methodologies. But at the same time as they attacked, they wrote themselves into the tradition. Although their methods, beliefs, and interests varied from those of their predecessors, they focused on a normative and "traditional" document, the Bible, which had been the source for interpretive theological inquiry throughout the history of Christianity to that point.

A scientific, comparative analysis of the Gospels through synopses resulted in a fundamental challenge to harmonies. Synopses are in large part responsible for the turn taken in biblical studies in the last two centuries. They demonstrate the differences among the Gospels and therefore also point to possible historical and social differences in the circumstances of their creation, the audiences for whom they were intended, and the intentions of their authors. On the other hand, the interest in a historical life of Jesus, based on actual verifiable data, resulted in a habit of looking at the Gospels as biographies or historical narratives. The consequence of this interest was to obscure dogmatic interest while promoting reading the Gospels as narratives. This in turn led to the increasing focus on the Bible as a literary and aesthetic model from the eighteenth century onward.[46]

The scientific interests of the eighteenth and nineteenth centuries spurred the search for the historical Jesus, promoted the endeavor to establish the accuracy of the biblical text, and encouraged scholars to look at the individual gospel texts and the oral sources lying behind them. Schweitzer's and Wrede's work,[47] though different in their aims, nevertheless were culminations of the first of these efforts. The second resulted in the 1881 *New Testament in the Original Greek,* the work of B. F. Westcott and F. J. A. Hort,[48] whose interest in the genealogical relationship between the manuscripts and whose careful analysis of internal and external evidence brought to fruition the work of J. A. Bengel (1763) and others in establishing an accurate text. This effort led to the monumental text-critical accomplishment of the nineteenth century, the 1898 edition of Eberhard Nestle, *Novum Testamentum Graece,* revised by Ervin Nestle in 1927, by Kurt Aland in 1963 and subsequently.[49] The third of these developments, the focus on the specific traits and goals of individual Gospels and their oral and written antecedents, has directed and defined much biblical scholarship in the twentieth century. With the growth of new disciplines in the university, totally new avenues of exploration of the Bible have been opened.

CHAPTER **6**

The Modern Period

"Mark is not Matthew's epitomizer"
J. J. Griesbach[1]

Though a gospel stepchild for most of its canonical history, Mark became the passion of biblical scholarship in the nineteenth century. The eighteenth-century synoptic approach to textual studies as a tool for academic readers facilitated a shift from "authority" as primary guide to the "subject-reader," accompanied by various philological tools, as principle guide. It also signaled a change from humanist philology, in the strict sense of establishing an accurate text, to history as primary guide in textual interpretation. The most important shift, however, was from the fourfold Gospels as a unified story to comparative analysis of each gospel, a comparison for historical and literary purposes rather than a purely theological one. Synopses, now recognized as essential for historical inquiry—particularly for a close analysis of the textual basis of arguments about gospel relationships, which has dominated biblical work for two centuries—made these studies possible. In featuring the gospels side by side, synopses underscore differences that verge on conflicts among the Gospels that the reader endeavors to reconcile or leaves unresolved.

Perception of gaps, expansions, and verbal contradictions among the Gospels fostered a critical approach to them, which in turn sustained the development of historically based gospel studies, including historical and literary approaches to the Gospels, source, form, tradition, and redaction criticism, which in the twentieth century have prompted an investigation into the unique aims and ideologies of the various New Testament writers. Synopses encourage a number of critical stances besides the more obvious theological ones. Instead of working to make all the biblical documents from Genesis to the Apocalypse fit into a single universal theology, as in medieval biblical exegesis and universal histories, recognition of the differences introduces tensions into the act of reading and interpreting that are not easily resolved. The contrasts fragment the unity implied by the harmonies that had supported a single theology, and these differences disrupt and dispel the illusion of cultural continuity harmonies seek to uphold. If the historical, social, and geographical differences of the period in which they were written (from the 60s to the 90s) and the communities they were addressed to (including Rome, Antioch, Jerusalem, or Ephesus, for example) are also taken into account, a unified interpretation of the Bible or even for the Gospels as a group becomes difficult to support. When the gaps among the Gospels are featured, they challenge the doctrinal convictions the Gospels undergird as a single communication. To recognize that the Gospels were written for distinct communities and that each one presents different theological, social, political, or literary interpretations of the story of Jesus is to undermine the claims to universality and catholicity that had determined the status of the Bible as a single harmonious theological communication.

An important feature of twentieth-century New Testament exegesis, therefore, is its focus on the unique contributions of the individual texts in the canon and on the specific contributions of individual Gospels rather than their shared features. Currently, the Gospels are read as separate texts, a habit of reading and interpreting that has led to the recognition of multiple theologies rather than to the single truth or story they were often made to represent.

With history as science emerging as the dominant epistemology in the humanities in the nineteenth century, biblical scholars searched for the historical Jesus while re-theorizing the chronological relationship among the gospels and their imagined precursor texts. These interrelated nineteenth-century goals were critical to Markan studies. To explore the relationship among the Gospels was to ask which came first. With the historical source taking on a privileged position, the oldest text became the most important. Just as the Fathers had done when they argued that Matthew was first, the new theory gave Mark "pride of place." As the "oldest" text, it offered a new version of the historical Jesus and a theology to match.[2] The importance of theories about the order of the Gospels cannot be underestimated, because the very nature of the "kerygma" and earliest traditions are linked to the oldest gospel.[3]

The argument for the priority of Mark developed gradually, beginning with G. C. Storr's (1786) radical thesis that Mark was a source for Matthew and Luke. Like G. E. Lessing (1778), J. B. Koppe (1782) argued that the synoptic gospels had a Hebrew/Aramaic source or sources, used by all the gospel writers. As discussed in the last chapter, though Griesbach radically questioned patristic convictions, he still held to the Augustinian theory on Matthew's priority, arguing that Luke had used Matthew and Mark had followed Matthew and Luke. Both Storr's proposal and G. Herder's 1797 hypothesis that an Aramaic proto-Mark lay behind Mark's text[4] were not generally accepted by biblical scholars. In 1835 Karl Lachmann, the first person to edit the Greek text of the New Testament using the evidence of manuscripts—with the order of the narrative as his primary criterion for judgment—argued in "The Order of the Narration of Events in the Synoptic Gospels" that it did not seem possible that Mark could have used Luke and Matthew in his version.[5] When Christian Hermann Weisse (1801–1866) formulated the two-source Markan hypothesis, he garnered the evidence to contradict the tradition upheld since Augustine's "Marcus eum subsecutus tamquam pedisequus et breviator eius videtur."

When Weisse's theory was adopted into Heinrich Holtzmann's (1832–1910) synoptic synthesis that an earlier form of Mark predated the canonical gospel (1863),[6] the long-held Matthean priority theory was definitively challenged.[7] In order for the two-source theory to be persuasive, large portions of Matthew and Luke that do not appear in Mark had to be accounted for. This led to the "Q-hypothesis" that Matthew and Luke had turned both to Mark and to a sayings collection, called "Q" (from German, Quelle) or "source" as their common sources. Although some scholars have introduced serious challenges, most scholars today still hold to the two-source theory and Markan priority.[8] Both the enormous attention to Mark and the nature of commentaries on the gospel in the last two centuries have depended to a great degree on Holtzmann's synthesis. R. H. Lightfoot writes, "the Gospel according to St. Mark has aroused more interest in the last century than at any other time," and this explosive attention doubtless stems from the Markan priority theory.[9] Testifying to the residual power of tradition, despite the eighteenth- and nineteenth-century scholarship systematically contradicting it, the Matthaean priority conviction was so influential that the Biblical Commission of the Roman Catholic Church reaffirmed the traditional authorship, date of composition, and historical character of the Gospel of Matthew by official decree on June 19, 1911.[10]

One phase of the search for the historical Jesus came to fruition in William Wrede's (1859–1907) *The Messianic Secret* (1901). Like earlier biblical scholars such as Valla, Erasmus, or Reimarus, who were radically dismantling conventional approaches to the Bible, Wrede, though working within an established historical framework, was interested in the "spirit" of particular accounts, "what the narrator in his own time intended to say to his readers."[11] Like Reimarus, he was interested in how the early Church, as represented by the Gospels, interpreted the life and teachings of Jesus. He was interested in history, not the canon, and certainly not in maintaining traditional dogmatic convictions. He held that scholars had read between the lines of the Gospel of Mark to make it reveal a development of Jesus in relationship to his mission, disciples, and supposed messiahship. In other words, he rejected the idea that Mark could be used as a historical source for establishing the life of Jesus. He took a skeptical position on all dogmatic interpretations, overturning traditional opinions in favor of a thorough and careful reading of the text, asking in fact for proof of anything historical in the gospel, and pointing out that the author of Mark had a primarily theological rather than historical agenda.

Like the interest in the agreement among the Gospels in the patristic era, the search for the historical Jesus in the nineteenth century also sought to establish a single story based on historical studies of the Gospels. Wrede's work disrupted this by focusing on what each gospel author contributed to an understanding of the "messianic secret," that is, the fact that Jesus had kept his messiahship secret. He chose Mark because he accepted Weisse's theory that Mark was the first gospel, and that the other evangelists adopted Mark's "secret." Although, true to his nineteenth-century scientific bias and narrowly defined reading strategies—reflecting the loss of "allegory" or the symbolic dimension of the text—he also believed that much of the Markan gospel was historically "untrue" (the baptism story, the raising of Jairus's daughter, miraculous feedings, the Transfiguration, the angel talking to the women at the tomb, for example).[12] With Mark as the primary text, Wrede's work contributed to the new and emerging emphasis on reading each of the Gospels as single stories with individual ideologies and rhetorical purposes. However, despite the fact that Wrede showed that Mark's own rhetorical purposes had to be distinguished from some objective "life of Jesus" or even from the beliefs of the early Church, scholars continued to use the gospel for these purposes.[13]

Recognizing the "either-or" thinking of the period, Schweitzer's still brilliant *The Quest for the Historical Jesus*, written in 1906, recounts the story of the nineteenth-century preoccupation with this historical epistemology in New Testament studies. These either-or oppositions were framed as "historical" or "eschatological," "synoptic or Johannine," and finally "eschatological or uneschatological." Schweitzer explored the range of contradictory attitudes characterizing the search for a Jesus of history, whether the rationalism of Reimarus, David Friedrich Strauss's demythologized "Life of Jesus" (1835), Bruno Bauer's Johannine-based skeptical version of Jesus' life (1840), Renan's popular literary "Vie de Jesus" (1863), or eschatological versions of Jesus' mission. Schweitzer felt that Mark impeded the search for the historical Jesus, and in the introduction to the sixth edition of *The Quest for the Historical Jesus*, he writes, "The key to understanding is provided by Matthew in the material he supplies beyond what is found in Mark."[14] In his appraisal of his own work, *The Secret of the Messiahship and the Passion*, which appeared simultaneously with Wrede's *Messianic Secret* (1901), Schweitzer sounds a warning about the inevitable clash between "history" and "eschatology," toward which nineteenth-century biblical scholarship had led:

The reader of Wrede's book cannot help feeling that here no quarter is given; and any one who goes carefully through the present writer's "Sketch" must come to see that between the modern historical and the eschatological Life of Jesus no compromise is possible.

Thoroughgoing skepticism and thoroughgoing eschatology may, in their union, either destroy, or be destroyed by modern historical theology; but they cannot combine with it and enable it to advance, any more than they can be advanced by it.[15] Schweitzer's discussion of the nineteenth-century reception of the Gospels and Mark's particular role highlighted how a shift in interpretive epistemology resulted in new theological views that conflicted with a view of an "eschatological" Jesus, under attack since Reimarus and Lessing over a century earlier.

Interest in objective knowledge, the program of the scientific era undergirded by eighteenth-century rationalism, motivated the kind of biblical scholarship typical of the nineteenth century. These scholars did not aim primarily to make the gospel interpretation conform with traditional teachings or to support doctrine. Rather the Bible became an "objective" text, whose history as text rather than as "Word of God" overturned the traditions of reading it and, as a consequence, revised opinions about what the text actually said.

After the two-source theory had become the "generally" accepted explanation of the relationship among the Gospels in the first part of the nineteenth century, scholars turned to an examination of earlier forms and sources predating the Gospels in their canonical forms. This kind of interest is remarkably similar to the effect of the synopsis-makers, for, like their work, attention to form and source further undermines the integrity of the text(s) as a unified whole. When scholars search out sources and scrutinize their underlying forms, they are forced to ask questions about the manner and reasons for the texts having been assembled as they were. Just as the synopses feature gaps among the four versions, source and form criticism features fragments brought together in the final gospel versions and draws attention to the scattered nature of the authors' oral and written resources. Even more, the idea of a single author or authority of even individual texts within the New Testament is called into question, as the text comes to be seen as a collection of pieces pulled together for various purposes, some the gospel writer's individual interests, and others a response to specific community needs or interests. Thus the twentieth-century reader has broken up the unity of the Bible, dismembering the whole in order to examine fragments that formerly had been made to serve as parts from which to construct an ideological unity.

Nineteenth-century scientific interests in the textual analysis of the

Bible led to form criticism. New Testament form criticism took as its model the work of Herman Gunkel (1862–1932) on the oral sources of the Hebrew Bible.[16] This model was applied to the New Testament by Rudolf Bultmann (1884–1976), Martin Dibelius (1891–1956), and Karl Ludwig Schmidt (1891–1956). Mark's apparent lack of a developed literary style and the gospel's many oral features convinced two of the twentieth century's most famous biblical scholars, Martin Dibelius and Rudolf Bultmann, that the Markan text was very close to its oral sources and that the author had merely recorded what he heard. Calling the Gospels "unliterary writings" for "the lower stratum" of society, who "accord no place to the artistic devices and tendencies of literary and polished writing," Dibelius assumed they were intended for readers who are not touched by literature "proper." Showing his nineteenth-century "romantic" bias about originality, he went even further than this with his claim that the evangelists' role in constructing the Gospels was confined to choosing, limiting, and shaping the material rather than creating a narrative whole.[17]

This fragmentation of the Gospels and their individual narrative authority followed from nineteenth-century historical interests, with history articulated according to contemporary scientific theories of history.[18] Historical questions, epitomized by Lightfoot's 1950 study, ruled biblical studies in the nineteenth century and continued to play an important role even up to the present.

Twentieth-century programs of form and redaction criticisms, like the work of Reimarus, Lessing, and Griesbach, have all tended to "objectify" the biblical texts. Given the tyrannical authority of tradition up to the eighteenth century and the millennium-and-a-half-long successful promotion of a single, universal, catholic teaching—which, despite the dissolution of Christianity into numerous sects, remained as an ideology even if not as a practice—the efforts of eighteenth-century scholars must be applauded as courageous and inspiring. They set the stage for all the developments in biblical scholarship in the nineteenth and twentieth centuries. Despite the fact that hermeneutical theorists from Dilthey and Schleiermacher to Gadamer have repudiated the claims of objectivity in inquiry, these scientific approaches emerged when the ideology of faith as an absolute cultural certainty collapsed. One could even argue that the new historical passion was the project of the loss of any conclusive subjective knowledge in an age of doubt. In the absence of this faith and the cultural absolutes supporting it, these methodologies of necessity took their place. The cultural agenda informing these methodologies as applied to the Bible assured its place in a civilization without the "single" faith that had preserved it in its previous history. In essence, the inspiration behind these methodologies, with their claims of objectivity, acted to save the story and all its possible or potential meanings.

As a text always open to an ever expanding reading audience, and because of its status as a canonical text, the Bible is constantly adapted to new cultural realities and preserved from possible loss. The threat to the Bible's survival as organizing cultural myth occurs when coercive social and economic developments lying outside the immediate realm of a biblical culture—and in the control of new, more powerful cultural forces in possession of their own narratives—challenge its central role. The scientific agenda of the nineteenth century was one of these historic challenges to the Bible. But when adopted by biblical scholars themselves as a methodology, the scientific approach to biblical scholarly activity of the last two centuries fragmented the canon as a single entity and disrupted the idea of a single uniform story and message. These new intellectual approaches made possible new understandings of the biblical texts conforming to current interests and cultural concerns, in essence keeping the stories alive when under the pressures and challenges of the modern era. Besides the intellectual and scientific forces, these challenges include, of course, replacing a traditional lifestyle that had supported Christian cultures but was now under siege by industrialization, urbanization, technologization, and consumerism. Unfortunately, the reaction to these forces in the late twentieth century appears to be a resurgence of fundamentalist religion.

The collapse of the old disciplines, with rhetoric and theology the heart of a liberal education in the universities in the nineteenth century, and their replacement with an emphasis on a scientific orientation of all academic studies in imitation of the model of the German university, led to still further developments in how the Bible would be read under the influence of modern disciplines, constituted along methodological lines (history, national literatures, psychology, sociology, anthropology, and so on). Both the dismantling of the Gospels into fragments and the attention to Jesus' historicity were challenged by redaction criticism, which was the first modern effort to examine the Gospels as integrated works written by specific authors with personal or community intentions and ideologies. Redaction criticism put attention back onto the author and the historical audience in the hermeneutical triangle, for as a form of rhetorical criticism, its primary interest is to ascertain a particular gospel's intention and strategy and the audience for whom it was intended. This is accomplished by comparing and contrasting what specific emphases the various evangelists express in their versions. Synopses are critical for redaction criticism because redaction critics, unlike Augustine and the harmonizers who wanted to show how the Gospels overlapped, chose to emphasize the unique theologies and narratives of the four evangelists.

Redaction criticism offers the synthesis between "history" and "eschatology" that Schweitzer feared was abandoned by the "scientific" epistemologies of the nineteenth-century biblical historians. We find hints of redaction-type criticism in Reimarus, and I would argue that the Griesbach synopsis is the essential foundation for redaction. Wrede in particular paved the way for redaction criticism and attention to Mark. Similarly, Lightfoot, while examining Mark, made redactional observations about the Gospels.[19] It is Willi Marxsen, however, who, with his *Mark the Evangelist: Studies in the Redaction History of the Gospel* (1956),[20] showed how the Markan author adapted his sources and how his creative understanding of the story imprinted itself on his version as distinct from the other Gospels. Studies like Marxsen's, which explore reading the gospel as a whole and examine the internal coherence structured to support its rhetorical strategy, have contributed to identifying the special qualities of the Markan version, characteristics not found in the other Gospels. This is the great contribution of redaction criticism, for it has been able to show that all the gospels represent different understandings and interpretations of Jesus' life and its meaning. This is a long road from Augustine's "Mark has nothing to add." This concentration on the uniqueness of the gospel theologies led to the final demise of the pride of place of Matthew, though this gospel still retained preeminence in the Catholic liturgy, for example, even until 1969. A result of five years of study, the work of many scriptural and liturgical experts, and a renewed Vatican interest in biblical studies, the *Ordo Lectionum Missae*,[21] finally gave Mark a place with the other Gospels in the lectionary.

The second half of the twentieth century has opened up the Bible to many other kinds of studies besides those directed by the proclaimed objective historical interests of the nineteenth century. The multidisciplinary academic environment of the twentieth century has contributed to yet another revolution in biblical studies, which, starting from redaction studies, moved to probe both implicit and explicit characteristics of the various biblical texts. Just as the old curriculum was ordered and organized according to certain tacit ideological convictions, the new curriculum is also undergirded by prejudices of inquiry. The overall organizing bias has been the conviction that a scientific outlook, as defined by nineteenth-century notions of science, should be the basis for knowledge, with each discipline possessing its own methods of inquiry. The new interest in a conscious hermeneutics of inquiry has led to an expansion of various kinds of self-conscious theoretical approaches to biblical interpretation in the last quarter of the century. Recent biblical studies show the imprint of the social and political theorizing so important to the nineteenth and twentieth centuries. As a consequence, we have, for example, Fernando Belo's Marxist study of the Gospel of Mark,[22] the biblical foundation for liberation theology,[23] sociological studies of the New Testament letters,[24] and feminist analyses of the Gospels,[25] all products of the theories and practices of the new disciplines and the new hermeneutics within these disciplines.

Also, more widespread literacy, the habit in the West since the eighteenth century of reading prose narrative fictional forms, and the literary theoretical scholarship of the twentieth century that has grown to help us appreciate these genres have all helped to develop sophisticated narrative readers. A revised interest in "literary" features has contributed to rediscovering what the church fathers meant by the "symbolic" dimension of the Bible.

In the last thirty years, literary interpretations divorced from specific theological interests have sought to uncover the symbolic and narratival communication of the Bible, which the rational-scientific orientation of the last two centuries tended to ignore. Augustine himself recognized this as the essential communication of the Bible when he remarked about his own early failure to understand that the Scriptures' low style hid their symbolic dimension and made them "lowly on one's entrance but lofty on further advance" (*Confessions*, 3.5). Interest in the style or aesthetics of the Gospels has been a unique focus of twentieth-century scholarship.

Erich Auerbach's discussion of the portrayal of Peter's denial—in his *Mimesis*, first published in 1946[26]—drew attention to the purely literary character of the biblical narratives. It has been followed by an explosion of such studies with diverse methodologies from structuralist to post-structuralist by those primarily trained in literature.[27] Also, the Gospel of Mark's inarticulateness about its generic status[28] has prompted scholars in the last one hundred and fifty years to identify it with a number of ancient forms, including memorabilia,[29] biography,[30] aretalogy,[31] history,[32] parable,[33] tragedy,[34] comedy,[35] popular novel,[36] and sacred narrative[37]—all efforts to expand the discussion of the gospel's genre, yet all failing to label it definitively. In fact, Frank Kermode's *Genesis of Secrecy* uses the Gospel of Mark to explore the complex literary features of narrative; drawing on the religious canonical status of the work, he shows the relationship between narrative technique and the secret of Jesus' messiahship.

Mark's greater prominence in biblical scholarship in this century, combined with the reassessment of established literary practice and new interests in literary theory and hermeneutics, has promoted an interest in the literary and rhetorical aspects of the Bible, leading biblical scholars to scrutinize Mark's literary character and rhetorical strategies.[38] Some connect this literary character to religious purpose, as Rudolf Pesch, for example, who pinpoints the literary structure of the Gospel of Mark with 8:27–30 as its central communication, thus showing the interconnection of literary feature and theological communication. F. Neirynck's analysis of the dualities in Mark connected this doubling strategy to the meaning of the gospel.[39] Daniel Via's emphasis on the Resurrection in his literary approach leads him to his conclusion that the gospel is a comedy. David Aune's interest in the literary features of Mark and his conclusion that it is a popular biography lead him to theorize the relationship between the gospel genre and its earliest community. More recently, in an effort to apply literary theory to Mark, Robert

Fowler, using reader-response criticism, has shifted the emphasis "away from the story of the Gospel narrative to the discourse of the narrative."[40] In all these examples, theologians attempt to align the literary character with the theological function and meaning of the gospel.

The persistent interest in hermeneutical and critical theory among both literary and biblical scholars continues to undermine the control of the religious authorities over the sacred texts that began in the eighteenth century. But the activities of literary scholars in particular expose the force of the Bible's purely literary and symbolic communication; these activities re-write the Gospels as literary discourse, which in turn unveils ideological and socio-cultural implications often obscured by more doctrinaire interpretations. These creative interpretive or supplementary activities expand our knowledge, appreciation, and enjoyment of the text, while raising questions about the positions of earlier scholarship. The break from harmonies, traditions, and univocal theological convictions has made radical new readings possible. In fact, it is ironically Cartesianism, which has been under siege in the contemporary theoretical environment, with its ideology of doubt and openness to dismantling *idees reçues,* that has made viable this renaissance of critical approaches to the Bible.

To bring Mark up to the present, one needs to consider the effect that the computer revolution has had on the gospel's reception. As Roger Chartier points out,

> Our current revolution is more extensive than Gutenberg's. It modifies not only the technology for reproduction of the text, but even the materiality of the object that communicates the text to readers. Until now, the printed book has been heir to the manuscript in its organization by leaves and pages, its hierarchy of formats, and its aids to reading (concordances, indices, tables). The substitution of screen for codex is a far more radical transformation because it changes methods of organization, structure, consultation, even the appearance of the written word.[41]

Furthermore, when one considers Erasmus's serendipitous discovery of Valla's *Collatio* in contrast to the contemporary instant access to "information," one is immediately made aware of how the new technology empowers readers and researchers in ways formerly impossible. A quick search on the World Wide Web will reveal well over a million sites for the Gospel of Mark on the Internet, in contrast to Matthew (a quarter of a million), Luke (one hundred and fifty thousand), and John, who surpasses even Mark in attention.

But this is not what is significant about the effect of computers on the reception of the gospel. The Mark home page declares for the whole world (or at least the world that has access to a computer) that Mark was the first Christian gospel, despite the fact that scholarly opinion is not uniform on this question. A Mark "chat room" allows those interested to exchange questions and findings worldwide instantly, and a hypertext version of the gospel invites readers to write comments alongside Mark's text. Again, as Chartier notes, "With the electronic text, matters will never again be the same. The reader can not only subject an electronic text to numerous processes (index it, annotate it, copy it, disassemble it, recompose it, move it), but, better yet, become its coauthor. The distinction that is highly visible in the printed book between writing and reading, between the author of the text and the reader of the book, will disappear in the face of an altogether different reality."[42] If this development does not bury forever the institutional authority that previously ruled the reading of the gospel, it will be because not everyone has access to this new technology.

Computer information systems further empower subjects, as readers and writers of texts (because screen or no, computers are merely a new reading/writing instrument). But the new technology poses a different kind of threat to the struggle to democratize the culture of the Bible that began with the translations into the vernacular languages in the early modern period, supported the *ordo laicorum,* and in the twentieth century has encouraged even women to engage in the discourse of theology. The anarchical Internet makes it possible for readers to bypass authorities, allowing readers to do more "extensive" searching than ever before. But because anyone can create a Website, computer technology makes it possible for an expansive proliferation of information, that may indeed be incorrect, to travel in electronic space.

The various approaches to the Bible informed by the ideology of doubt from the eighteenth century onward, whether textual or interpretive, were all attempts to objectify the texts, and the consequence of this was the loss of their symbolic communication.[43] Nevertheless, without this objectification, deceptive as its methods may ultimately be, it is unlikely that the texts could have been scrutinized with the same openness and freedom from doctrinal constraints. New methodologies, combined with a radical shift in patronage—from the institutional Church in the patristic period to religious orders in the Middle Ages, to oversight by autocratic monarchs from the Renaissance to the Enlightenment, and to universities in the modern era—have worked to redefine what texts are read, how the text would be read, what makes it worth reading, and who, indeed, could participate in biblical scholarship. In fact, one could argue that because Cartesianism assaulted subjective knowledge and objectified external phenomena, it made possible the examination of the Bible as a literary artifact. The current intellectual revolt against Cartesianism,[44] on the other hand, is in some ways another Cartesian

assault against tradition. It underlies the revised interest in the Bible's political, social, and symbolic or literary communication, as distinguished from
questions about dogma, textual problems, or historical accuracy.[45] Patronage
has played an important role in these changes as well, and the contemporary
emergence of the secular university as a new patron of biblical studies has no
doubt contributed to the redirection in critical inquiry by biblical scholars
who, for the first time in history, include women.

The uneven reception of the Gospel of Mark throughout this long
time span forces the question about why it was unappealing in some eras and
has become important in the last two centuries. For the Fathers, trained in
the requirements of classical rhetoric, the gospel was anomalous. In contrast
to Matthew, it lacks many of the desirable details for a harmonized and
"complete" life of Jesus. It provides no clear material for any of the Fathers'
doctrinal interests (for example, primacy of the authority of the disciples,
legitimacy of the Church of Rome, the Trinity, the sacraments); to the contrary, it is close to silent on these issues. In terms of literary style, the gospel
appears on the surface to be the least sophisticated. It is paratactic, has re-
dundancies, pleonasms, and even grammatical flaws. Its narrative is disjunc-
tive because its presentation of the story includes embedded narratives,
juxtapositions, intercalations and parallelisms, and folktale simplicity (trebling, journey motif, and wonder-working hero).[46] All of these complement
the gospel's paradoxical content, which our own era, trained to be sophisticated readers of prose fiction in an intellectual culture thriving on suspicion,
relativity, and ambiguous open-endedness, has found so interesting.

As to its content, recent studies have argued that Mark's elusive "kerygma" is intentional. He refuses to make judgments. Like the "J" writer in
Hebrew Scriptures, he leaves such moral interpretations to his audience. He
also leaves many empty spaces in his gospel, and, particularly, his tomb is
empty. He does not provide the ethical norms of Matthew's Sermon on the
Mount, valued by theologians seeking a firm grounding for the Gospels'
teachings. These absences in Mark's version and his primacy in the historical
quests of the nineteenth century contributed to the skeptical theological climate of the period. It was precisely this parsimony of detail in the Markan
text that undergirded Schweitzer's concerns about the gospel's emerging importance in the nineteenth century:

> Mark knows nothing of any development in Jesus, he knows
> nothing of any paedagogic considerations which are supposed to
> have determined the conduct of Jesus towards the disciples and
> the people; he knows nothing of any conflict in the mind of Jesus
> between a spiritual and a popular, political Messianic ideal; he
> does not know, either, that in this respect there was any differ-
> ence between the view of Jesus and that of the people . . . he does

not know, either, that Jesus explained the secret of the passion to the disciples, nor that they had any understanding of it. . . .

All these things of which the Evangelist says nothing—and they are the foundations of the modern view—should first be proved, if proved they can be; they ought not to be simply read into the text as something self-evident. For it is just those things which appear so self-evident to the prevailing critical temper which are in reality the least evident of all.[47]

The strong preference for Matthew until the nineteenth century resulted partly from his fuller account of the Jesus story, a fact that ranked the gospel before Mark in the opinion of the Fathers. But Matthew and John also appealed to the literary tastes of the ruling readers throughout this period. In contrast, they found Mark deficient. The Gospels of Matthew and John communicated to a receptive audience because they appealed to already established theological convictions as well as ecclesiastical and stylistic prejudices. In an era when Church authorities were searching for authoritative texts that could be used to support an orthodox creedal formulation, the Gospel of Mark offered only vagueness on these issues. It is precisely these gaps and paradoxes, as well as Mark's interest in and representation of the marginalized, that our own age has found so provocative. As Belo's Marxist study has shown, Mark's narrative is attentive to the poor, the hungry, and the powerless (whether women, the disabled, the poor, minorities, aliens, or other outsiders from power), while the rich and the powerful are subtly repudiated. Since the twentieth century has witnessed more mass displacement of people than former centuries, and since the Gospel of Mark collects a whole series of stories about the marginalized (as in the focus on miracles that transform marginalized sufferers, whether blind, lame, bleeding, deaf, sick, mad, or dead), in contrast to the other Gospels, this may also help explain our interest in the gospel. Ending Mark at 16:8 with the empty tomb, the consensus of modern textual scholars but which editions and harmonies had suppressed for sixteen hundred years, is an example of the kind of tantalizing frame Mark offers contemporary commentators. Mark's fragments, enigmas, and elusive mode of communication invite reader intervention, which modern readers, trained to read literary texts that are not transparent, find stimulating.

A study such as this, which documents the reception of a normative or canonical text in different historical periods and diverse social-literary settings, must confront the problems of validity in interpretation, literary and theological value and conviction, and historical "prejudice." Major shifts in reading methods, rhetorical standards or expectations, and cultural interests have led to different attitudes toward the Gospel of Mark. As I have shown, different social and cultural situations affecting academic and ecclesiastical convictions and decisions have played a decisive role in the changing attitudes toward biblical texts. The authority of powerful voices, whether Augustine's dismissal of the Gospel of Mark or the now prevalent two-source theory, have directed and sometimes controlled work on this gospel and all other biblical texts. These differences over time are the results of scholarly methods and interests of certain periods. Reigning ideologies and convictions in particular time frames form the interpretive climate and rule how canonical texts are read. The material examined in this study shows how documents can and are molded to suit often divergent interests. It also reveals how controlling, whether accurate or inaccurate, patterns of reading are in the discoveries made by interpreters. A two-thousand-year history of scholarly and popular responses likewise militates against any claims of absoluteness in scholarly interpretation. Rather than opening up the arena of literary discussion to "play" as an end in itself,[48] this extended story of hermeneutical practice emphasizes how interpretation and interpreters are bound by their historical time.

Finally, at the root of this study of the Gospel of Mark is a consideration of what it means for a normative literary work to be included in a canon of revered documents and how that work is to be read once included. Canonicity is a formidable power. Even if a literary document is ignored, its existence within a canon guarantees that it will not disappear into oblivion. Though it might be ignored for centuries, its resurrection, depending on the cultural and social temper of the times, is always possible. I have examined the role of authority, historically determined interpretive methods, literary and rhetorical prejudice, and contemporary cultural, social, and subjective interests in the reception of the Gospel of Mark, urging that these methods and attitudes are forceful instruments that direct and control our communal reading habits.

Notes

List of Abbreviations

BAV   Vatican City, Biblioteca Apostolica Vaticana
CCSL Corpus Christianorum Series Latina
EETS Early English Text Society
PG   *Patrologia Graeca,* ed. J.-P. Migne, 161 vols. Paris, 1857–66.
PL   *Patrologia Latina,* ed. J.-P. Migne, 217 and 4 index vols. Paris, 1841–61.
SBL   Society of Biblical Literature
SC   *Sources Chretiennes*

Preface

1. Origen, *De Principiis,* in *SC* (Rome: Pontificium Institutum Studiorem Orientalium, 1990), 252–53, 268–69, 312; Origen, *On First Principles,* trans. G. W. Butterworth, intro. Henri de Lubac (New York: Harper Torchbooks, 1966); Jerome, *Commentary on Ezekiel,* in *CCSL* 75, 13 (Turnhout: Brepols, 1954), 42, 13 (615–16).

2. Jacques Le Goff, *Medieval Civilization,* trans. Julia Barrow (Oxford: Basil Blackwell, 1988).

3. Thomas S. Kuhn, *The Structure of Scientific Revolutions* (Chicago: University of Chicago Press, 1962).

4. *Aristotle on Rhetoric: A Theory of Civic Discourse,* trans. George A. Kennedy (New York: Oxford University Press, 1991), 1:3.

5. Roger Chartier, *Forms and Meanings: Texts, Performances, and Audiences from Codex to Computer* (Philadelphia: University of Pennsylvania Press, 1995).

6. This is Hans-Georg Gadamer's idea of spontaneous interpretation, undirected by hermeneutical principles. *Truth and Method* (New York: Crossroad, 1986), 191f.

Introduction

1. For the role of rhetoric in biblical studies, see Amos N. Wilder, *Early Christian Rhetoric: The Language of the Gospel* (Cambridge, Mass.: Harvard University Press, 1971); George Kennedy, *New Testament Interpretation through Rhetorical Criticism* (Chapel Hill: University of North Carolina Press, 1984); David Rhoads and Donald Michie, *Mark as Story: An Introduction to the Narrative of a Gospel* (Philadelphia: Fortress Press, 1982); Vernon K. Robbins, *Jesus the Teacher: A Socio-Rhetorical Interpretation of Mark* (Philadelphia: Fortress Press, 1984); T. Boomershine, "Mark, the Storyteller: A Rhetorical-Critical Investigation of Mark's Passion and Resurrection Narrative" (Ph.D. diss., Union Theological Seminary, New York, 1974); Burton L. Mack and Vernon K. Robbins, *Patterns of Persuasion in the Gospels* (Sonoma, Calif.: Polebridge Press, 1989); Burton L. Mack, *Rhetoric and the New Testament* (Minneapolis: Fortress Press, 1990). For hermeneutics and history, see Gadamer, *Truth and Method;* Hans-Georg Gadamer, *Reason in the Age of Science,* trans. Frederick G. Lawrence (Cambridge, Mass.: MIT Press, 1981); Kathy Eden, *Hermeneutics and the Rhetorical Tradition: Chapters in the Ancient Legacy and Its Humanist Reception* (New Haven: Yale University Press, 1997).
2. Gerard Genette, *Palimpsestes: La Litterature au Second Degre* (Paris: Editions du Seuil, 1982).
3. Jacques Derrida, "From/Of the Supplement to the Source: The Theory of Writing," in his *Of Grammatology,* trans. Gayatri Chakravorty Spivak (Baltimore: Johns Hopkins University Press, 1974), 269–316.
4. Michel Foucault, "The Prose of the World," in *The Order of Things: An Archaeology of the Human Sciences* (New York: Vintage Books, 1973), 17–45.
5. "Supplement" is Derrida's term for the commentaries on written works.
6. Genette, *Palimpsestes,* 7–14.
7. Wolfgang Iser, *The Act of Reading: A Theory of Aesthetic Response* (Baltimore: Johns Hopkins University Press, 1978); Hans Robert Jauss, *Aesthetic Experience and Literary Hermeneutics,* trans. Michael Shaw (Minneapolis: University of Minnesota Press, 1982); Jane P. Tompkins, "The Reader in History: The Changing Shape of Literary Response," in *Reader-Response Criticism,* ed. Tompkins (Baltimore: Johns Hopkins University Press, 1980), 201–32.
8. Harold Bloom, *The Anxiety of Influence* (New York: Oxford University Press, 1973).
9. Stanley Fish, *Is There a Text in This Class?* (Cambridge, Mass.: Harvard University Press, 1980).
10. Frank Kermode, *History and Value* (Oxford: Clarendon, 1988), and *Forms of Attention* (Chicago: University of Chicago Press, 1985).
11. Michael Riffaterre, *La Production du Texte* (Paris: Editions du Seuil, 1979), 9.
12. *Aristotle on Rhetoric.* See Gadamer, *Reason in the Age of Science,* and Kennedy, *New Testament Interpretation through Rhetorical Criticism.*

13. For elaboration of this idea, see Kathy Eden, "Hermeneutics and the Ancient Rhetorical Tradition," *Rhetorica* 5 (1987): 59–86. Also see Eden, *Hermeneutics and the Rhetorical Tradition.*

14. As developed in John Guillory, *Cultural Capital: The Problem of Literary Canon Formation* (Chicago: University of Chicago Press, 1993).

15. Gerard Genette, *Narrative Discourse: An Essay in Method,* trans. Jane E. Lewin (Ithaca: Cornell University Press, 1980), 25–27.

16. Christian Hermann Weisse, *Die Evangelienfrage in ihrem gegenwartigen Stadium* (Leipzig: Breitkopf und Hartel, 1856). See chapter 6 for a summary of the precedents that led to Weisse's formulation of the Markan priority two-source theory.

17. For a reader-response discussion of Mark's reception in light of the Markan priority theory, see Robert M. Fowler, *Let the Reader Understand: Reader-Response Criticism and the Gospel of Mark* (Minneapolis: Fortress Press, 1991).

18. These notions of absence, presence, and parsimony of expression I have borrowed from Paul Ricoeur, "Interpretative Narrative," trans. David Pellauer, in Regina Schwartz, ed., *The Book and the Text: The Bible and Literary Theory* (London: Basil Blackwell, 1990), 237–57. The idea of "absent-presence" in Mark's rendition of the gospel story is developed in John D. Crossan, *Cliffs of Fall* (New York: Seabury Press, 1980).

19. See Chartier, *Forms and Meanings,* 6–24.

20. See Erasmus's *Annotations on the New Testament. Facsimile of the Final Latin Text (1535) with All Earlier Variants (1516, 1519, 1522, 1527),* ed. Anne Reeve (London: Gerald Duckworth, 1986).

21. *Synopsis of the Four Gospels,* ed. Kurt Aland (Stuttgart: Biblia-Druck, 1972).

22. *Synopsis Quattuor Evangeliorum: Locis parallelis evangeliorum apocryphorum et patrum adhibitis,* ed. Kurt Aland (Stuttgart: Deutsche Bibelgesellschaft, 1985).

23. For theoretical discussions of the reader's role in constructing the meaning or noting its absence in texts, see Derrida, "From/Of the Supplement to the Source: The Theory of Writing," in *Of Grammatology;* Iser, *The Act of Reading;* Jauss, *Aesthetic Experience and Literary Hermeneutics;* Tompkins, ed., *Reader-Response Criticism,* for theoretical discussions of the reader's role in constructing the meaning or noting its absence in texts.

24. Foucault, "The Prose of the World," 17–45. Augustine, *De Doctrina Christiana,* in *CCSL* 32 (Turnhout: Brepols, 1962), 1–167.

25. Gadamer, *Truth and Method,* 239–45.

26. "Interpretive community" is Stanley Fish's term for the group that imposes or fails to impose a particular interpretation on a literary work. See *Is There a Text in This Class?,* 14.

27. Wayne Meeks, *The First Urban Christians* (New Haven: Yale University Press, 1983), 54.

28. For some background in the development of the idea of leisure, see Josef Pieper, *Leisure: The Basis of Culture,* with intro. T. S. Eliot, trans. Alexander Dru (London: Faber and Faber, 1952); and Michael O'Loughlin, *The Garlands of Repose: The Literary Celebration of Civic and Retired Leisure* (Chicago: University of Chicago Press, 1978).

29. John Guillory, "Canonical and Non-Canonical: A Critique of the Current Debate," *ELH* 54, no. 3 (fall 1987), 483–527; also see Guillory, *Cultural Capital*. The ideas about tradition to which I allude throughout this book are influenced by those of Jaroslav Pelikan, *The Vindication of Tradition* (New Haven: Yale University Press, 1984), and Gadamer, *Truth and Method*.

30. Jan Mukarovsky, *Aesthetic Function, Norm, and Value as Social Facts*, trans. Mark Suino (Ann Arbor: University of Michigan Press, 1970), 88.

31. Jane P. Tompkins, *Sensational Designs: The Cultural Work of American Fiction, 1790–1860* (New York: Oxford University Press, 1985), xiv; Barbara Herrnstein Smith, *Contingencies of Value: Alternative Perspectives for Literary Theory* (Cambridge, Mass.: Harvard University Press, 1988); Henry Louis Gates, Jr., "The Master's Pieces: On Canon Formation and the African-American Tradition," *South Atlantic Quarterly* 89 (1990): 89–111.

32. As examined by Guillory in "The Discourse of Value," in *Cultural Capital*, 269–340.

33. Kermode, *Forms of Attention*, 74.

34. I. Lønning, *"Kanon im Kanon": zum dogmatischen Grundlagen problem des neutestamentlichen Kanons* (Munich: C. Kaiser; Oslo: Universitetsforlaget, 1972).

35. For discussion of Hebraic patterns of intertextual reference, see Michael Fishbane, *The Garments of Torah: Essays in Biblical Hermeneutics* (Bloomington: Indiana University Press, 1989); Jacob Neusner, *Canon and Connection: Intertextuality in Judaism* (Lanham, Md.: University Press of America, 1987). For New Testament uses of Hebrew Scriptures, see Northrop Frye, *The Great Code: The Bible and Literature* (New York: Harcourt Brace Jovanovich, 1983). Harold Bloom asserts that Christians like Northrop Frye have made the Hebrew Bible the "captive prize of the Gentiles"; *The Book of J*, trans. David Rosenberg and interp. Harold Bloom (New York: Grove and Weidenfeld, 1990), 14.

36. It is not in the scope of this study to discuss what these conditions might have been, but the following authors explore the occasions for the creation of specific New Testament documents: Gerd Theissen, *The Social Setting of Pauline Christianity*, ed. and trans. John H. Schutz (Philadelphia: Fortress Press, 1982); John H. Elliott, *Home for the Homeless* (Philadelphia: Fortress Press, 1981); Werner H. Kelber, *The Oral and the Written Gospel* (Philadelphia: Fortress Press, 1983); Meeks, *The First Urban Christians*.

37. Henry Y. Gamble, *The New Testament Canon* (Philadelphia: Fortress Press, 1985), 67–68.

38. Brevard Childs, *The New Testament as Canon: An Introduction* (Philadelphia: Fortress Press, 1985), 41.

39. Edgar Hennecke, *New Testament Apocrypha*, ed. Wilhelm Schneemelcher, trans. R. McL. Wilson (Philadelphia: Westminster Press, 1963), 1:25–26.

40. I base these opinions on my own reading of the *Nag Hammadi Library*, ed. James M. Robinson (San Francisco: Harper and Row, 1978); Elaine Pagels, *The Gnostic Gospels* (New York: Vintage, 1979); and John Dominic Crossan, *Four Other Gospels: Shadows on the Contours of Canon* (Minneapolis: Winston Press, 1985).

41. Childs, *The New Testament as Canon*, 21–24.

Chapter 1

1. "Markos men hermeneutes Petrou genomenos," Eusebius of Caesarea, *Histoire Ecclesiastique*, ed. Gustave Bardy, in *SC* 31 (Paris: Editions du Cerf, 1952), 3.39.15. All translations are the author's unless a translation is cited.

2. "Marcus eum subsecutus tamquam pedisequus et breviator eius videtur," Augustine, *De Consensu Evangelistarum*, ed. Franciscus Weihrich in *Corpus Scriptorum Ecclesiasticorum Latinorum* 43 (Vindobonae: F. Tempsky, 1904), 1.2.

3. Ireneus of Lyon, *Contre les Heresies*, ed. Adelin Rousseau and Louis Doutreleau, S.J., in *SC* 211 (Paris: Editions du Cerf, 1974).

4. These prologues are printed in *Synopsis Quattuor Evangeliorum: Locis parellelis evangeliorum apocryphorum et patrum adhibitis*.

5. Eusebius, *Histoire Ecclesiastique*, ed. Gustave Bardy, in *SC* 41 (Paris: Editions du Cerf, 1955), 6.14, 5–7.

6. Eusebius, *Histoire Ecclesiastique*, in *SC* 41, 6.25, 4–5. The first nine chapters are missing from Origen's commentary on Matthew.

7. Tertullian, *Adversus Marcionem*, Bks. IV–V, vol. 2, ed. and trans. Ernest Evans (Oxford: Clarendon, 1972), 270–71.

8. John Chrysostom, *In Matthaeum Homil*, in *PG* 57.

9. Jerome, "Preface," in *Commentaire sur S. Matthieu 1 (1–2)*, Latin text, intro., trans., and notes Emile Bonnard, in *SC* 242 (Paris: Editions du Cerf, 1977), 63; Jerome, *Liber de Viris illustribus*, in *PL* 23, Col. 609.

10. "Marcus fuit a Deo ordinatus scribere evangelium, et instructus a Petro, cui fuit familiaris, de veritate gestorum Christi." As quoted in Fridericus Stegmuller, *Repertorium Biblicum Medii Aevi 3* (Barcelona: Instituto Francisco Suarez, 1949; rpt. Barcelona: Graficas Marina, 1955), 349, 456.

11. "Marcus abbreviator Matthaei, ea quae in itinere ad rationem vitae regendae docebat Petrus," in Isidore of Seville, *In Libros Veteris ac Novi Testamenti Praemia*, in *PL* 83, Col. 175.

12. Gamble, *The New Testament Canon*.

13. For an overview of this omission, see R. H. Lightfoot, *The Gospel Message of Mark* (Oxford: Oxford University Press, 1950), 1–14.

14. Bruce M. Metzger, *The Canon of the New Testament* (Oxford: Clarendon, 1987), 211–12, 235, 237. St. Athanasius's Easter Letter, 367, lists the four Gospels; and at the councils of Hippo (393) and Carthage (397), the book canon of the New Testament was listed as it is today. The Council of Hippo records read: "The canonical books of the New Testament are the four books of the evangelists, the acts of the apostles, thirteen letters of Paul, one letter to the Hebrews, two letters of Peter, three of John, one of James, one of Jude and the Apocalypse of John," in Charles Joseph Hefele, *History of the Councils of the Church II: A.D. 326–A.D. 429*, trans. Henry Nutcombe Oxenham (Edinburgh: T. and T. Clark, 1876), 89. See also Sean P. Kealy, *Mark's Gospel: A History of Its Interpretation* (New York: Paulist Press, 1982), 23.

15. This is according to Clement, as reported in Eusebius, *H.E.*, see footnote 5; Gamble, *The New Testament Canon;* William R. Farmer and Denis M. Farkasfalvy, *The Formation of the New Testament Canon* (New York: Paulist Press, 1983), 17–19.

16. See, for example, William O. Walker, Jr., ed., *The Relationship among the Gospels* (San Antonio: Trinity University Press, 1978); *J. J. Griesbach: Synoptic and Text—Critical Studies 1776–1976*, ed. Bernard Orchard and Thomas R. W. Longstaff (Cambridge: Cambridge University Press, 1978); Bruce Corley, ed. and intro., *Colloquy on New Testament Studies: A Time for Reappraisal and Fresh Approaches* (Macon, Ga.: Mercer University Press, 1983); Arthur J. Bellinzoni, ed., *The Two-Source Hypothesis: A Critical Appraisal* (Macon, Ga.: Mercer University Press, 1985); William R. Farmer, *The Synoptic Problem: A Critical Analysis* (New York: Macmillan, 1964).

17. "Tract. In Marci Evangelium," in Jerome, *Presbyteri Opera,* in *CCSL* 78 (Turnhout: Brepols, 1958), 449–500.

18. For a thorough study of the role of Matthew's gospel in the first two centuries of the Church, see Edouard Massaux, *Influence de l'Evangile de saint Matthieu sur la litterature chretienne avant saint Irenee* (Louvain: Publications Universitaires, 1950; rpt. Louvain University Press, 1986).

19. Peter Brown, *Augustine of Hippo* (Berkeley: University of California Press, 1969), 21.

20. George Kennedy, *Classical Rhetoric and Its Christian and Secular Tradition from Ancient to Modern Times* (Chapel Hill: University of North Carolina Press, 1980), 146; George Kennedy, *Greek Rhetoric under Christian Emperors* (Princeton: Princeton University Press, 1983).

21. Augustine, *De Doctrina Christiana,* and Jerome, "Prologus Sancti Hieronymi Presbyteri in Pentateucho," *Biblia Sacra Iuxta Vulgatam Versionem* (Stuttgart: Wurttembergische Bibelanstalt, 1969), 1:3–4.

22. Mark D. Jordan, "Words and Word: Incarnation and Signification in Augustine's *De Doctrina Christiana,*" *Augustinian Studies* 11 (1980): 177–96. See introduction, Brian Stock, *Augustine the Reader: Meditation, Self-Knowledge, and the Ethics of Interpretation* (Cambridge, Mass.: Harvard University Press, 1996), 1–19.

23. Stock, *Augustine the Reader,* 18.

24. Ibid., 39.

25. Gadamer, *Truth and Method,* 191–92.

26. Johannes Quasten, *Patrology. 2: The Ante-Nicene Literature after Irenaeus* (Westminster, Md.: Newman Press, 1953), 45–51.

27. Hilary of Poitiers, *Sur Matthieu,* intro., critical text, trans., and notes Jean Doignon, in *SC* 254 (Paris: Editions du Cerf, 1978).

28. Johannes Quasten, *Patrology. 3: Golden Age of Greek Patristic Literature* (Westminster, Md.: Newman Press, 1960), 361.

29. Ambrose of Milan, in *CCSL* 14 (Turnhout: Brepols Editores, 1957).

30. See note 9.

31. Cyril of Alexandria, *Commentarium in Evangelium Joannis,* in *PG* 73.

32. Cyril of Alexandria, *Commentarii in Matthaeum fragmenta,* in *PG* 72, Col. 365–474.

33. Cyril of Alexandria, *Commentarii in Lucam,* in *PG* 72, Col. 475–950; see Quasten, *Patrology,* 3:124.

34. See note 8.

35. John Chrysostom, in *PG* 59, 24–382.

36. *Commentarius in Evangelium Iohannis Apostoli*, ed. J.-M. Voste. Scriptores Syrii, Series Quarta, III (Paris: E. Typographeo Republicae, 1940). See also Robert Devreesse, *Essai sur Theodore de Mopsueste* (Vatican City: BAV, 1948); Rowan A. Greer, *Theodore of Mopsuestia: Exegete and Theologian* (London: Faith Press, 1961), 112–52.

37. Augustine, *Homelies sur l'Evangile de Saint Jean*, 60–79, in *Oeuvres de Saint Augustin* 73A, 73B, 74A, ed. M.-F. Berouard (Perpignan: Institut des Etudes Augustiniennes, 1988, 1989, 1993).

38. See note 2.

39. Augustine, *Questiones evangeliorum*, in *CCSL* 44B (Turnhout: Brepols, 1980).

40. For a brief summary and discussion of this and later commentaries, see Kealy, *Mark's Gospel*, 28–57. Augustine's comment that Mark was Matthew's epitomizer dominates the history of the gospel until the eighteenth century.

41. *Biblia Patristica: Index des Citations et Allusions Bibliques dans la Litterature Patristique. 1: Des Origines a Clement d'Alexandrie et Tertullien* (Paris: Editions du Centre National de la Recherche Scientifique, 1975).

42. *Biblia Patristica: Index des Citations et Allusions Bibliques dans la Litterature Patristique. 2: Le Troisieme siecle (Origene excepte)* (Paris: Editions du Centre National de la Recherche Scientifique, 1977).

43. Clement of Alexandria, *Quis dives salvetur?*, ed. K. Koster (Frankfurt: Unveranderter Nachdruck, 1968).

44. Morton Smith, *Clement of Alexandria and a Secret Gospel of Mark* (Cambridge, Mass.: Harvard University Press, 1973); Morton Smith, *The Secret Gospel: The Discovery and Interpretation of the Secret Gospel According to Mark* (San Francisco: Harper and Row, 1973).

45. *Biblia Patristica: Index des Citations et Allusions Bibliques dans la Litterature Patristique. 3: Origene* (Paris: Editions du Centre National de la Recherche Scientifique, 1980).

46. Augustine, *De Trinitate*, ed. W. J. Mountain, in *CCSL* 50A (Turnhout: Brepols, 1968).

47. *Confessionum* libri XIII, in *CCSL* 27 (Turnhout: Brepols, 1961). Specifically, he refers to Mark 7:37 in I.l.13. There are two other references, but they are also found in Matthew (Mark 10:28 and Mark 12:30).

48. Mark 1:2 (Bk. XV, Ch. 23); 1:24 (Bk. IX, Ch. 21); 3:5 (Bk. XIV, Ch. 9); 3:27 (Bk. XX, Ch. 7); 9:43–48 (Bk. XXI, Ch. 9).

49. See G. G. Willis, *St. Augustine's Lectionary* (London: S.P.C.K, 1962).

50. See *Holy and Sacred Gospel* (Brookline, Mass.: Holy Cross Orthodox Press, 1993). In the Orthodox lectionary, John is read from Easter to Pentecost, Matthew from Pentecost to the Exaltation of the Cross, Luke from then to Lent, and Mark during Lent. For the Coptic Church, see *St. Mark and the Coptic Church* (Cairo: Coptic Orthodox Patriarchate, 1968), which records that according to early witnesses, "St. Mark being in close contact with St. Paul and St. Peter, composed the liturgy known by his name, i.e., 'The Liturgy of St. Mark'" (56). But this liturgy, which "is one of the oldest" and was used regularly in the early church both in Egypt and Ethiopia, has been rarely used in recent times (56–57).

51. See *The Revised Common Lectionary: The Consultation of Common Texts* (Nashville: Abingdon, 1992), 7, for a list of all the churches that today share the same lectionary—which of course includes Mark as part of the three-year cycle. See also *Lectionary for Mass* (New York: Catholic Book Publishing, 1970).

Chapter 2

1. Jerome, "Ad Eustochium," *Lettres* I, text and trans. Jerome Labourt (Paris: Societe d'Edition "Les Belles Lettres," 1949), 146.

2. For discussions of these literary standards, see Erich Auerbach, *Mimesis: The Representation of Reality in Western Literature*, trans. Willard R. Trask (Princeton: Princeton University Press, 1953), 35–43, and *Literary Language and Its Public in Late Latin Antiquity and in the Middle Ages*, trans. Ralph Manheim (New York: Pantheon Books, 1965).

3. For example, in *Alethes Logos*, Celsus (c.180) wrote that the gospels told an untrue story. *On the True Doctrine: A Discourse against the Christians/Celsus*, trans. and intro. R. Joseph Hoffman (New York: Oxford University Press, 1987). See Tjitze Baarda, "Diaphonia-Sumphonia, Factors in the Harmonization of the Gospels. Especially the *Diatessaron* of Tatian," in *Essays on the Diatessaron* (Kampen, The Netherlands: Kok Pharos Publishing, 1994), 29.

4. Tertullian, *Adversus Marcionem Books I–III*, vol. 1, ed. and trans. Ernest Evans (Oxford: Clarendon, 1972), intro., ix–xvi.

5. Hennecke, *New Testament Apocrypha*, vol. 1.

6. William L. Peterson, *Tatian's Diatessaron. Its Creation, Dissemination, Significance and History in Scholarship* (Leiden: E. J. Brill, 1994), 1.

7. For a brief history of Tatian, the impetus for the harmony, and the *Diatessaron*, see Baarda, "Diaphonia-Sumphonia," 29–47.

8. See introduction to *The Earliest Life of Jesus Ever Compiled from the Four Gospels Being the Diatessaron of Tatian*, trans. J. Hamlyn Hill (Edinburgh: T. and T. Clark, 1910), vii–xiv. This version dates from the twelfth through the fourteenth century, is translated from Arabic, and is supposed to have been written in Egypt.

9. *Diatessaron*, ed. Ignatius Ortiz de Urbina (Madrid: Matriti, Consejo de Investigaciones Cientificas, 1967).

10. For a thorough discussion of the early versions of the *Diatessaron*, see William L. Peterson, *Tatian's Diatesseron; "The Diatessaron of Tatian," in Bruce M. Metzger, *The Early Versions of the New Testament: Their Origin, Transmission, and Limitations* (Oxford: Clarendon, 1987), 10–36. For its dissemination, see G. Quispel, *Tatian and the Gospel of Thomas* (Leiden: E. J. Brill, 1975); *The Liege Diatessaron*, ed. D. Plooij, C. A. Phillips, and A. H. A. Bakker, English trans. A. J. Barnouw, Pt. I–V (Amsterdam: Uitgave N. V. Noord–Hollandsche Uitgevers MIJ, 1929–1938); *Diatessaron Persiano*, ed. Giuseppe Messina (Rome: Pontificio Instituto Biblico, 1951); *Il Diatessaron in volgare italiano*, testi inediti dei secoli XIII–XIV, eds. Venanzio Todesco, P. Alberto Vaccari, and Mons. Marco Vattasso (BAV, 1937).

11. Madeleine Moreau, "Lecture du *De Doctrina Christiana*," in Anne-Marie la Bonnardiere, ed., *Saint Augustin et la Bible* (Paris: Beauchesne, 1986), 253–85 (256).

12. Stock, *Augustine the Reader,* 190.

13. "Inter omnes divinas auctoritates, quae sanctis litteris continentur, evangelium merito excellit. quod enim lex et prophetae futurum praenuntiaverunt, hoc redditum adque completum in evangelio demonstratur," Augustine, *De Consensu Evangelistarum,* 1.1. "In the entire number of those divine records which are contained in the sacred writings, the gospel deservedly stands pre-eminent. For what the law and the prophets aforetime announced as destined to come to pass, is exhibited in the gospel in its realization and fulfilment," in *The Sermon on the Mount and the Harmony of the Gospels,* in *The Works of Aurelius Augustine,* ed. Marcus Dods (Edinburgh: T. and T. Clark, 1873), 8:139.

14. Augustine, *The Harmony of the Gospels,* 142; Augustine, *De Consensu Evangelistarum,* 1.2. Marcus eum subsecutus tamquam pedisequus et breviator eius videtur. cum solo quippe Iohanne nihil dixit, solus ipse perpauca, cum solo Luca pauciora, cum Mattheo vero plurima et multa paene totidem adque ipsis verbis sive cum solo sive cum ceteris consonante.

15. See Bk. 4, *The Harmony of the Gospels,* 482, 484, 490. Writing about Augustine's treatment of Mark 4:35–41, one of the rare occasions when he singled out a Markan pericope, Anne-Marie la Bonnardiere writes that this is characteristic of Augustine's style, whose primary interest is what the text can tell us about Jesus-Christ. See "La tempete apaise," in her *Saint Augustin et la Bible,* 145–48.

16. Anne-Marie la Bonnardiere, "Augustin a-t-il utilise la *Vulgate* de Jerome," in *Saint Augustin et la Bible,* 303–12, argues that to the end of his career, Augustine preferred the Latin *Septuagint* version of the Hebrew Scriptures over Jerome's translation.

17. Augustine, *De Consensu Evangelistarum,* 1.2–6.

18. Hayden V. White, *The Content of the Form: Narrative Discourse and Historical Representation* (Baltimore: Johns Hopkins University Press, 1987).

19. Stock, *Augustine the Reader,* presents Augustine's theory of reading as innovative. For Augustine, reading the Bible is not merely reciting words, but interpreting them, and then changing as a consequence of experiencing these new words.

20. See Jordan, "Words and Word."

21. Stock, *Augustine the Reader,* 2.

22. Eusebius introduced the device for showing which passages in each gospel have parallel passages. "In his letter to Carpianus he explains the entire system and mentions that it was suggested to him by the Gospel Harmony or Sections of Ammonius of Alexandria, which arrange the Gospels in four parallel columns. He developed the plan of Ammonius still further, wishing to remedy the disadvantage of the system, which permitted only the Gospel of Matthew to be read continuously." He constructed ten columns, which came to be known as the *Eusebian Canons* or *Eusebian Sections,* so the Gospels could be seen in relationship to each other. Quasten, *Patrology,* 3:335. These are included in the Greek Text of the Nestle-Aland 26th edition of the New Testament.

23. For a survey of the early witnesses as well as an assessment of the longer endings of Mark and their textual and ecclesiological implications, see William R. Farmer, *The Last Twelve Verses of Mark* (Cambridge: Cambridge University Press, 1974); Joseph Hug, *La finale de l'Evangile de Marc (Mc 16,9–20)* (Paris: J. Gabalda, 1978); see also J. D. Crossan, "Empty Tomb and Absent Lord (Mark 16:1–8)," in Werner H. Kelber, ed., *The Passion in Mark* (Philadelphia: Fortress Press, 1976), 135–52.

24. See *De Consensu Evangelistarum*, 3.24; *The Harmony of the Gospels*, 449–50.

25. See Rita Copeland, *Rhetoric, Hermeneutics, and Translation in the Middle Ages* (Cambridge: Cambridge University Press, 1991), and her "The Fortunes of 'Non Verbum pro Verbo': Or Why Jerome Is Not a Ciceronian," in Roger Ellis, ed., *The Medieval Translator: The Theory and Practice of Translation in the Middle Ages* (Cambridge: D. S. Brewer, 1989), 1:15–35.

26. Willis, *St. Augustine's Lectionary*, 10.

27. See G. G. Willis, *A History of the Early Roman Liturgy: To the Death of Pope Gregory the Great* (London: Boydell and Brewer, 1994), which lists the Gospels attested in the homilies of Gregory the Great, 112–13. Mark appears twice, for Easter (16: 1–7) and Ascension (16:14–20), in contrast to numerous references to the other Gospels.

28. Willis, *St. Augustine's Lectionary*, 5–9; see also Augustine, *Sermons pour la Paque*, intro. and notes Suzanne Poque (Paris: Editions du Cerf, 1966), 352–65, for Augustine's Easter sermons.

29. See Augustine, *Sermons pour la Paque*, 352–65.

30. Willis, *A History of the Early Roman Liturgy*, 78, 126–27.

31. Willis, *St. Augustine's Lectionary*, 64–100; Walter Howard Frere, *Studies in the Early Roman Liturgy: The Roman Lectionary* (Oxford: Oxford University Press, 1934).

32. *The Liturgy of St. Mark*, ed. Geoffrey J. Cuming (Rome: Pontificium Institutum Studiorem Orientalium, 1990); see also *St. Mark and the Coptic Church*.

33. Eusebius, *Histoire Ecclesiastique*, in *SC* 31, 2.15–16.

34. R. B. Tollinton, *Clement of Alexandria*, vol. 2 (London: Williams and Norgate, 1914).

35. Smith, *Clement of Alexandria*, 186; Smith, *The Secret Gospel*.

36. Willis, *St. Augustine's Lectionary*, 94–95.

37. *Biblia Patristica*, 1:293–319.

38. "Qui autem Iesum separant a Christo et impassibilem perseverasse Christum, passum vero Iesum dicunt, id quod secundum Marcum est praeferentes Evangelium, cum amore veritatis legentes illud corrigi possunt." *Contre les Heresies*, ed. Rousseau and Doutreleau, S.J., in *SC* 211, 3.11.7.

39. "Et ei qui dixisset illi: 'Magister bone, eum qui vere bonus esset Deus confessum esse respondentem: Quid me dicis bonum? unus est bonus, Pater in Caelis,'" *Contre les Heresies*, in *SC* 264 (Paris: Editions du Cerf, 1979), 20.2.

40. W. H. C. Frend, *Rise of Christianity* (London: Darton, Longman, and Todd, 1984), 282.

41. "Tales arbitros infans Dominus expertus non alios habuit et adultus. Petrum solum invenio maritum, per socrum. Monogamum praesumo per ecclesiam,

qua super illum." Tertullian, *De Monogamia*, ed. Paul Mattei, in *SC* 343 (Paris: Editions du Cerf, 1988), 8.4.

42. Origen, *Commentaire sur Saint Jean* 1–4, Greek text, preface, trans., and notes Cecile Blanc, in *SC* 120, 157, 222, 290, 385 (Paris: Editions du Cerf, 1970, 1975, 1982, 1992, 1996).

43. See Augustine, *Letters* I (1–82), trans. Sr. Wilfrid Parsons, S.N.D. (New York: Fathers of the Church, 1951), particularly 28, 71, 72, 73, 75, 81, and 82, which include both Augustine's and Jerome's letters.

44. "Praeparatio ad novissimum diem. Fratres, quod audistis modo monentem Scripturam atque dicentem, ut propter diem novissimum vigilemus, unusquisque de novissimo suo die cogitet: ne forte cum senseritis vel putaveritis longe esse novissimum saeculi diem, dormitetis ad novissimum vestrum diem, dormitetis ad novissimum vestrum diem." Augustine, in *PL* 38, Col. 590.

45. "Mundum non amemus. Premit amatores suos, non eos ad bonum adducit" (97, 4). Augustine, in ibid.

46. "Septem panes significant septiformen operationem Spiritus sancti: quattuor millia hominum, Ecclesiam sub quattuor Evangeliis constitutam: septem sportae fragmentorum, perfectionem Ecclesiae." Augustine, in ibid., Col. 582.

47. *St. Jerome's Homilies 2*, Homilies 60–96, trans. Sister Marie Liguori Ewald, in *The Fathers of the Church* 57 (Washington, D.C.: Catholic University of America, 1966), 152; "Debemus enim scire venas ipsas carnesque scripturarum, ut cum intellexerimus ipsam scripturam, postea sensum videre possum" (4, I.12–14); Jerome, *Tractatus in Marci Evangelium*, *CCSL* 78 (Turnhout: Brepols, 1958), 473.

48. Homily 76, *St. Jerome's Homilies*, 2:132; "Historia manifesta est, et absque nostra interpretatione audientibus patet," Jerome, in *Marci Evangelium*, 460.

49. *St. Jerome's Homilies*, 2:154; "Considerate quid dicitur. Historia manifesta est, littera patet: spiritus requiratur." Jerome, *Marci Evangelium*, 474.

50. Homily 76 (2), *St. Jerome's Homilies*, 2:132.

51. Jerome, *Marci Evangelium*, 473.

52. *St. Jerome's Homilies*, 152; "Non debemus igitur scripturas neglegenter legere," Jerome, *Marci Evangelium*, 473.

53. See Eugene F. Rice, Jr., *Saint Jerome in the Renaissance* (Baltimore: Johns Hopkins University Press, 1985), 173–99.

54. For example, in Homily 27, on Matthew 8:14–15, he remarks, referring to Mark 1:31: "But Mark also adds 'immediately,' to show the time as well." ("Ho de Markos kai eutheos, prosetheke, boulomenos kai ton chronon delosai.") *Homiliae in Matthaeum*, in *PG* 57, Col. 343. In Homily 45, on Matthew 13:10–11, he again notes a stylistic characteristic of Mark: "ho Markos auto saphesteron parestesen, eipon hoti kat' idian proselthon auto." *Homiliae in Matthaeum*, *PG* 57, Col. 472 ("Mark expressed it more distinctly") (Mark 4:10).

55. See, for example, Kennedy, *Classical Rhetoric and Its Christian and Secular Tradition*.

56. Frend, *Rise of Christianity*, 604–5.

57. "A bishop shall read no heathen books, and heretical books only when necessary," Hefele, *History of the Councils of the Church*, 412.

58. Kennedy, *Classical Rhetoric and Its Christian and Secular Tradition,* 146.

59. Kennedy, *Greek Rhetoric under Christian Emperors,* 255.

60. For example, Henri-Irenee Marrou writes of the Fathers and the Bible: "Mais essayons de nous representer ce que penser ces lettres sortis de Donat, si preoccupes de la purete grammaticale, du *bene latine dicere,* en face de ces traductions ou le souci de transcrire litteralement la parole divine avait bouleverse toutes les habitudes de la latinite, vocabulaire, syntaxe, morphologie. Si le grec des Septante et du Nouveau Testament etait deja un sujet d'etonnement pour des Hellenes habitues a l'atticisme, combien plus devaient choquer les versions latines anterieures a saint Jerome, oeuvres sorties du peuple, dues a des traducteurs a demi-illettres." In the chapter "La Bible et les lettres de la decadence," *Saint Augustin et la fin de la culture antique* (Paris: Editions E. de Boccard, 1958), 474–75.

61. The long-standing connection between rhetoric and philosophy is made by Hans-Georg Gadamer in several works, including *Reason in the Age of Science, Rhetorik und Hermeneutik* (Gottingen: Vandenhoeck and Ruprecht, 1976), and *Truth and Method*; Gadamer argues that this connection resides first in Aristotle and is continued through the Latin rhetorical tradition. A special issue of *Poetique* (23, 1975), titled *Rhetorique et Hermeneutique* and edited by Tzvetan Todorov, also took up this relation. Kathy Eden, "Hermeneutics and the Ancient Rhetorical Tradition," 59–86 and "The Rhetorical Tradition and Augustinian Hermeneutics in *De doctrina christiana,*" *Rhetorica* 8 (1990): 45–63, argue for the early connection between ancient rhetoric and the development of hermeneutics. See also Eden, *Hermeneutics and the Rhetorical Tradition.*

62. Augustine, "Itaque institui animum intendere in scripturas sanctas et videre, quales essent. Et ecce video rem non compertam superbis neque nudatam pueris, sed incessu humilem, successu excelsam et velatam mysteriis, et non eram ego talis, ut intrare in eam possem aut inclinare cervicem ad eius gressus. Non enim sicut modo loquor, ita sensi, cum attendi ad illam scripturam, sed visa est mihi indigna, quam Tullianae dignitati compararem. Tumor enim meus refugiebat modum eius et acies mea non penetrabat interiora eius. Verum autem illa erat, quae cresceret cum paruulis, sed ego dedignabar esse paruulus et turgidus fastu mihi grandis videbar." Augustine, *Confessionum,* III.V.9, in *CCSL* 27 (Turnhout: Brepols, 1981), 30. "I accordingly decided to turn my mind to the Holy Scriptures and see what they were like. And behold, I see something within them that was neither revealed to the proud nor made plain to children, that was lowly on one's entrance but lofty on further advance, and that was veiled over in mysteries. None such as I was at that time could enter into it, nor could I bend my neck for its passageways. When I first turned to the Scripture, I did not feel towards it as I am speaking now, but it seemed to me unworthy of comparison with the nobility of Cicero's writings. My swelling pride turned away from its humble style, and my sharp gaze did not penetrate into its inner meaning. But in truth it was of its nature that its meaning would increase together with your little ones, whereas I disdained to be a little child and, puffed up with pride, I considered myself to be a great fellow." *Confessions,* trans. John K. Ryan (New York: Doubleday, 1960), 82; Jerome, Letter 22, "Ad Eustochium," 144–46.

63. See Alastair Fowler, *Kinds of Literature: An Introduction to the Theory of Genres and Modes* (Cambridge, Mass.: Harvard University Press, 1982), and Gerard Genette, *Introduction a l'Architexte* (Paris: Editions du Seuil, 1979).

64. David Edward Aune, *The New Testament in Its Literary Environment* (Philadelphia: Westminster Press, 1987), 17–76; Richard A. Burridge, *What Are the Gospels? A Comparison with Graeco-Roman Biography* (Cambridge: Cambridge University Press, 1992).

65. Hermogenes, *Ars Rhetorica*, ed. L. Spengel (Leipzig: B. G. Teubner, 1854).

66. Quasten, *Patrology*, 3:214–15. As George L. Kustas writes, "No-one among the Church fathers is more sensitive to the message [the importance of psychic and somatic delivery of speeches] from the old pagan world than Basil." "Basil and the Rhetorical Tradition," in *Basil of Caesarea: Christian, Humanist, Ascetic*, ed. Paul Jonathan Fedwick (Toronto: PIMS, 1981), 230 (221–79).

67. "Nam mihi carmen erit Christi vitalia gesta,/ Divinum in populis falsi sine crimine donum./ Nec metus, ut mundi rapiant incendia secum/ Hoc opus" (*Praefatio*, 19–22). C. Vettii Aquilini Iuvenci, *Libri Evangeliorum IIII*, ed. Carolus Marold (Lipsiae: B. G. Teubner, 1886), 2–3. Author's paraphrase.

68. Quasten, *Patrology*, 3:380.

69. Harald Hagendahl, *Augustine and the Latin Classics. 1: Testimonia* (Stockholm: Almquist and Wiksell, 1967), 387.

70. *Augustine and the Latin Classics*, 430–63.

71. See note 62.

72. See *Biblical Interpretation in the Early Church*, trans. and ed. Karlfried Froehlich (Philadelphia: Fortress Press, 1984), 3–8; James L. Kugel and Rowan A. Greer, *Early Biblical Interpretation* (Philadelphia: Westminster Press, 1986), 52–72; Greer, *Theodore of Mopsuestia*; Devreesse, *Essai sur Theodore de Mopsueste*.

73. Hayden White's *The Content of the Form* explores this idea, as does his earlier essay, "Historical Text as Literary Artifact," in his *Tropics of Discourse: Essays in Cultural Criticism* (Baltimore: Johns Hopkins University Press, 1978), 81–100. The "at" versus "through" distinction is discussed in depth by Richard Lanham, *Analyzing Prose* (New York: Scribner, 1979), and *Literacy and the Survival of Humanism* (New Haven: Yale University Press, 1983).

74. This has been fully discussed by Frank Kermode in *Genesis of Secrecy* (Cambridge, Mass.: Harvard University Press, 1979); also Ernest Best, *Mark: The Gospel as Story* (Edinburgh: T. and T. Clark, 1983), explores this literary aspect of the Gospel.

75. ". . . sciat ambiguitatem scripturae aut in verbis propriis esse aut in translatis," *De Doctrina Christiana*, III.1.1. ". . . know that the ambiguity of Scripture arises either from words used literally or figuratively." *On Christian Doctrine*, trans. D. W. Robertson, Jr. (Indianapolis: Bobbs-Merrill, 1958), 78. See also Jordan, "Words and Word"; Stock, *Augustine the Reader*; Brenda Deen Schildgen, "Augustine's Answer to Jacques Derrida in the *De Doctrina Christiana*," *New Literary History* 25 (spring 1994): 382–97; Joseph Mazzeo, "St. Augustine's Rhetoric of Silence: Truth vs. Eloquence and Things vs. Signs," in his *Renaissance and Seventeenth-Century Studies* (New York: Columbia University Press, 1964), 1–28; for Augustine's contribution to the history of the four meanings in

scripture, see Henri de Lubac, *Exégèse Médievale: Les Quatre Sens de l'Ecriture*, 4 vols. (Paris: Aubier, 1954–1964).

76. Jerome, *Lettres* III (Paris: Societe d'edition "Les Belles Lettres," 1953), "quia Hebraei non solum habent *arthra* sed et *proarthra*, ille *kakotzelos* et syllabas interpretetur et litteras, dicatque *sun ton ouranon kai sun ten gen*, quod Graeca et Latina omnino lingua non recipit? huius rei exemplum ex nostro sermone capere possumus. Quanta enim apud Graecos bene dicuntur quae, si ad verbum transferamus, in Latino non resonant, et e regione, quae apud nos placent si vertantur iuxta ordinem, apud illos displicebunt," 71. "Because Hebrew has not only articles but prefixes as well, he must with tiresome zeal translate syllable by syllable and letter by letter thus: 'with *the* heaven and with *the* earth' Gn. 1:1; what neither Greek nor Latin admits. We can take analogous examples from our own language. How many phrases are charming in Greek which, translated literally have no euphony in Latin. Inversely, how many are pleasing to us in Latin, that if we translate according to the order of the words would not please the Greek."

77. "Quid igitur? Damnamus veteres? Minime; sed post priorum studia in domo Domini quod possumus laboramus. Illi interpretati sunt ante adventum Christi et quod nesciebant dubiis protulere sententiis, nos post passionem et resurrectionem eius non tam prophetiam quam historiam scribimus; aliter enim audita, aliter visa narrantur; quod melius intellegimis, melius et proferimus." Jerome, "Prologus in Pentateucho," in *Biblia Sacra Iuxta Vulgatam* I (Stuttgart: Wurttembergische Bibelstalt, 1969).

78. A recent essay on the inadequacies of the disciples in the Gospel of Mark that reviews scholarly work on the subject is F. J. Matera, "The Incomprehension of the Disciples and Peter's Confession (Mark 6:14–8:30)," *Biblica* 70 (1989): 153–72.

79. A topic to be taken up in the final chapter, but Kermode, *The Genesis of Secrecy*, is an outstanding example of this kind of interest.

Chapter 3

1. See Giuseppe Mazzotta, *Dante's Vision and the Circle of Knowledge* (Princeton: Princeton University Press, 1992), for this theory of the medieval approach to learning.

2. De Lubac, *Exégèse Médievale*; Beryl Smalley, *The Gospels in the Schools c.1100– c.1280* (London and Ronceverte: Hambledon Press, 1985).

3. Jeanine Sauvanon, *Les métiers au Moyen Âge: Leurs "signatures" dans les vitraux* (Le Coudray: Houvet, 1993); see also Wolfgang Kemp, *The Narratives of Gothic Stained Glass*, trans. Caroline Dobson Saltzweld (Cambridge: Cambridge University Press, 1997).

4. See, for example, Ezio Franceschini, "La Bibbia nell'alto medio evo," in *La Bibbia nell'Alto Medioevo* (Spoleto: Presse la Sede del Centro, 1963), and numerous other essays in this collection that testify to the widespread use of the Bible in the period. See also *The Bible in the Middle Ages: Its Influence on Literature and Art*, ed. Bernard S. Levy (Binghamton, N.Y.: State University of New York, 1992); David C. Fowler, *The Bible in Early English Literature* (Seattle:

University of Washington Press, 1976); James H. Morey, "Peter Comestor, Biblical Paraphrase, and the Medieval Popular Bible," *Speculum* 68 (January 1993): 6–35; Guy de Poerck, with Rita Van Deyck, "La Bible et l'activité traductrice dans les pays romans avant 1300," in *La Litterature Didactique, Allegorique et Satirique* I, ed. Hans Robert Jauss (Heidelberg: Carl Winter, 1968), 21–48; Jean Robert Smeets, "Les traductions, adaptations et paraphrases de la Bible en vers," in ibid., 1:48–57; H. H. Glunz, *History of the Vulgate in England from Alcuin to Roger Bacon* (Cambridge: Cambridge University Press, 1933); Hugh Pope, *English Versions of the Bible*, rev. and amplified Sebastian Bullough (London: B. Herder, 1952); Samuel Berger, *La Bible romane au moyen âge* (Geneva: Slatkine, 1977; rpt. *Romania* XVIII [1889], XIX [1890], XXIII [1894], XXVIII [1899]); Emmanuel Petavel, *La Bible en France ou les Traductions Françaises des Saintes Ecritures* (Paris, 1864; rpt. Geneva: Slatkine, 1970); Samuel Berger, *La Bible française au moyen age: Etude sur les plus anciennes versions de la Bible ecrites en prose de langue d'oïl* (Paris: Champion, 1884); Jean Bonnard, *Les Traductions de la Bible en Vers Français au Moyen Âge* (Paris, 1884; rpt. Geneva: Slatkine, 1967); *The Cambridge History of the Bible. 2: The West from the Fathers to the Reformation*, ed. G. W. H. Lampe (Cambridge: Cambridge University Press, 1969), 338–491. Most important for the official reception of the Bible, see Beryl Smalley, *The Study of the Bible in the Middle Ages* (Oxford: Clarendon press, 1941); Fridericus Stegmuller's compendious *Repertorium Biblicum Medii Aevi 1–11* (Barcelona: Instituto Francisco Suarez, 1940–1980). G. R. Evans, *The Language and Logic of the Bible: The Road to the Reformation* (Cambridge: Cambridge University Press, 1985); G. R. Evans, *The Language and Logic of the Bible: The Earlier Middle Ages* (Cambridge: Cambridge University Press, 1984); Katherine Walsh and Diana Wood, eds., *The Bible in the Medieval World: Essays in Memory of Beryl Smalley* (Oxford: Basil Blackwell, 1985); Robert E. McNally, *The Bible in the Early Middle Ages* (Westminster, Md.: Newman Press, 1959).

5. *PL* 30, Col. 589–644; Kealy, *Mark's Gospel*, 36–37, ascribes this to Cummeanus, as does McNally, *The Bible in the Early Middle Ages*, 107.

6. *PL* 103, Col. 279–86.

7. *PL* 30, Col. 560–67.

8. Venerable Bede, *In Marci Evangelium Expositio*, ed. D. Hurst, in *CCSL* 120 (Turnhout: Brepols, 1960), 427–648.

9. Albertus Magnus, *Secundum Marcum*, in *Enarrationes in Matthaeum (XXI–XXVIII)- in Marcum*, in *Opera Omni* 21 (Paris: Apud Ludovicum Vives, Bibliopolam Editorem, 1894), 339–761.

10. *Catena Aurea: Commentary on the Four Gospels, collected out of the Works of the Fathers. St Mark*, vol. 2 (Oxford and London: John Henry and James Parker, 1865).

11. *PG* 129 has all the commentaries; for Mark, see Col. 767–852.

12. *PG* 123 has all the commentaries, and Mark at Col. 491–682.

13. *Paraphrase on Mark*, trans. and annotated Erika Rummel, in *Collected Works of Erasmus* (Toronto: University of Toronto Press, 1988).

14. *La Bible de Jehan Malkaraume*, ed. J. R Smeets, 2 vols. (Assen: Van Gorcum, 1978).

15. Alfonso X el Sabio, *General Estoria*, ed. Antonio G. Solalinde (Madrid: Alvarez de Castro, 1930); *General Estoria 2*, ed. Antonio Solalinde, Lloyd Kasten, Victor R. B. Oelschlager (Madrid: Alvarez de Castro, 1961). Francisco Rico, *Alfonso el Sabio y La General Estoria* (Barcelona: Ediciones Ariel, 1972), discusses how Alfonso's work fits into the tradition of other medieval universal histories.

16. Paul Orosius, *Histoires I and II*, ed. Marie-Pierre Arnaud-Lindet (Paris: Les Belles Lettres, 1990).

17. "Peter Comestor, Biblical Paraphrase, and the Medieval Popular Bible," 6–35.

18. See chapter 2, note 10.

19. In speaking of narrative units, I am referring, for example, to theories of narrative as developed by Gerard Genette, *Narrative Discourse*, or Mieke Bal, *Narratology: Introduction to the Theory of Narrative*, trans. Christine van Boheemen (Toronto: University of Toronto Press, 1985). Biblical scholars who examine the structure of the Markan narrative include Rudolf Pesch, *Das Markus-evangelium*, 2 vols. (Freiburg: Herder, 1976–1977), a model of a contemporary theological commentary on the gospel. He is attentive to how the narrative features of the gospel support theological convictions. Also see David Rhoads's "Narrative Criticism and the Gospel of Mark," *Journal of the American Academy of Religion* 50, no. 3 (1982): 411–34; David Rhoads and Donald Michie, *Mark as Story: An Introduction to the Narrative of a Gospel* (Philadelphia: Fortress Press, 1982); Brenda Deen Schildgen, *Crisis and Continuity: Time in the Gospel of Mark* (Sheffield: Sheffield Academic Press, 1998); Ricoeur, "Interpretative Narrative," in *The Book and the Text*, 237–57; and of course, Kermode, *Genesis of Secrecy*.

20. Arnaldo Momigliano, *The Development of Greek Biography* (Cambridge, Mass.: Harvard University Press, 1971).

21. *Otfrids Evangelienbuch*, ed. Oskar Erdmann (1882; rpt. Tübingen: Verlag von Max Niemeyer, 1957).

22. *Heliand und genesis*, ed. Otto Behaghel (Halle: Max Niemeyer, 1910); *The Heliand: The Saxon Gospel*, trans. G. Ronald Murphy, S.J. (Oxford: Oxford University Press, 1992).

23. See G. Ronald Murphy, *The Saxon Savior: The Germanic Transformation of the Gospel in the Ninth-Century Heliand* (Oxford: Oxford University Press, 1989) for a full discussion of how the *Heliand* represents a "Germanic Christ."

24. *Aurora Petri Rigae Biblia Versificata*, ed. Paul E. Beichner (South Bend: Notre Dame University Press, 1965), 2 vols. See introduction, 1:xi–lv, for the historical background to the *Aurora*.

25. Berger, *La Bible romane au moyen âge; Cambridge History of the Bible*, 2:436–52.

26. Bonnard, *Les Traductions de la Bible*.

27. In *Sourcebook of Texts for Comparative Study of the Gospels* (Missoula, Mont.: SBL, 1973), 11–26, later published as *Documents for the Study of the Gospels*, ed. and trans. David R. Cartlidge and David L. Dungan (Philadelphia: Fortress Press, 1980), 107–16.

28. In *The Other Bible*, ed. Willis Barnstone (San Francisco: Harper and Row, 1984), 362–80.

29. *Sourcebook of Texts for Comparative Study of the Gospels*, 35–40.

30. This is the point made by Ina Spiele in her introduction to Herman de Valenciennes, *Li Romanz de Dieu et de sa Mere*, ed. Ina Spiele (Leiden: University Press of Leiden, 1975). See also Smeets, "Les traductions, adaptations et paraphrases de la Bible en vers," 48–57.

31. Geufroi de Paris, *La Passion des Jongleurs*, ed. Anne Joubert Amari Perry (Paris: Beauchesne, 1981).

32. *La Bible de Mace de la Charite VI Evangiles, Actes des Apostres*, ed. J. R. Smeets (Leiden: Leiden University Press, 1986).

33. *La Bible anonyme du Ms. Paris B.N.f. fr.763*, ed. Julia C. Szirmai (Amsterdam: Rodopi, 1985).

34. See Spiele, intro. to *Li Romanz de Dieu et sa Mere*, 37–45.

35. See introduction to *La Passion*, 18–20.

36. See introduction to *La Bible de Mace de la Charite* for the history of and influences on the text, particularly 96–97.

37. See the synoptic tables from *Aurora*, Mace de la Charite, and the four gospels, in *La Bible de Mace de la Charite* for the overlaps and Mark's absence, 77–91.

38. Ludolphus de Saxony, *Vita Jesu Christi*, ed. L.-M. Rigollot (Paris: Victorem Palme, 1878); for a thorough discussion of the *Vita Christi*, see Sister Mary Immaculate Bodenstedt, *The Vita Christi of Ludolphus the Carthusian* (Washington, D.C.: Catholic University of America Press, 1944).

39. See O. B. Hardisson, *Christian Rite and Christian Drama in the Middle Ages* (Baltimore: Johns Hopkins University Press, 1965), and Benjamin Hunningher, *The Origin of the Theater* (New York: Hill and Wang, 1955). Hunningher argues for the ritual origin of all drama, and Hardisson provides a history of the role of the *quem quaeritis* trope in the development of medieval drama.

40. For development of this idea, see Victor Turner, *The Ritual Process* (Ithaca: Cornell University Press, 1969).

41. Interrogatio. "Quem quaeritis in sepulchro, o Christicolae?" Responsio. "Jesum Nazarenum crucifixum, o caelicolae."

Angeli. "Non est hic; surrexit, sicut praedixerat. Ite, nuntiate quia surrexit de sepulchro." "The Quem Quaeritis Trope" from the introit of the Mass at Easter found in the monastery of St. Gall. Reprinted in *Medieval and Tudor Drama*, ed. John Gassner (New York: Bantam Books, 1963), 35.

42. See *Medieval Church Music-Dramas, A Repertory of Complete Plays*, trans. and ed. Fletcher Collins, Jr. (Charlottesville: University Press of Virginia, 1976).

43. "Christ's Resurrection," in *The Late Medieval Religious Plays of Bodleian Mss. Digby 133 and E Museo 160*, ed. Donald C. Baker, John L. Murphy, and Louis B. Hall. EETS 283 (Oxford: Oxford University Press, 1982).

44. See Walter Howard Frere, *Studies in the Early Roman Liturgy: The Roman Lectionary* (Oxford: Oxford University Press, 1934). This is a study of Mass-lessons in gospel books over four centuries, from 700 onward.

45. Amalarii Episcopi, *Liber Officialis*, in *Opera Liturgica Omnia II*, ed. Ioanne Michaele Hanssens (Vatican City: BAV, 1948).

46. *Liber Officialis* I.I, 31, 160–61.

47. See introduction, *Aurora*, xxx–xxxiii.

48. See McNally, *The Bible in the Early Middle Ages*, 105–9, for lists of these commentaries.

49. Copeland, "Translation and Interlingual Commentary," in her *Rhetoric, Hermeneutics, and Translation*, 87–126.

50. Isidore of Seville, *Etimologías: Edicion Bilingue I*, ed. Jose Oroz Reta and Manuel-A. Marcos Casquero (Madrid: Biblioteca de Autores Cristianos, 1982), 1.30.1.

51. See Evans, "A Standard Commentary: The *Glossa Ordinaria*," in his *The Language and Logic of the Bible: The Earlier Middle Ages*, 37.

52. Ibid., 37–47. Also Smalley, *The Study of the Bible in the Middle Ages*, provides a brief history of the development of the *Glossa* that became the *Glossa ordinaria* (35–45); and see Ermenegildo Bertola, "La 'Glossa Ordinaria' biblica ed I suoi problemi," *Recherches de Theologie ancienne et medievale* 45 (1978): 34–78.

53. Bertola, "La 'Glossa Ordinaria,' " 35–36.

54. Petrus Comestor, *Historia Scholastica*, in *PL* 198, Col. 1049–1722. For a full discussion of the role of Peter Comestor's *Historia* in biblical paraphrases and the popular medieval Bible, see Morey, "Peter Comestor," and David Luscombe, "Peter Comestor," in Walsh and Wood, eds., *The Bible in the Medieval World*, 109–129.

55. Brian Stock, *The Implications of Literacy: Written Language and Models of Interpretation in the Eleventh and Twelfth Centuries* (Princeton: Princeton University Press, 1983), 90–91, 522–31.

56. See note 5.

57. Bede, *In Marci Evangelium Expositio*, "Initium evangelii Iesu Christi filii Dei. Sicut scriptum est in Esaia propheta. Conferendum hoc evangelii Marci principium principio Mathei quo ait, Liber generationis Iesu Christi filii David filii Abraham," I.i, 1–2.

58. Bede, *In Marci Evangelium Expositio*, "Evigilate iusti et nolite peccare," IV.xiv, 71–72.

59. Ibid., IV.xiv, 10.

60. Ibid., I.ii, 14.

61. Ibid., IV.xiv, 35–36.

62. Ibid., IV.xiv, 69–70.

63. See de Lubac, *Exegese Medievale*, 2:305; see also Evans, *The Language and Logic of the Bible: The Road to the Reformation*, 42–50, for the renewed interest in the "literal sense."

64. "tres theologicas, spem, fidem, charitatem: et quatuor cardinales, prudentiam, justitiam, fortitudinem, temperantiam" (513) (the three theological, hope, faith, and charity: and the four cardinal, prudence, justice, fortitude, and temperance).

65. See de Lubac, *Exegese Medievale*, 2:304–7.

66. See *Paraphrase on Mark*, xii.

67. *Paraphrase on Mark*, 18.

68. See translator's note to *Paraphrase on Mark*, xi. Erasmus explains in his dedicatory letter to Francis, King of France, that having completed *paraphrases* of the other three gospels, he has left Mark to the last; spurred on by symmetry, he says, he chose to dedicate each to the leading monarchs of the day (2).

69. See Chartier, *Forms and Meanings,* 42.

70. "I find further evidence of the large numbers who now read the New Testament in the fact that, although the printers put so many thousands of volumes on the market every year, yet all those presses cannot keep up with the eager demand of the purchasers. Anything written by anyone on the gospel is a very saleable object nowadays." From Erasmus, "Dedicatory letter," *Paraphrase on Mark,* 10–11.

71. See W. P. Stevens, "The Bible," in his *The Theology of Huldrych Zwingli* (Oxford: Clarendon, 1986), 56 (51–79, 313).

72. Wyclif quotes John more frequently than either Matthew or Luke, and Mark not even half as often as these others. In Wyclif's Sunday and festival sermons, Matthew takes first place, Luke second, John third, and Mark—with only five sermons—a very distant fourth. See *Select English Works of John Wyclif. 1: Sermons on the Gospels for Sundays and festivals,* ed. Thomas Arnold (Oxford: Clarendon, 1869); and *2: Sermons on the Ferial Gospels and Sunday Epistles. Treatises,* ed. Thomas Arnold (Oxford: Clarendon, 1871).

73. *The Gospel according to St. John, 1–10,* trans. T. H. L. Parker, in *Calvin's Commentaries 4,* ed. David W. Torrance and Thomas F. Torrance (Edinburgh and London: Oliver and Boyd, 1959), 6. John Calvin wrote *A Harmony of the Gospels: Matthew, Mark and Luke,* vol. 1, trans. A. W. Morrison, ed. David W. Torrance and Thomas F. Torrance (Edinburgh: Saint Andrew Press, 1972); *A Harmony of the Gospels: Matthew, Mark and Luke,* vol. 2, trans. H. L. Parker, ed. David W. Torrance and Thomas F. Torrance (Edinburgh: Saint Andrew Press, 1972); *A Harmony of the Gospels: Matthew, Mark and Luke,* vol. 3, trans. A. W. Morrison, ed. David W. Torrance and Thomas F. Torrance (Edinburgh: Saint Andrew Press, 1972). But he also produced two volumes on John's gospel and the First Epistle of John.

74. Timothy J. Wengert, *Philip Melanchthon's Annotationes in Johannem in Relation to Its Predecessors and Contemporaries* (Geneva: Librairie Droz, 1987), 23–56.

75. See *Luther's Works,* vols. 1–55, ed. Jaroslav Pelikan (vols. 1–30) and Helmut T. Lehmann (vols. 31–55) (Philadelphia: Fortress Press, 1958–1986).

76. "Against the Roman Papacy, an Institution of the Devil," in *Luther's Works 41: Church and Ministry III,* ed. Eric W. Gritsch, intro. G. Gordon Rupp (Philadelphia: Fortress Press, 1966), 325.

77. John Colet, *An Exposition of St. Paul's First Epistle to the Corinthians,* ed. and trans. J. H. Lupton (London, 1874; rpt. Ridgewood, N.J.: Gregg Press, 1965); *An Exposition of St. Paul's Epistle to the Romans,* ed. and trans. J. H. Lupton (London, 1873; rpt. Ridgewood, N.J.: Gregg Press, 1965).

Chapter 4

1. Jerome, *Lettres* III. Jerome discusses how Hilary the Confessor translated homilies on Job and the Psalms from Greek. He writes that Hilary, far from attaching himself to the words or producing a tortured translation, "quasi captivos sensus in suam linguam victoris jure transposuit."

2. "Ex quo factum est, ut etiam scriptura divina, . . . ab una lingua profecta, qua

opportune potuit per orbem terrarum disseminari, per varias interpretum linguas longe lateque diffusa innotesceret gentibus ad salutem."

3. "Sociosemantic" is a term used in Jan de Waard and Eugene A. Nida, *From One Language to Another: Functional Equivalence in Bible Translating* (Nashville: Thomas Nelson, 1986), 60–77.

4. See, for example, Martin McNamara, *Studies on Texts of Early Irish Latin Gospels (A.D. 600–1200)* (Dordrecht: Kluwer Academic Publishers, 1990).

5. Glunz, *History of the Vulgate in England*, 24–29.

6. H. F. D. Sparks, "The Latin Bible," in *The Bible in the Early Church*, ed. and intro. Everett Ferguson (New York: Garland, 1993), 360–61 (342–69).

7. Nicholas de Lyra, *Postilla* (Venice: Hertzog, 1494); a 1492 Strassburg edition is reprinted as *Postilla Super Totam Bibliam* (Frankfurt: Minerva Gmb. H., 1971). The prologues to the *Postilla*, in which Nicholas explains his methodology, are translated into French with an introduction by Yves Delegue, *Les Machines du Sens: Textes de Hugues de Saint-Victor, Thomas d'Aquin, et Nicolas de Lyre* (Paris: Editions des Cendres, 1987), 95–118.

8. Lorenzo Valla, *Collatio Novi Testamenti*, ed. Alessandro Perosa (Florence: Sansoni Editore, 1970). The *Collatio* was first published in Paris by Erasmus in 1505 from a version completed in 1449–1450.

9. *Novum Instrumentum Omne*, diligiter ab Erasmo Roterodamo recognitum emendatum (Basileae in laedibus Ioannis Frobenij Hammelburgensis, Februario, 1516).

10. Glunz, *History of the Vulgate in England*, 24.

11. Jerry H. Bentley, *Humanists and Holy Writ: New Testament Scholarship in the Renaissance* (Princeton: Princeton University Press, 1983).

12. See de Lubac, "Nicolas de Lyre," in his *Exegese Medievale* 2:344–67.

13. Nicolas de Lyre, "Postilles sur toute la Bible," in Delegue, *Les Machines du Sens*, 106–9.

14. See Evans, *The Language and Logic of the Bible: The Road to the Reformation*, xxii.

15. Other variations of this saying are "Si Lyra non lyrasset, / Totus mundus delirasset. Or Si Lyra non lyrasset, / Ecclesia Dei non saltasset," as quoted in de Lubac, *Exegese Medievale*, 2:353. A paraphrase might read, "If Lyra had not done his kind of work, the whole world would be foolish," or "If Lyra had not done his kind of work, the Church of God would not have danced."

16. For a history of Jerome's reception in the Renaissance, see Rice, *Saint Jerome and the Renaissance*.

17. See Walter J. Ong, *Orality and Literacy: The Technologizing of the Word* (London: Methuen, 1982), for the impact of this technological revolution. For a thorough picture of the evolution from manuscript to book, see Lucien Febvre and Henri-Jean Martin, *L'Apparition du Livre* (Paris: Edition Albin Michel, 1958), especially 3–4; also see 162–92 for the mercantile value of books and 326–71 for the commercial aspects of bookmaking. Also "Representations of the Written Word," Chartier, *Forms and Meanings*, 6–24.

18. *Collatio*, 7–10.

19. "Verum si post quadringentos solum annos ita turbidus a fonte fluebat rivus,

quid mirum si rursus post mille annos—tot enim ab Hieronymo ad hoc evum sunt—hic rivus nunquam repurgatus aliqua in parte limum sordesque contraxit?" *Collatio*, 9.

20. "Better two codices, though set down rarely, where one reads, *emisit* for *expellere* . . . ; in addition, it is in the present tense not the past." "Melius ii codices, quanquam rari sint, quibus legitur 'emisit,' nam 'expellere'. . . ; preterea est temporis presentis non preteriti." *Collatio*, 74.

21. "Magister, non ad te pertinet quod perimus?", he writes, "Proprie est grece: 'non est cure tibi' sive 'non curas quod perimus?' " *Collatio*, 77.

22. See Marjorie O'Rourke Boyle, *Erasmus on Language and Method in Theology* (Toronto: University of Toronto Press, 1977), 117–27, for a discussion of Erasmus's approach to allegory. In contrast to other scholars who have argued that Erasmus rejected allegory, O'Rourke Boyle shows how he expanded its meaning to include metaphor and all figurative language.

23. For a discussion of the relation between Augustine's and Erasmus's humanism, see Charles Bene, *Erasme et Saint Augustin ou l'influence de Saint Augustin sur l'humanisme d'Erasme* (Geneva: Librairie Droz, 1969), 78–95; also see Kathy Eden, "Rhetoric in the Hermeneutics of Erasmus' Later Works," *Erasmus of Rotterdam Society* 11 (1991): 88–104.

24. Erasmus, *Paraphrase on Mark*, xii.

25. Hugh of St. Cher, *Postillae in universa Biblia juxta quadruplicem sensum litteralem, allegoricum, moralem, anagogicum*, 8 vols. (Lyon, 1645).

26. Boyle, *Erasmus on Language and Method in Theology*, 3–31.

27. Erasmus, *Annotations on the New Testament: The Gospels*, ed. Anne Reeve (London: Duckworth, 1986). Since Erasmus continued to add and delete from the *Annotations* through the several editions between 1516 and 1535 (1519, 1522, 1527), this edition includes all modifications, constituting what Reeve calls a "spiritual and scholarly diary" (xi). Also see Erika Rummel, *Erasmus' Annotations on the New Testament: From Philologist to Theologian* (Toronto: University of Toronto Press, 1986), 12–13. For a history of these dramatic developments in the textual criticism of the Bible, see Bentley, *Humanists and Holy Writ*.

28. Erasmus, *Annotations*, 113.

29. Ibid., 113.

30. Ibid., 147.

31. Ibid., 114.

32. Boyle, *Erasmus on Language and Method in Theology*, 117–27.

33. For the impact of this shift, see Robert Coogan, *Erasmus, Lee and the Correction of the Vulgate: The Shaking of the Foundations* (Geneva: Droz, 1992).

34. The Council of Trent decreed the *Vulgate* was the only official Bible, and every biblical text, whether commentary or otherwise, had to be scrutinized. "Sessio Quarta: Decretum de Canonicis Scripturis," *Canones et Decreta Concilii Tridentini* (Naples: Joseph Pelella, 1859), 11–12. See *The Canons and Decrees of the Sacred and Oecumenical Council of Trent*, trans. Rev. J. Waterworth (1848, Verbatim; rpt. Chicago: Christian Symbolic Publication Society, n.d.), 19–20.

35. *Biblia Sacrae Vulgatae Editionis Sixti V. et Clementis VIII* (Paris: 1618).

36. *Nova Vulgata Bibliorum Editione* (BAV, 1970).

37. See note 39 to Johann Griesbach, "Commentatio," in *J. J. Griesbach*, 205.

38. Books that discuss the theory and practice of translation include Jacques Derrida, *Difference in Translation*, trans. and ed. Joseph F. Graham (Ithaca: Cornell University Press, 1985); George Steiner, *After Babel: Aspects of Language and Translation* (Oxford: Oxford University Press, 1975; rpt. 1977); Louis Kelly, *The True Interpreter: A History of Translation Theory and Practice in the West* (Oxford: Basil Blackwell, 1979); Copeland, *Rhetoric, Hermeneutics, and Translation*, and her essay "The Fortunes of 'Non Verbum pro Verbo': Or Why Jerome Is Not a Ciceronian," in Ellis, ed., *The Medieval Translator: The Theory and Practice of Translation in the Middle Ages*, 1:15–35. Books on medieval translation theory that do not deal specifically with biblical translations include Jeanette Beer, ed., *Medieval Translators and Their Craft* (Studies in Medieval Culture XXV) (Kalamazoo, Mich.: Western Michigan University, Medieval Institute Publications, 1989); Ellis, ed., *The Medieval Translator: The Theory and Practice of Translation in the Middle Ages*, vol. 1; Roger Ellis, ed., *The Medieval Translator: The Theory and Practice of Translation in the Middle Ages*, vol. 2 (London: Center for Medieval Studies, 1991). For biblical translations, see Eugene A. Nida, *Toward a Science of Translating* (Leiden: E. J. Brill, 1964), especially 11–29, for an overview of the cultural issues involved in translations.

39. See Copeland, "Roman Theories of Translation," 9–36, and "From Antiquity to the Middle Ages I: The Place of Translation and the Value of Hermeneutics," 37–62, in her *Rhetoric, Hermeneutics, and Translation*; Gadamer, *Truth and Method*, 346–51; *"De Optimo Genere Oratorum,"* in *Cicero* II, trans. H. M. Hubbell (Cambridge, Mass.: Harvard University Press; London: Heinemann, 1976), 354–73.

40. In this work Cicero distinguishes between translating as an interpreter and translating as an orator, based on his conviction that eloquence is comprised of both "verbis et sententiis" (words and sense) (*De Optimo*, II, 356). His understanding of oratory as opposed to interpretation allowed him to maintain the style, metaphors, and force of the original, in contrast to what he called interpretation, which would have required him to follow word for word (*De Optimo*, V, 364–68). Copeland, *Rhetoric, Hermeneutics, and Translation*, discusses this Ciceronian preconception in her study of translation and hermeneutics in the Middle Ages (9–36).

41. "Prologus Sancti Hieronymi Presbyteri in Pentateucho," in the *Biblia Sacra* I, 3–4; also see "Ad Pammachium," in Jerome, *Lettres* III.

42. For analyses of Augustine's purposes in the *De Doctrina*, see Gerald A. Press, "The Subject and Structure of Augustine's *De Doctrina Christiana*," *Augustinian Studies* 11 (1980): 99–124; Jordan, "Words and Word"; Duane W. H. Arnold and Pamela Bright, eds., *The De Doctrina Christiana: A Classic of Western Culture* (South Bend: Notre Dame University Press, 1995); Brenda Deen Schildgen, "Rhetoric and the Body of Christ: Augustine, Jerome, and the Classical *Paideia*," in Brenda Deen Schildgen, ed., *The Rhetoric Canon* (Detroit: Wayne State University Press, 1997), 151–73.

43. See Glunz, *History of the Vulgate in England*, for a history of this development (1–71).

44. Derrida, *De la Grammatologie.*
45. "Si enim latinis exemplaribus fides est adhibenda, respondeant quibus: tot sunt paene quot codices. Sin autem veritas est quaerenda de pluribus, cur non ad graecam originem revertentes ea quae vel a vitiosis interpretibus male edita vel a praesumptoribus imperitis emendata perversius vel a librariis dormitantibus aut addita sunt aut mutata corrigimus?" "Epistula ad Damasum," "Praefatio," *Biblia Sacra,* II, 1515.
46. *On Christian Doctrine,* II.9, 44. "Qui enim scripturas ex hebraea in graecam verterunt, numerari possunt, latini autem interpretes nullo modo. Ut enim cuique primis fidei temporibus in manus venit codex graecus, et aliquantum facultatis sibi utriusque linguae habere videbatur, ausus est interpretari," *De Doctrina Christiana* II.9.16.
47. Bonifatius Fischer, *Beitrage zur Geschichte Der Lateinischen Bibeltexte* (Freiburg: Verlag Herder, 1986).
48. "Ad Pammachium," in Jerome, *Lettres* III.57, 5. "Ego enim non solum fateor, sed libera voce profiteor me in interpretatione Graecorum absque scripturis sanctis, ubi et verborum ordo mysterium est, non verbum e verbo sed sensum exprimere de sensu."
49. *Horace on Poetry: The "Ars Poetica,"* ed. C. O. Brink (Cambridge: Cambridge University Press, 1971), ll. 133–34.
50. "nec verbum verbo curabis reddere fidus interpres." Jerome, *Lettres* III.57, 5. Rita Copeland's conviction that "interpreter" in this context is a reference to grammar or philological understanding rather than to rhetoric/hermeneutics is evident. See "From Antiquity to the Middle Ages I," in her *Rhetoric, Hermeneutics, and Translation,* 37–62.
51. Jerome, *Lettres* III.57, 6.
52. Metzger, *The Early Versions of the New Testament,* 323–24: "Parallel with the adoption of Greek words there went the creation of many neologisms in Latin. These were made with no concern for the purity of the language." Mlle. Christine Mohrmann has observed that Greek terms were kept on the whole for the concrete aspects—institutions (e.g., *eucharistia, baptismus*) and the hierarchy (e.g., *episcopus, presbyter, diaconus*)—while Latin neologisms were created, or old words used in a new sense, to express abstract or spiritual ideas like redemption and salvation. See also, G. Q. A. Meershoeck, *Le Latin Biblique d'apres Saint Jerome: Aspects Linguistiques de la Rencontre entre la Bible et le Monde Classique* (Utrecht: Dekker and Van de Vegt N.V. Nijmegen, 1966), 31–32.
53. Cicero, *De Oratore,* Bk. III. 37, trans. H. Rackham (Cambridge, Mass.: Harvard University Press, 1968), 118–20.
54. Erika Rummel, "The Task and Its Execution," in *Erasmus' Annotations on the New Testament: From Philologist to Theologian,* 89–121, discusses Jerome and Erasmus's changes.
55. See Eligius Dekkers, "L'eglise devant la bible en langue vernaculaire," in W. Lourdaux and D. Verhelst, eds., *The Bible and Medieval Culture* (Louvain: Louvain University Press, 1979), 1–15.
56. This is the argument taken up by Derrida in "Des Tours de Babel," 165–207, and "Appendix Des Tours de Babel," 209–48, in *Difference in Translation.*

57. Bruce Metzger's *The Early Versions of the New Testament* is a thorough history of the creation, quality, textual remains, and assessment of these versions of the New Testament. For a synopsis of the Gothic, Anglo-Saxon, Wyclif, and Tyndale versions, see *The Gothic and Anglo-Saxon Gospels in Parallel Columns with the Versions of Wycliffe and Tyndale*, ed. Rev. Joseph Bosworth (London: John Russell Smith, 1874). For an edition of Ulfilas's Gothic Bible, see *Die Gotische Bibel*, ed. Wilhelm Streitberg (Heidelberg: Carl Winter, 1919; rpt. 1960). For the Anglo-Saxon and Middle English versions, see F. F. Bruce, *The English Bible: A History of Translations* (New York: Oxford University Press, 1961), and Pope, *English Versions of the Bible*. For an edition of the Anglo-Saxon version of the Gospel of Mark, see *The Gospel of Saint Mark, in Anglo-Saxon and Northumbrian Versions*, EETS 304, ed. Walter Skeat (Cambridge: Cambridge University Press, 1871). Also *The Cambridge History of the Bible. 1: From the Beginnings to Jerome*, ed. P. R. Ackroyd and C. F. Evans (Cambridge: Cambridge University Press, 1969), and *2: The West from the Fathers to the Reformation*, provide an overview of the translations from the Apostolic to the Reformation periods. See also Lourdaux and Verhelst, eds., *The Bible and Medieval Culture*.

58. See Petavel, *La Bible en France*; Berger, *La Bible française au moyen âge*; and Bonnard, *Les Traductions de la Bible*.

59. See Klaus Reinhardt and Horacio Santiago-Otero, *Biblioteca Bíblica Ibérica Medieval* (Madrid: Consejo Superior de Investigaciones Científicas, 1986), for a list of the Iberian peninsula vernacular bibles, 21–46; *El Nuevo Testamento segun el manuscrito escurialense 1–1-6*, ed. T. A. Montgomery and Spurgeon W. Baldwin, Anejos del BRAE 22 (Madrid: Real Academia Espanola, 1970).

60. *Bíblia Medieval Portuguesa*, ed. Serafim da Silva Neto (Rio de Janeiro: Instituto Nacional do Livro, 1958).

61. *Il Diatessaron in volgare italiano*. These are harmonies, but nonetheless they represent contributions to the vernacularization of the Bible in the Middle Ages. See Kenelm Foster's essay in *Cambridge History of the Bible*, vol. 2; Foster supports Berger's nineteenth-century conclusion that "the whole Bible had probably been translated into Italian, by the mid-thirteenth century or a little later" (2:457).

62. Ian J. Kirby, *Bible Translation in Old Norse* (Geneva: Librairie Droz, 1986).

63. *The Liege Diatessaron*.

64. See Quispel, "The Origin of the Codex," "The Old High German Version of the Codex Ludgerianus," and "The Old High German and Jewish-Christian Gospel Tradition," 50–107, in his *Tatian and the Gospel of Thomas*; Metzger, *Early Versions*, 455–60.

65. Typical of this kind of prejudice is the recent Harry M. Orlinsky and Robert G. Bratcher, *A History of Bible Translation and the North American Contribution* (Atlanta: Scholars Press, 1991). The first chapter, titled "The First Great Age of Bible Translation, 200 B.C.E.–Fourth Century C.E." and the second, similarly titled "The Second Great Age of Biblical Translation, Fourth Century–1500" completely overlook the medieval translations, going from the *Vulgata* to Wyclif with a passing reference to the Anglo-Saxon translation as a gloss. See

Margaret Deanesly's *The Lollard Bible and Other Medieval Biblical Versions* (Cambridge: Cambridge University Press, 1920; rpt. 1966), which also reflects a similar bias. Leonard Boyle tries to set the record straight in "Innocent III and Vernacular Scripture," in Walsh and Wood, eds., *The Bible in the Medieval World*, 97–107, writing that "Innocent has been much maligned by historians who see a denunciation of translations, or of the reading or study of the Scriptures by the laity" (106).

66. For the condition of Jerome's version of the Bible during the Middle Ages, see the preface to Samuel Berger's *Histoire de la Vulgate pendant les premiers siecles du moyen age* (Paris, 1893; rpt. New York: Burt Franklin, 1958), vii–xxi, still an accurate description of how subject this most copied text was to errors of all kinds; Glunz, *The History of the Vulgate in England*, 5–71; "Medieval History of the Latin Vulgate," in *Cambridge History of the Bible*, 2:102–54.

67. In *De Schematibus et Tropis*, in *PL* 90, Col. 175–86. Bede clearly demonstrated his interest in philological issues for biblical study; using Roman and Carolingian rhetoric books, he identified lists of figures, many of which he located in the Bible.

68. See *Cambridge History of the Bible*, 2:133–40 for a brief history of this text.

69. Richard Kieckhefer, *Magic in the Middle Ages* (Cambridge: Cambridge University Press, 1990), 47, 70–71.

70. Murphy, *The Saxon Savior*, 75–94.

71. See Murphy, "Magic in the *Heliand*," in *The Heliand*, 205–20.

72. For a thorough discussion of Ulfilas's style, see G. W. S. Friedrichsen, *The Gothic Version of the Gospels: A Study of Its Style and Textual History* (London: Humphrey Milford, Oxford University Press, 1926); Georges Cuendet, *L'Ordre des Mots dans le texte grec et dans les versions gotique, armenienne, et vieux slave des evangiles* (Paris: Librairie Ancienne Honore Champion, 1929); Carlo Alberto Mastrelli, "La Tecnica delle Traduzioni della Bibbia nell'Alto Medioevo," in *Bibbia nell'Alto Medioevo*, 657–81.

73. *Die gothische Bibel*; Friedrich Ludwig Stamm, *Ulfilas oder die uns erhaltenen Denkmaler der gotischen Sprache*, ed. Moritz Heyne and Ferdinand Wrede (Paderborn: Druck und Verlag von Ferdinand Schoningh, 1903); *The Gothic and Anglo-Saxon Gospels in Parallel Columns*; Metzger, *Early Versions*, 375–88; *Cambridge History of the Bible*, 2:338–62.

74. Metzger, *Early Versions*, 376–77.

75. Friedrichsen, *The Gothic Version of the Gospels*, 15–16.

76. Cuendet, *L'Ordre des Mots*, 171.

77. Metzger, *Early Versions*, 446–47; Pope, *English Versions of the Bible*, 31–51; Skeat, *The Gospel of Mark*, i–iv.

78. See David Fowler, chapter 3, "Old English Translations and Paraphrases," *The Bible in Early English Literature*, 79–124 (87); *The Lindisfarne and Rushworth Gospels: The Gospel of Mark*, ed. George Waring, Publications of the Surtees Society 39 (London: Whittaker, 1861).

79. Pope, *English Versions of the Bible*, 41–44.

80. *The Old English Version of the Gospels*, ed. R. M. Liuzza, in EETS 304 (Oxford: Oxford University Press, 1994).

81. See Anne Hudson, *The Premature Reformation: Wycliffite Texts and Lollard History* (Oxford: Clarendon, 1988).

82. Ibid.; also Deanesly's *The Lollard Bible and Other Medieval Biblical Versions* deals with this history.

83. For some corrections to Berger, see Clive R. Sneddon, "The 'Bible du XIIIᵉ siecle': Its Medieval Public in Light of Its Manuscript Tradition," in Lourdaux and Verhelst, eds., *The Bible and Medieval Culture*, 127–40.

84. *Cambridge History of the Bible*, 2:458–59.

85. Ibid., 441, 451.

86. As quoted in Berger, *La Bible français au moyen âge*, 239.

87. Dante Alighieri, *De vulgari eloquentia*, ed. Steven Botterill (Cambridge: Cambridge University Press, 1996), 1.X.2.

88. See de Poerck, with Van Deyck, "La Bible et l'activite traductrice dans les pays romans avant 1300," 1:21–48; also Christine Thouzellier, "L'Emploi de la Bible par les Cathares," in Lourdaux and Verhelst, eds., *The Bible and Medieval Culture*, 141–56; *Cambridge History of the Bible*, 2:451.

89. Reinhardt and Santiago-Otero, *Biblioteca Biblica Iberica Medieval*.

Chapter 5

1. *Das Messianitats und Leidensgeheimnis: Eine Skizze des Lebens Jesu* (Tubingen and Leipzig, 1901; rpt. Leipzig: J. C. B. Mohr, 1956); *The Mystery of the Kingdom of God: The Secret of the Messiahship and Passion*, trans. Walter Lowrie (New York: Dodd, Mead, 1914). Albert Schweitzer explored the history of this primary focus of eighteenth- and nineteenth-century biblical scholarship in *The Quest of the Historical Jesus: A Critical Study of Its Progress from Reimarus to Wrede*, trans. W. Montgomery (*Von Reimarus zu Wrede*. Tubingen, 1906; New York: Macmillan, 1968, intro. James M. Robinson).

2. *Das Messiasgeheimnis in den Evangelien* (Gottingen: Vandenhoeck and Ruprecht, 1901); *The Messianic Secret in the Gospels*, forming a contribution also to the understanding of the Gospel of Mark, trans. J. C. G. Greig (Greenwood, S.C.: Attic Press, 1971).

3. Peter Gay, *The Enlightenment: An Interpretation* (New York and London: W. W. Norton, 1977), 3–12.

4. Edgar Krentz, *The Historical-Critical Method* (London: S.P.C.K., 1975), 34.

5. Weisse, *Die Evangelienfrage in ihrem gegenwartigen Stadium*.

6. Schweitzer, *Quest of the Historical Jesus*, 8.

7. Ibid., 14.

8. Ibid., 24.

9. Hermann Samuel Reimarus, *The Goal of Jesus and His Disciples*, intro. and trans. George Wesley Buchanan (Leiden: E. J. Brill, 1970).

10. *Lessing's Theological Writings: Selections in Translation with an Introduction*, ed. Henry Chadwick (Stanford: Stanford University Press, 1959).

11. Wilson H. Coates, Hayden V. White, and J. Salwyn Schapiro, *The Emergence of Liberal Humanism: An Intellectual History of Western Europe. 1: From the Renaissance to the French Revolution* (New York: McGraw Hill, 1966), 269.

12. Reprinted in Latin with an English translation in *J. J. Griesbach*, 74–135.

13. Heinrich Greeven, "Gospel Synopsis from 1776 to the Present," in *J. J. Griesbach*, 24–26.

14. The source for this assertion is Jh. Alb. Fabricius, *Bibliotheca Graeca* (Hamburg, 1790–1809), 4:882–89, in Greeven, "Gospel Synopsis from 1776 to the Present," *J. J. Griesbach*, 24.

15. Reimarus, *The Goal of Jesus and His Disciples*, 37. In Lessing's version, published as the final fragment, he wrote, "We will now, however, step nearer and more directly to the subject in question, and examine both systems according to the sayings and doings of Jesus himself, so far as they are handed down to us. It is evident that with regard to the old system, all depends upon whether the evangelists, in their history of Jesus, left unintentionally and through sheer carelessness, a few remaining traces of the reasons which influenced them at first in attributing to their master the object of becoming a worldly deliverer of Israel." *Fragments from Reimarus*, trans. and ed. Rev. Charles Voysey (London and Edinburgh: Williams and Norgate, 1879), 9.

16. *Lessing's Theological Writings*, 65.

17. As quoted in "A Demonstration that Mark was written after Matthew and Luke" (translation of J. J. Griesbach's *Commentatio qua Marci Evangelium totum e Matthaei et Lucae commentariis decerptum esse monstratur*), in *J. J. Griesbach*, 103.

18. Reimarus, *Apologie oder Schutzschrift für die vernunftigen Verehrer Gottes*, vols. 1 and 2, ed. Gerhard Alexander (Frankfurt: Insel Verlag, 1972).

19. *Lessing's Theological Writings*, 14–15.

20. Ibid., 26.

21. Lessing, *Fragments from Reimarus*, 10–11. See also the entire section, 6–68, for a complete version of Reimarus's attack on traditional views of Jesus' messianic odyssey according to Lessing's version.

22. Lessing, *Fragments from Reimarus*, 86. In the "Worldly Ambitions of the Apostles," Reimarus pursued his attack of the sacred readings of the Bible, arguing for the simplicity and worldly corruption of the apostles, who, in Reimarus's version, were almost self-seeking frauds.

23. Lessing, *Fragments from Reimarus*, 25.

24. For a full discussion of this development, see Schweitzer, *Quest of the Historical Jesus*, 13–26.

25. *Lessing's Theological Writings*, 65–81.

26. "I do not for one moment deny that in Christ prophecies were fulfilled; I do not for one moment deny that Christ performed miracles. But . . . I deny that they can and should bind me in the least to a faith in the other teachings of Christ. These other teachings I accept on other grounds." *Lessing's Theological Writings*, 53.

27. For example, "For Eusebius writes (H.E.3.24.5): Matthew preached the Gospel to the Hebrews in Palestine. . . . Of this strictly speaking only half can be true." Or "When Epiphanius for example says that the Nazarenes possessed the Gospel of Matthew . . . in Hebrew: what can be said of this which avoids all objections? . . . And how could Origen and Jerome treat these additions so

indulgently? Only after my interpretation of this matter have Epiphanius' words their proper force." *Lessing's Theological Writings*, 71, 73.

28. "New Hypothesis Concerning the Evangelists Regarded as Merely Human Historians," *Lessing's Theological Writings*, 78–79.

29. "Since Matthew's translation could not be stamped with any unmistakable sign of divinity, and since it only attained canonical status through examination and comparison, and so was confirmed by the Church and preserved—what was more natural than that several others who either did not know or did not entirely approve of Matthew's work, because they wished it contained this or that story or because they would have preferred this or that story to be told differently, should undertake the same work, and should carry it out as each individual's powers enables him." *Lessing's Theological Writings*, 75.

30. *Lessing's Theological Writings*, 81.

31. Gadamer, *Truth and Method*, 241.

32. "A Demonstration," in *J. J. Griesbach*, 106.

33. From the preface to the second edition of J. J. Griesbach, *Synopsis evangeliorum Matthaei, Marci et Lucae una cum iis Joannis Pericopis quae historiam passionis et resurrectionis Jesu Christi complectuntur* (Halle, 1797). As quoted in Greeven, "Gospel Synopsis from 1776 to the Present," in *J. J. Griesbach*, 27.

34. See C. M. Tuckett, *The Revival of the Griesbach Hypothesis: An Analysis and Appraisal* (Cambridge: Cambridge University Press, 1983), for an assessment of the viability of the Griesbach theory of the relationship among the Gospels.

35. Greeven, in *J. J. Griesbach*, 27.

36. Bo Reicke, "Griesbach's Answer to the Synoptic Question," trans. Ronald Walls, in *J. J. Griesbach*, 51.

37. "A Demonstration," in *J. J. Griesbach*, 105.

38. Ibid., 106.

39. Ibid., 108–13.

40. Ibid., 114–18 (115).

41. Ibid., 120.

42. "We are fully persuaded that the whole series of events (Mark 11:11–27) happened in the order and time in which Mark has arranged them in his Gospel. He has deliberately chosen to differ from Matthew because he had acquired for himself from another source more accurate information about the whole affair than Matthew had." "A Demonstration," in *J. J. Griesbach*, 133.

43. "Whether our hypothesis, built up on the comparison of the three Gospels, lacks proof and compelling force, is a matter we gladly leave to the judgement of those who are not blinded by prejudice. For the scholars, who, prior to us, had publicly propounded with regard to the Gospel of Mark other hypotheses which collapsed of their own accord when ours was put forward, though they are exceedingly clever and estimable persons, hardly seem to be unbiased judges." "A Demonstration," in *J. J. Griesbach*, 114.

44. Hans W. Frei, *The Eclipse of Biblical Narrative* (New Haven: Yale University Press, 1974), 9.

45. From G. E. Lessing, "Gegensätze des Herausgebers," in *Gesammelte Werke*, ed. Paul Rilla (Berlin: Aufbau-Verlag, 1954–1958), 7:813.

46. See Stephen Prickett, *Origins of Narrative: The Romantic Appropriation of the Bible* (Cambridge: Cambridge University Press, 1996).
47. See note 1.
48. *The New Testament in the Original Greek*, the text revised by Brooke Foss Westcott, D.D., and Fenton John Anthony Hort, D.D. (New York: Macmillan, 1957; reproduced from the second and corrected impression of the larger edition of the text, issued in December 1881.)
49. The latest edition is *Novum Testamentum Graece* (Stuttgart: Deutsche Bibelgesellschaft, 1983).

Chapter 6

1. J. J. Griesbach, "Commentatio," in *J. J. Griesbach*, 74. (Marcum non esse Matthaei epitomatorem.)
2. For a discussion of how Markan priority theory affected theology in the period, see H. U. Meyboom, *A History and Critique of the Origin of the Marcan Hypothesis 1835–1866: A Contemporary Report Rediscovered* (Groningen, 1866), trans. and ed. John J. Kiwiet (Macon, Ga.: Mercer University Press, 1993).
3. For an explanation of this phenomenon in gospel studies, see Bellinzoni, introduction to *The Two-Source Hypothesis*, 1–19.
4. *J. J. Griesbach*, 52.
5. Stephen Neill and Tom Wright, *The Interpretation of the New Testament 1861–1986* (Oxford: Oxford University Press, 1988), 117.
6. See Farmer, *The Synoptic Problem*, for an overview of Holtzmann's hypothesis, a brief history of the development of the two-source theory, and Farmer's case against it.
7. See Schweitzer, *Quest of the Historical Jesus*, for this history.
8. See *L'Evangile selon Marc: Tradition et Redaction*, new edition augmented by M. Sabbe (Louvain: Louvain University Press, 1971; rpt. 1988), for an overview of the continuing debates. For arguments against Markan priority, see Sherman E. Johnson, *The Griesbach Hypothesis and Redaction Criticism* (Atlanta: Scholars Press, 1991). Bernard Orchard and Harold Riley, *The Order of the Synoptics: Why Three Synoptic Gospels* (Macon, Ga.: Mercer University Press, 1987), write, "all theories of Markan Priority rely either on hypothetical sources or questionable conjectures" that date "the gospels later than the Apostolic Age." They do not take into consideration the fact that Mark's shared pericopes are longer and fuller than Matthew's and Luke's; that Mark "zigzags" between Matthew and Luke; and that the patristic sources are unanimous in favoring Matthean priority (p. x). Arguments for and against the two-source theory are made in Walker, ed., *The Relationship among the Gospels*. For cases for and against Markan priority, see "The Case for the Priority of Mark," 21–93, and "The Case against the Priority of Mark," 97–217, in Bellinzoni, ed., *The Two-Source Hypothesis;* and of course, Farmer, *The Synoptic Problem*.
9. "The Reception of St. Mark's Gospel in the Church and a Survey of Its Contents," in *The Gospel of St. Mark*, 1–14 (1).
10. See B. C. Butler, "The Synoptic Problem," in Bellinzoni, ed., *The Two-Source*

Hypothesis, who explains the Pontifical Biblical Commission's interrogation of the theory in 1911–1912 at 101–2 (97–118).

11. Wrede, *The Messianic Secret*, 5–6.

12. Ibid., 9–10.

13. See James J. Robinson, *The Problem of History in Mark* (Philadelphia: Fortress Press, 1982), for a discussion of this issue.

14. As quoted in James M. Robinson, "Introduction," in Schweitzer, *Quest of the Historical Jesus*, xv–xvi.

15. Schweitzer, *Quest of the Historical Jesus*, 331.

16. *The Legends of Genesis*, trans. W. H. Carruth, intro. William F. Albright (New York: Schocken, 1964).

17. Rudolf Bultmann, *The History of the Synoptic Tradition*, trans. John Marsh (New York: Harper and Row, 1963) (originally *Die Erforschung der synoptischen Evangelien* [Giessen: Topelman, 1925]); Karl Ludwig Schmidt, *Le probleme du Christianisme primitif; quatre conferences sur la forme et la pensee du Nouveau Testament* (Paris: E. Leroux, 1938); and Martin Dibelius, *From Tradition to Gospel*, trans. and rev. ed. Bertram Lee Woolf (Cambridge and London: James Clarke, 1971), 1–2.

18. For an extended discussion of the nature of this theory of history writing as well as its pitfalls and blindness to its own rhetorical biases, see Hayden V. White, *Metahistory: The Historical Imagination of Nineteenth-Century Europe* (Baltimore: Johns Hopkins University Press, 1973), and his *The Content of the Form*.

19. Lightfoot, *The Gospel Message of Mark*.

20. Willi Marxsen, *Mark the Evangelist: Studies on the Redaction History of the Gospel*, trans. James Boyce and others (Nashville: Abingdon, 1969), and Marxsen, *Der Evangelist Markus: Studien zur Redaktionsgeschichte des Evangeliums* (Gottingen: Vandenhoeck and Ruprecht, 1956).

21. *Ordo Lectionem Missae* (BAV, 1969). The Presbyterian, Episcopal, and Lutheran churches all adopted lectionaries based on this *Ordo* because of their respect for its erudition and careful scholarship.

22. Fernando Belo, *Lecture materialiste de l'evangile de Marc; recit, pratique, ideologie* (Paris: Editions du Cerf, 1975); English edition, *A Materialist Reading of the Gospel of Mark*, trans. Matthew J. O'Connell (Maryknoll, N.Y.: Orbis Books, 1981).

23. For example, see Jon Sobrino, *Christology at the Crossroads*, trans. John Drury (New York: Orbis Books, 1978); Leonardo Boff, *Jesus Christ Liberator: A Critical Christology of Our Time* (New York: Orbis Books, 1980); or Herman C. Waetjen, *A Reordering of Power: A Socio-Political Reading of Mark's Gospel* (Minneapolis: Fortress Press, 1989).

24. Elliott, *Home for the Homeless;* Theissen, *The Social Setting of Pauline Christianity;* John R. Donohue, *The Theology and Setting of Discipleship* (Milwaukee: Marquette University Press, 1983).

25. Elizabeth Schussler Fiorenza, *In Memory of Her: A Feminist Theological Reconstruction of Christian Origins* (New York: Crossroad, 1983); Marla J. Selvidge, *Woman, Cult, and Miracle Recital: A Redactional Critical Investigation on Mark 5:24–34* (Lewisburg, Pa.: Bucknell University Press, 1990).

26. "Fortunata," in Auerbach, *Mimesis*, 35–43.

27. These include Frye, *The Great Code;* Kermode, *The Genesis of Secrecy;* James L. Kugel, *The Idea of Biblical Poetry* (New Haven: Yale University Press, 1981); Kenneth R. R. Gros Louis with James S. Ackerman, eds., *Literary Interpretations of the Biblical Narrative II* (Nashville: Abingdon, 1982); Robert Alter and Frank Kermode, eds., *Literary Guide to the Bible* (Cambridge, Mass.: Harvard/Belknap, 1987); Schwartz, ed., *The Book and the Text;* George Aichele, *Jesus Framed* (London: Routledge and Kegan Paul, 1996); and George Aichele, *The Postmodern Bible: The Bible and Culture Collective* (New Haven: Yale University Press, 1995).

28. Charles H. Talbert, *What Is a Gospel?: The Genre of the Canonical Gospels* (Philadelphia: Fortress Press, 1977).

29. Robbins, *Jesus the Teacher,* 60–67.

30. Ernest Renan, *Vie de Jesus* (Paris: Michel Levy, 1863), assumed the Gospels were biographies, as did Clyde Weber Votaw, in "The Gospels and Contemporary Biographies" *American Journal of Theology* 19 (1915): 45–73 and 217–49 (rpt. Philadelphia: Fortress Press, 1970, intro. John Reumann). Votaw tried to show that the Gospels have parallels in the lives of "philosopher-teachers like Socrates, Epictetus, and the miracle-worker-teacher Apollonius of Tyana" (iii). Recent additions to the discussion of this generic classification include Aune, *The New Testament in Its Literary Environment;* Adela Yarbro Collins, *Is Mark's Gospel a Life of Jesus?: The Question of Genre* (Milwaukee: Marquette University Press, 1990); Burridge, *What Are the Gospels?;* and Christopher Bryan, *A Preface to Mark: Notes on the Gospel and Its Literary and Cultural Settings* (New York: Oxford University Press, 1993).

31. Moses Hadas and Morton Smith, *Heroes and Gods* (New York: Harper and Row, 1965).

32. Robinson, *The Problem of History in Mark.*

33. Kermode, *The Genesis of Secrecy;* James G. Williams, *Gospel against Parable: Mark's Language of Mystery* (Sheffield: Almond Press, 1985).

34. Gilbert Bilezikian, *The Liberated Gospel: The Gospel of Mark Compared with Greek Tragedy* (Grand Rapids, Mich.: Baker Book House, 1977), 52–55.

35. Daniel Otto Via, *Kerygma and Comedy in the New Testament* (Philadelphia: Fortress Press, 1975).

36. Mary Ann Tolbert, *Sowing the Gospel: Mark's World in Literary-Historical Perspective* (Minneapolis: Fortress, 1989); Mary Ann Tolbert, "The Gospel in Greco-Roman Culture," in Schwartz, ed., *The Book and the Text,* 258–275; also Schildgen, "The Gospel of Mark as Picaresque Novella," *Genre* 29 (1996): 297–323.

37. Best, *Mark: The Gospel as Story,* 141–43.

38. For example, Norman Perrin, "The Christology of Mark: A Study in Methodology," *Journal of Religion* 51 (1971): 173–87; Via, *Kerygma and Comedy in the New Testament;* Rudolf Pesch, *Das Markus-evangelium;* Norman Perrin, *The New Testament: An Introduction: Proclamation and Parenesis, Myth and History* (New York: Harcourt Brace Jovanovich, 1982); and J. D. Crossan, *The Dark Interval: Towards a Theology of Story* (Niles, Ill.: Argus Communications, 1975).

A general study applying structuralism to the New Testament is Alfred M. Johnson, ed. and trans., *The New Testament and Structuralism* (Pittsburgh: Pickwick Press, 1976). Also see Elizabeth Struthers Malbon, *Narrative Space and Mythic Meaning in Mark* (San Francisco: Harper and Row, 1986); Tolbert, *Sowing the Gospel*; Bilezikian, *The Liberated Gospel*; Norman Peterson, *Literary Criticism for New Testament Critics* (Philadelphia: Fortress Press, 1978); Rhoads, "Narrative Criticism and the Gospel of Mark"; Rhoads and Michie, *Mark as Story*; Crossan, *Cliffs of Fall*; Gert Luderitz, "Rhetoric, Poetik, Kompositiontechnik im Markusevangelium," in *Markus Philologie*, ed. Hubert Cancik (Tübingen: J. C. B. Mohr, 1984), 165–203; Kelber, *The Oral and the Written Gospel*; Best, *Mark: The Gospel as Story*; Robert Funk, *The Poetics of Biblical Narrative* (Sonoma, Calif.: Polebridge Press, 1988); Walker, ed., *The Relationship among the Gospels*; Aune, *The New Testament in Its Literary Environment*; and Childs, *The New Testament as Canon*. Stephen Moore, *Literary Criticism and the Gospels* (New Haven: Yale University Press, 1989), provides a complete bibliography of these studies. See also Jerry Camery-Hoggatt, *Irony in Mark's Gospel: Text and Subtext* (Cambridge: Cambridge University Press, 1992); Stephen D. Moore, *Mark and Luke in Poststructuralist Perspectives* (New Haven: Yale University Press, 1992); Walter Brueggemann, *Texts under Negotiation: The Bible and Postmodern Imagination* (Minneapolis: Fortress Press, 1993); Edgar McKnight, *Postmodern Use of the Bible: The Emergence of Reader-oriented Criticism* (Nashville: Abingdon, 1988); and Schildgen, *Crisis and Continuity*.

39. F. Neirynck, *Duality in Mark* (Louvain: Louvain University Press, 1972).

40. R. Fowler, *Let the Reader Understand*, 2.

41. Chartier, *Forms and Meanings*, 15; see also *Bible et Informatique: "Materiel et matière". L'impact de l'informatique sur les etudes bibliques* (Paris: Honore Champion, 1995), which lays out how computers have and can be used as tools in philological studies of biblical texts.

42. Chartier, *Forms and Meanings*, 20.

43. Andrew Louth, *Discerning the Mystery* (Oxford: Clarendon, 1983), examines the Fathers' use of allegory. He uses Gadamerian hermeneutics to argue that in contrast to the patristic era, modern reading habits have been prejudiced against the symbolic meaning of the biblical texts.

44. I have in mind the vast range of phenomenologists, including Heidegger, Sartre, Gadamer, Habermas, and Derrida, among others.

45. In addition to sociological and political studies already cited, Kermode, *The Genesis of Secrecy*; Robert Alter, *Art of Biblical Poetry* (New York: Basic Books, 1985), and his *Art of Biblical Narrative* (New York: Basic Books, 1981); and Bloom, *The Book of J*, among many other current works, are examples of this tendency.

46. These literary traits are fully explored in a number of works, including Pesch, *Das Markus-evangelium*; Kermode, *The Genesis of Secrecy*; Neirynck, *Duality in Mark*; Aune, *The New Testament in Its Literary Environment*; Tolbert, *Sowing the Gospel*; and Schildgen, *Crisis and Continuity*.

47. Schweitzer, *Quest of the Historical Jesus*, 332.

48. For this concept of "play" in literary discourse, see Derrida, *Of Grammatology*, 16: "L'avenement de l'ecriture est l'avenement du jeu; le jeu aujourd'hui se rend a lui meme, effaçant la limite depuis laquelle on a cru pouvoir regler la circulation des signes." Despite this apparent criticism, the influence of Prof. Derrida's work is evident throughout this study.

Bibliographies

Bibles, Harmonies, and Lectionaries

Biblia Latina, cum postillis Nicolai de Lyra. Nuremberg: Anton Koberger, 1487.

Biblia Medieval Portuguesa. Ed. Serafim da Silva Neto. Rio de Janeiro: Instituto Nacional do Livro, 1958.

Biblia Sacra Iuxta Vulgatam Versionem I and II. Stuttgart: Württembergische Bibelanstalt, 1969.

Biblia Sacrae Vulgatae Editionis Sixti V. et Clementis VIII. Paris, 1618.

Diatessaron. Ed. Ignatius Ortiz de Urbina. Madrid: Matriti, Consejo de Investigaciones Cientificas, 1967.

Diatessaron Persiano. Ed. Giuseppe Messina. Rome: Pontificio Instituto Biblico, 1951.

Il Diatessaron in Volgare Italiano. Ed. Venanzio Todesco, P. Alberto Vaccari, and Mons. Marco Vattaso. Vatican City: BAV, 1937.

The Earliest Life of Jesus Ever Compiled from the Four Gospels Being the Diatessaron of Tatian. Trans. J. Hamlyn Hill. Edinburgh: T. and T. Clark, 1910.

Erasmus, Desiderius. *Annotationes in Novum Testamentum.* 1522.

―――. *Novum Instrumentum Omne.* Diligiter ab Erasmo Roterodamo recognitum emendatum. Basileae in laedibus Ioannis Frobenij Hammelburgensis, Februario 1516.

The Gospel of Saint Mark, in Anglo-Saxon and Northumbrian Versions. Ed. Walter Skeat. EETS 304. Cambridge: Cambridge University Press, 1871.

The Gothic and Anglo-Saxon Gospels in Parallel Columns with the Versions of Wycliffe and Tyndale. Ed. Rev. Joseph Bosworth. London: John Russell Smith, 1874.

Die Gotische Bibel. Ed. Wilhelm Streitberg. Heidelberg: Carl Winter, 1919. Rpt. 1960.

The Greek New Testament. Ed. Kurt Aland, Matthew Black, Carlo M. Martini, Bruce M. Metzger, and Allen Wikgren. 3d ed. New York: United Bible Societies, 1975.

Holy and Sacred Gospel. Brookline, Mass.: Holy Cross Orthodox Press, 1993.

Lectionary for Mass. New York: Catholic Book Publishing, 1970.

The Liege Diatessaron. Ed. D. Plooij, C. A. Phillips, and A. H. A. Bakker. Trans. A. J. Barnouw. Pts. I–V. Amsterdam: Uitgave N. V. Noord-Hollandsche Uitgevers MIJ, 1929–1938.

The Lindisfarne and Rushworth Gospels: The Gospel of Mark. Ed. George Waring. Publications of the Surtees Society 39. London: Whittaker, 1861.

Ordo Lectionem Missae, Editio Typica. Vatican City: Typis Polyglotis Vaticanis, 1969.

The New Testament in the Original Greek. Text revised by Brooke Foss Westcott, D. D. and Fenton John Anthony Hort, D. D. Reproduced from the second and corrected impression of the larger edition of the text, issued in December 1881. New York: Macmillan, 1957.

Nova Vulgata Bibliorum Editione. Vatican City: Libreria Editrice Vaticana, 1970.

El Nuevo Testamento segun el manuscrito escurialense 1–1–6. Ed. T. A. Montgomery and Spurgeon W. Baldwin. Anejos del BRAE 22. Madrid: Real Academia Espanola, 1970.

The Old English Version of the Gospels. Ed. R. M. Liuzza. EETS 304. Oxford: Oxford University Press, 1994.

The Revised Common Lectionary: The Consultation of Common Texts. Nashville: Abingdon, 1992.

Reference Texts

Biblia Patristica: Index des Citations et Allusions Bibliques dans la Litterature Patristique 1: Origines a Clement d'Alexandrie et Tertullien. Paris: Editions du Centre National de la Recherche Scientifique, 1975.

Biblia Patristica: Index des Citations et Allusions Bibliques dans la Litterature Patristique 2: Le Troisieme siecle (Origene excepte). Paris: Editions du Centre National de la Recherche Scientifique, 1977.

Biblia Patristica: Index des Citations et Allusions Bibliques dans la Litterature Patristique 3: Origene. Paris: Editions du Centre National de la Recherche Scientifique, 1980.

The Cambridge History of the Bible 1: From the Beginnings to Jerome. Ed. P. R. Ackroyd and C. F. Evans. Cambridge: Cambridge University Press, 1970.

The Cambridge History of the Bible 2: The West from the Fathers to the Reformation, ed. G. W. H. Lampe. Cambridge: Cambridge University Press, 1969.

Canones et Decreta Concilii Tridentini. Naples: Joseph Pelella, 1859.

The Canons and Decrees of the Sacred and Oecumenical Council of Trent. Trans. Rev. J. Waterworth. 1848. Rpt. Chicago: Christian Symbolic Publication Society.

Hefele, Charles Joseph. *History of the Councils of the Church II:* A.D. 326–A.D. 429. Trans. Henry Nutcombe Oxenham. Edinburgh: T. and T. Clark, 1876.

Hennecke, Edgar. *New Testament Apocrypha 1.* Ed. Wilhelm Schneemelcher, English trans. R. McL. Wilson. Philadelphia: Westminster Press, 1963.

Nag Hammadi Library. Ed. James L. Robinson. San Francisco: Harper and Row, 1978.

Quasten, Johannes. *Patrology 2: The Ante-Nicene Literature after Irenaeus.* Westminster, Md.: Newman Press, 1953.

———. *Patrology 3: Age of Greek Patristic Literature.* Westminster, Md.: Newman Press, 1960.

Stegmuller, Fridericus. *Repertorium Biblicum Medii Aevi.* 5 vols. Barcelona: Instituto Francisco Suarez, 1949. Rpt. Barcelona: Graficas Marina, 1955.

Synopsis of the Four Gospels. Ed. Kurt Aland. Stuttgart: Biblia-Druck, 1972.

Synopsis Quattuor Evangeliorum: Locis parallelis evangeliorum apocryphorum et patrum adhibitis. Ed. Kurt Aland. Stuttgart: Deutsche Bibelgesellschaft, 1985.

Primary Texts

PATRISTIC PERIOD

Ambrose of Milan, *Expositio Evangelii secundum Lucam.* In *CCSL* 14. Turnhout: Brepols, 1957.

Augustine. *Confessionum* libri XIII. Ed. Martin Skutella. In *CCSL* 27. Turnhout: Brepols, 1961.

———. *Confessions.* Trans. John K. Ryan. New York: Doubleday, 1960.

———. *De Consensu Evangelistarum.* Ed. Franciscus Weihrich. In *Corpus Scriptorum Ecclesiasticorum Latinorum* 43. Vindobonae: F. Tempsky, 1904.

———. *De Doctrina Christiana.* Ed. Joseph Martin. In *CCSL* 32. Turnhout: Brepols, 1962. 1–167.

———. *On Christian Doctrine.* Trans. D. W. Robertson, Jr. Indianapolis: Bobbs-Merrill, 1958.

———. *De Trinitate.* Ed. W. J. Mountain. In *CCSL* 50 and 50A. Turnhout: Brepols, 1968.

———. *Homelies sur l'Evangile de Saint Jean* LV–LXXIX. In *Oeuvres de Saint Augustin* 73A, 73B, 74A. Ed. M.-F Berouard. Perpignan: Institut des Etudes Augustiniennes, 1988, 1989, 1993.

———. *Opera Omnia.* In *PL* 38. Paris, 1841.

———. *Questiones evangeliorum.* In *CCSL* 44B. Turnhout: Brepols, 1980.

———. *St. Augustine's Letters 1–82.* Trans. Sr. Wilfred Parsons. New York: Fathers of the Church, 1951.

———. *The Sermon on the Mount and the Harmony of the Gospels.* In *The Works of Aurelius Augustine.* Ed. Marcus Dods. Edinburgh: T. and T. Clark, 1873.

———. *Sermons pour la Paque.* Intro. and notes by Suzanne Poque. Paris: Editions du Cerf, 1966.

Celsus. *On the True Doctrine: A Discourse against the Christians/Celsus.* Trans. and intro. R. Joseph Hoffman. New York: Oxford University Press, 1987.

Chrysostom, John. *Homilies on John.* In *PG* 59. Paris, 1859. Col. 24–382.

———. *In Matthaeum Homil.* In *PG* 57. Paris, 1860.

Clement of Alexandria. *Quis dives salvetur?* Ed. K. Koster. Frankfurt: Unveranderter Nachdruck, 1968.

Cyril of Alexandria. *Commentarium in Evangelium Joannis.* In *PG* 73. Paris, 1859.

———. *Commentarii in Lucam.* In *PG* 72. Paris, 1859. Col. 475–950.

———. *Commentarii in Matthaeum fragmenta.* In *PG* 72. Paris, 1859. Col. 365–474.

Eusebius of Caesarea. *Commentary on Matthew.* In *SC* 41. Paris: Editions du Cerf, 1955.

———. *Histoire Ecclesiastique.* Ed. Gustave Bardy. In *SC* 31. Paris: Editions du Cerf, 1952.

Hilary of Poitiers. *Sur Matthieu.* Intro., critical text, trans., and notes Jean Doignon. In *SC* 254. Paris: Editions du Cerf, 1978.

Ireneus of Lyon. *Contre les Heresies.* Ed. Adelin Rousseau and Louis Doutreleau, S.J. In *SC* 34. Paris: Editions du Cerf, 1974.

Iuvencus, C. Vettii Aquilini. *Libri Evangeliorum* IV. Ed. Carolus Marold. Lipsiae: G. G. Teubner, 1886.

Jerome. *Commentaire sur S. Matthieu* I (Bks. I–II). Latin text, intro., trans., and notes Emile Bonnard. In *SC* 242. Paris: Editions du Cerf, 1977.

———. *Commentary on Ezekiel.* In *CCSL* 75. Turnhout: Brepols, 1954.

———. *Lettres* I. Text and trans. Jerome Labourt. Paris: Societe d'Edition "Les Belles Lettres," 1949.

———. *Lettres* III. Text and trans. Jerome Labourt. Paris: Societe d'Edition "Les Belles Lettres," 1953.

———. *Liber de Viris illustribus.* In *Opera Omnia.* In *PL* 23. Paris, 1845. Col. 601–722.

———. *St. Jerome's Homilies* 2. Trans. Sister Marie Liguori Ewald. In *The Fathers of the Church* 57. Washington, D.C.: Catholic University of America, 1966.

———. *Tractatus in Marci Evangelium.* In *CCSL* 78. Turnhout: Brepols, 1958. 449–500.

The Liturgy of St. Mark. Ed. Geoffrey J. Cuming. Rome: Pontificium Institutum Studiorem Orientalium, 1990.

Origen. *Commentaire sur Saint Jean.* Greek text, preface, trans. and notes Cecile Blanc. In *SC* 120, 157, 222, 290, and 385. Paris: Editions du Cerf, 1970, 1975, 1982, 1992, 1996.

———. *De Principiis.* Intro. and ed. Rufin. Trans. H. Crouzel and M. Simonetti. In *SC* 252–53, 268–69, 312. Paris: Editions du Cerf, 1978–1984.

———. *On First Principles.* Trans. G. W. Butterworth, intro. Henri de Lubac. New York: Harper Torchbooks, 1966.

Orosius, Paul. *Histoires I and II.* Ed. Marie-Pierre Arnaud-Lindet. Paris: Les Belles Lettres, 1990.

Tertullian. *Adversus Marcionem.* 1 and 2. Ed. and trans. Ernest Evans. Oxford: Clarendon, 1972.

———. *De Monogamia.* Ed. Paul Mattei. In *SC* 343. Paris: Editions de Cerf, 1988.

Theodore of Mopsuestia. *Commentarius in Evangelium Iohannis Apostoli.* Ed. J.-M. Voste. Scriptores Syrii, Series Quarta, III. Paris: E. Typographeo Reipublicae, 1940.

MEDIEVAL/RENAISSANCE

Albertus Magnus. *Secundum Marcum.* In *Enarrationes in Matthaeum (XXI–XXVIII)—in Marcum.* In *Opera Omni 21.* Paris: Apud Ludovicum Vives, Bibliopolam Editorem, 1894. 339–761.

Alfonso X el Sabio. *General Estoria.* Ed. Antonio G. Solalinde. Madrid: Alvarez de Castro, 1930.

———. *General Estoria 2.* Ed. Antonio G. Solalinde, Lloyd Kasten, and Victor R. B. Oelschlager. Madrid: Alvarez de Castro, 1961.

Alighieri, Dante. *De vulgari eloquentia.* Ed. Steven Botterill. Cambridge: Cambridge University Press, 1996.

Amalarii Episcopi. *Liber Officialis.* In *Opera Liturgica Omnia* II. Ed. Ioanne Michaele Hanssens. Vatican City: BAV, 1948.

Aquinas, Thomas. *Catena Aurea: Commentary on the Four Gospels, Collected out of the Works of the Fathers.* II: *St. Mark.* Oxford and London: John Henry and James Parker, 1865.

Aurora Petri Rigae Biblia Versificata, 2 vols. Ed. Paul E. Beichner. South Bend: Notre Dame University Press, 1965.

Bede, Venerable. *De Schematibus et Tropis.* In *PL* 90. Paris, 1862. Col. 175–86.

———. *In Marci Evangelium Expositio.* Ed. D. Hurst. In *CCSL* 120. Turnhout: Brepols, 1960. 427–648.

La Bible anonyme du Ms. Paris B.N.f. fr.763. Ed. Julia C. Szirmai. Amsterdam: Rodopi, 1985.

La Bible de Jehan Malkaraume. Ed. J. R. Smeets. 2 vols. Assen: Van Gorcum, 1978.

La Bible de Mace de la Charite VI Evangiles, Actes des Apostres. Ed. J. R. Smeets. Leiden: Leiden University Press, 1986.

Calvin, John. *The Gospel According to St. John, 1–10.* Trans. T. H. L. Parker, in *Calvin's Commentaries 4.* Ed. David W. Torrance and Thomas F. Torrance. Edinburgh and London: Oliver and Boyd, 1959.

———. *A Harmony of the Gospels: Matthew, Mark and Luke.* Vol. 1. Trans. A. W. Morrison, ed. David W. Torrance and Thomas F. Torrance. Edinburgh: Saint Andrew Press, 1972.

———. *A Harmony of the Gospels: Matthew, Mark and Luke.* Vol. 2. Trans. H. L. Parker, ed. David W. Torrance and Thomas F. Torrance. Edinburgh: Saint Andrew Press, 1972.

———. *A Harmony of the Gospels: Matthew, Mark and Luke.* Vol. 3. Trans. A. W. Morrison, ed. David W. Torrance and Thomas F. Torrance. Edinburgh: Saint Andrew Press, 1972.

Colet, John. *An Exposition of St. Paul's Epistle to the Romans.* Ed. and trans. J. H. Lupton. London, 1873. Rpt. Ridgewood, N.J.: Gregg Press, 1965.

———. *An Exposition of St. Paul's First Epistle to the Corinthians.* Ed. and trans. J. H. Lupton. London, 1874. Rpt. Ridgewood, N.J.: Gregg Press, 1965.

Cummeanus. In *PL* 30. Paris, 1846. Col. 589–644.

Erasmus, Desiderius. *Annotations on the New Testament. Facsimile of the Final Latin Text (1535) with All Earlier Variants (1516, 1519, 1522, 1527).* Ed. Anne Reeve. London: Gerald Duckworth, 1986.

———. *Annotations on the New Testament: The Gospels.* Ed. Anne Reeve (London: Duckworth, 1986).

———. *Paraphrase on Mark.* Trans. and annotated Erika Rummel. In *Collected Works of Erasmus.* Toronto: University of Toronto Press, 1988.

Euthymius. "Mark." In *PG* 129. Paris, 1898. Col. 765–852.

Geufroi de Paris. *La Passion des Jongleurs.* Ed. Anne Joubert Amari Perry. Paris: Beauchesne, 1981.

The Heliand: The Saxon Gospel. Trans. G. Ronald Murphy, S.J. Oxford: Oxford University Press, 1992.

Heliand und genesis. Ed. Otto Behaghel. Halle a.S.: Verlag von Max Niemeyer, 1910.

Herman de Valenciennes. *Li Romanz de Dieu et de sa Mere.* Ed. Ina Spiele. Leiden: University Press of Leiden, 1975.

Hugh of St. Cher. *Postillae in universa Biblia juxta quadruplicem sensum litteralem, allegoricum, moralem, anagogicum.* 8 vols. Lyon, 1645.

Isidore of Seville. *Etimologias: Edicion Bilingue* I. Ed. Jose Oroz Reta and Manuel-A. Marcos Casquero. Madrid: Biblioteca de Autores Cristianos, 1982.

———. *In Libras Veteris Ac Novi Testamenti Præmia.* In *PL* 83. Paris, 1850. Col. 155–80.

The Late Medieval Religious Plays of Bodleian Mss. Digby 13 and E. Museo 160. Ed. Donald C. Baker, John L. Murphy, and Louis B. Hall. EETS 283. Oxford: Oxford University Press, 1982.

Ludolphus of Saxony. *Vita Jesu Christi.* Ed. L.-M. Rigollot. Paris: Victorem Palme, 1878.

Luther, Martin. *Luther's Works 41: Church and Ministry III.* Ed. Eric W. Gritsch, intro. G. Gordon Rupp. Philadelphia: Fortress Press, 1966.

———. *Luther's Works* 1–55. Ed. Jaroslav Pelikan (1–30), and Helmut T. Lehmann (31–55). Philadelphia: Fortress Press, 1958–1986.

Medieval and Tudor Drama. Ed. John Gassner. New York: Bantam Books, 1963.

Medieval Church Music-Dramas, A Repertory of Complete Plays. Trans. and ed. Fletcher Collins, Jr. Charlottesville: University Press of Virginia, 1976.

Nicholas de Lyra. *Postilla.* Venice. Hertzog, 1494.

———. *Postilla Super Totam Bibliam.* Strasbourg 1492. Rpt. Frankfurt: Minerva Gmb. H., 1971.

Otfrids Evangelienbuch. Ed. Oskar Erdmann. 1882. Rpt. Tübingen: Verlag von Max Niemeyer, 1957.

Petrus Comestor. *Historia Scholastica.* In *PL* 198. Paris. 1049–1722.

Pseudo-Jerome. "Expositio Quatuor Evangeliorum Marcus." In *PL* 30. Paris, 1846. Col. 560–67.

Sedulius Scotus. "Argumentum Secundum Markum." In *PL* 103. Paris, 1864. Col. 279–86.

Theophylactus. "Enarratio in Evangelium Marci." In *PG* 123. Paris, 1883. Col. 491–682.

Valla, Lorenzo. *Collatio Novi Testamenti.* Ed. Alessandro Perosa. Florence: Sansoni Editore, 1970.

Wyclif, John. *Select English Works of John Wyclif 1: Sermons on the Gospels for Sundays and Festivals.* Ed. Thomas Arnold. Oxford: Clarendon, 1869.

———. *Select English Works of John Wyclif 2: Sermons on the Ferial Gospels and Sunday Epistles. Treatises.* Ed. Thomas Arnold. Oxford: Clarendon, 1871.

Eighteenth–Nineteenth Centuries

Griesbach, J. J. *J. J. Griesbach: Synoptic and Text—Critical Studies 1776–1976.* Ed. Bernard Orchard and Thomas R. W. Longstaff. Cambridge: Cambridge University Press, 1978.

——. *Synopsis evangeliorum Matthaei, Marci et Lucae una cum iis Joannis pericopis quae historiam passionis et resurrectionis Jesu Christi complectuntur.* Halle, 1797.

Lessing, G. E. *Fragments from Reimarus.* Trans. and ed. Rev. Charles Voysey. London and Edinburgh: Williams and Norgate, 1879.

——. "Gegensatze des Herausgebers." In *Gesammelte Werke.* 7. Ed. Paul Rilla. Berlin: Aufbau-Verlag, 1954–1958.

——. *Lessing's Theological Writings: Selections in Translation with an Introduction.* Ed. Henry Chadwick. Stanford: Stanford University Press, 1959.

Meyboom, H. U. *A History and Critique of the Origin of the Marcan Hypothesis 1835–1866: A Contemporary Report Rediscovered.* Trans. and ed. John J. Kiwiet. Macon, Ga.: Mercer University Press, 1993.

Reimarus, Hermann Samuel. *Apologie oder Schutzschrift für die vernunftigen Verehrer Gottes.* Vols. 1 and 2. Ed. Gerhard Alexander. Frankfurt: Insel Verlag, 1972.

——. *The Goal of Jesus and His Disciples.* Intro. and trans. George Wesley Buchanan. Leiden: E. J. Brill, 1970.

Renan, Ernest. *Vie de Jesus.* Paris: Michel Levy, 1863.

Schweitzer, Albert. *Das Messianitats und Leidensgeheimnis: eine Skizze des Lebens Jesu.* Tubingen and Leipzig, 1901. Rpt. Leipzig: J. C. B. Mohr, 1956.

——. *The Mystery of the Kingdom of God: The Secret of the Messiahship and Passion.* Trans. Walter Lowrie. New York: Dodd, Mead, 1914.

——. *The Quest of the Historical Jesus: A Critical Study of Its Progress from Reimarus to Wrede.* Trans. W. Montgomery (*Von Reimarus zu Wrede.* Tubingen, 1906). New York: Macmillan, 1968, intro. James M. Robinson.

Tuckett, C. M. *The Revival of the Griesbach Hypothesis: An Analysis and Appraisal.* Cambridge: Cambridge University Press, 1983.

Weisse, Christian Hermann. *Die Evangelienfrage in ihrem gegenwartigen Stadium.* Leipzig: Breitkopf und Hartel, 1856.

Wrede, Wilhelm. *Das Messiasgeheimnis in den Evangelien.* Gottingen: Vandenhoeck and Ruprecht, 1901.

——. *The Messianic Secret in the Gospels.* Forming a contribution also to the understanding of the Gospel of Mark. Trans. J. C. G. Greig. Greenwood, S.C.: Attic Press, 1971.

Rhetoric and Cultural, Literary, and Philosophical Theory

Aristotle on Rhetoric: A Theory of Civic Discourse. Trans. George A. Kennedy. New York: Oxford University Press, 1991.

Auerbach, Erich. *Literary Language and Its Public in Late Latin Antiquity and in the Middle Ages.* Trans. Ralph Manheim. New York: Oxford University Press, 1987.

——. *Mimesis: The Representation of Reality in Western Literature.* Trans. Willard R. Trask. Princeton: Princeton University Press, 1953.

Bloom, Harold. *The Anxiety of Influence.* New York: Oxford University Press, 1973.

Chartier, Roger. *Forms and Meanings: Texts, Performances, and Audiences from Codex to Computer.* Philadelphia: University of Pennsylvania Press, 1995.

Cicero. *De Optimo Genere Oratorum.* In *Cicero* II. Trans. H. M. Hubbell. Cambridge, Mass.: Harvard University Press, and London: Heinemann, 1976. 354–73.

———. *De Oratore*. Bk. III. In *Cicero* IV. Trans. H. Rackham. Cambridge, Mass.: Harvard University Press, 1968.

Derrida, Jacques. *Difference in Translation*. Trans. and ed. Joseph F. Graham. Ithaca: Cornell University Press, 1985.

———. *Of Grammatology*. Trans. Gayatri Chakravorty Spivak. Baltimore: Johns Hopkins University Press, 1974.

Eden, Kathy. "Hermeneutics and the Ancient Rhetorical Tradition." *Rhetorica* 5 (1987): 59–86.

———. *Hermeneutics and the Rhetorical Tradition: Chapters in the Ancient Legacy and Its Humanist Reception*. New Haven: Yale University Press, 1997.

———. "The Rhetorical Tradition and Augustinian Hermeneutics in *De Doctrina Christiana*," *Rhetorica* 8 (1990): 45–63.

Febvre, Lucien, and Henri-Jean Martin. *L'Apparition du Livre*. Paris: Edition Albin Michel, 1958.

Fish, Stanley. *Is There a Text in This Class?* Cambridge, Mass.: Harvard University Press, 1980.

Foucault, Michel. *The Order of Things: An Archaeology of the Human Sciences*. New York: Vintage Books, 1973.

Fowler, Alastair. *Kinds of Literature: An Introduction to the Theory of Genres and Modes*. Cambridge, Mass.: Harvard University Press, 1982.

Gadamer, Hans-Georg. *Reason in the Age of Science*. Trans. Frederick G. Lawrence. Cambridge, Mass.: MIT Press, 1981.

———. *Rhetoric und Hermeneutick*. Gottingen: Vanderhoeck and Ruprecht, 1976.

———. *Truth and Method*. New York: Crossroad, 1986.

Gates, Henry Louis, Jr. "The Master's Pieces: On Canon Formation and the African-American Tradition." *South Atlantic Quarterly* 89 (1990): 89–111.

Genette, Gerard. *Introduction a l'architexte*. Paris: Editions du Seuil, 1979.

———. *Narrative Discourse: An Essay in Method*. Trans. Jane E. Lewin. Ithaca: Cornell University Press, 1980.

———. *Palimpsestes: La Litterature au Second Degre*. Paris: Editions du Seuil, 1982.

Guillory, John. "Canonical and Non-Canonical: A Critique of the Current Debate." *ELH* 54, no. 3 (fall 1987): 483–527.

———. *Cultural Capital: The Problem of Literary Canon Formation*. Chicago: University of Chicago Press, 1993.

Hermogenes. *Ars Rhetorica*. Ed. L. Spengel. Leipzig: B. G. Teubner, 1854.

Horace. *Horace on Poetry: The "Ars Poetica."* Ed. C. O. Brink. Cambridge: Cambridge University Press, 1971.

Iser, Wolfgang. *The Act of Reading: A Theory of Aesthetic Response*. Baltimore: Johns Hopkins University Press, 1978.

Jauss, Hans Robert. *Aesthetic Experience and Literary Hermeneutics*. Trans. Michael Shaw. Minneapolis: University of Minnesota Press, 1982.

Kelly, Louis. *The True Interpreter: A History of Translation Theory and Practice in the West*. Oxford: Basil Blackwell, 1979.

Kennedy, George. *Classical Rhetoric and Its Christian and Secular Tradition from Ancient to Modern Times*. Chapel Hill: University of North Carolina Press, 1980.

———. *Greek Rhetoric under Christian Emperors*. Princeton: Princeton University Press, 1983.

———. *New Testament Interpretation through Rhetorical Criticism.* Chapel Hill: University of North Carolina Press, 1984.

Kermode, Frank. *Forms of Attention.* Chicago: University of Chicago Press, 1985.

———. *History and Value.* Oxford: Clarendon, 1988.

Kuhn, Thomas S. *The Structure of Scientific Revolutions.* Chicago: University of Chicago Press, 1962.

Lanham, Richard. *Analyzing Prose.* New York: Scribner, 1979.

———. *Literacy and the Survival of Humanism.* New Haven: Yale University Press, 1983.

Lubac, Henri de. *Exégèse Médiévale: Les Quatre Sens de l'Écriture.* Paris: Aubier, 1954–1964.

Mukarovsky, Jan. *Aesthetic Function, Norm, and Value as Social Facts.* Trans. Mark Suino. Ann Arbor: University of Michigan Press, 1970.

O'Loughlin, Michael. *The Garlands of Repose: The Literary Celebration of Civic and Retired Leisure.* Chicago: University of Chicago Press, 1978.

Ong, Walter J., S.J. *Orality and Literacy: The Technologizing of the Word.* London: Methuen, 1982.

Pelikan, Jaroslav. *The Vindication of Tradition.* New Haven: Yale University Press, 1984.

Pieper, Josef. *Leisure: The Basis of Culture.* Intro. T. S. Eliot. Trans. Alexander Dru. London: Faber and Faber, 1952.

Rhetorique et Hermeneutique. Ed. Tzvetan Todorov. *Poetique* 23 (1975).

Riffaterre, Michael. *La Production du Texte.* Paris: Editions du Seuil, 1979.

Smith, Barbara Herrnstein. *Contingencies of Value: Alternative Perspectives for Literary Theory.* Cambridge, Mass.: Harvard University Press, 1988.

Steiner, George. *After Babel: Aspects of Language and Translation.* Oxford: Oxford University Press, 1975. Rpt. 1977.

Stock, Brian. *Augustine the Reader: Meditation, Self-Knowledge, and the Ethics of Interpretation.* Cambridge, Mass.: Harvard University Press, 1996.

Tompkins, Jane P., ed. *Reader-Response Criticism.* Baltimore: Johns Hopkins University Press, 1980.

———. *Sensational Designs: The Cultural Work of American Fiction, 1790–1860.* New York: Oxford University Press, 1985.

White, Hayden V. *The Content of the Form: Narrative Discourse and Historical Representation.* Baltimore: Johns Hopkins University Press, 1987.

———. *Metahistory: The Historical Imagination of Nineteenth-Century Europe.* Baltimore: Johns Hopkins University Press, 1973.

———. *Tropics of Discourse: Essays in Cultural Criticism.* Baltimore: Johns Hopkins University Press, 1978.

General Bibliography

Aichele, George. *Jesus Framed.* London: Routledge and Kegan Paul, 1996.

———. *The Postmodern Bible: The Bible and Culture Collective.* New Haven: Yale University Press, 1995.

Alter, Robert. *The Art of Biblical Narrative.* New York: Basic Books, 1981.

————. *The Art of Biblical Poetry.* New York: Basic Books, 1985.

Alter, Robert, and Frank Kermode, eds. *Literary Guide to the Bible.* Cambridge, Mass.: Harvard/Belknap, 1987.

Arnold, W. H., and Pamela Bright, eds. *The De Doctrina Christiana: A Classic of Western Culture.* South Bend: Notre Dame University Press, 1995.

Aune, David Edward. *The New Testament in Its Literary Environment.* Philadelphia: Westminster Press, 1987.

Baarda, Tjitze. "Diaphonia-Sumphonia, Factors in the Harmonization of the Gospels. Especially the *Diatessaron* of Tatian," 29–47. In *Essays on the Diatessaron.* Kampen, The Netherlands: Kok Pharos Publishing, 1994.

Bal, Mieke. *Narratology: Introduction to the Theory of Narrative.* Trans. Christine van Boheemen. Toronto: University of Toronto Press, 1985.

Barnstone, Willis, ed. *The Other Bible.* San Francisco: Harper and Row, 1984.

Beer, Jeanette, ed. *Medieval Translators and Their Craft.* Studies in Medieval Culture XXV. Kalamazoo, Mich.: Western Michigan University, Medieval Institute Publications, 1989.

Bellinzoni, Arthur J., Jr., ed. *The Two-Source Hypothesis: A Critical Appraisal.* Macon, Ga.: Mercer University Press, 1985.

Belo, Fernando. *Lecture materialiste de l'evangile de Marc; recit, pratique, ideologie.* Paris: Editions du Cerf, 1975. English ed., *A Materialist Reading of the Gospel of Mark.* Trans. Matthew J. O'Connell. Maryknoll, N.Y.: Orbis Books, 1981.

Bene, Charles. *Erasme et Saint Augustin ou l'influence de Saint Augustin sur l'humanisme d'Erasme.* Geneva: Librairie Droz, 1969.

Bentley, Jerry H. *Humanists and Holy Writ: New Testament Scholarship in the Renaissance.* Princeton: Princeton University Press, 1983.

Berger, Samuel. *La Bible française au moyen age: Etude sur les plus anciennes versions de la Bible ecrites en prose de langue d'oil.* Paris: Champion, 1884.

————. *La Bible romane au moyen age.* Rpt. Geneva: Slatkine, 1977. Rpt. *Romania* XVIII (1889), XIX (1890), XXIII (1896), XXVIII (1899).

————. *Histoire de la Vulgate pendant les premiers siecles du moyen age.* Paris 1893. Rpt. New York: Burt Franklin, 1958.

Bertola, Ermenegildo. "La 'Glossa Ordinaria' biblica ed i suoi problemi." *Recherches de Theologie ancienne et medievale* 45 (1978): 34–78.

Best, Ernest. *Mark: The Gospel as Story.* Edinburgh: T. and T. Clark, 1983.

La Bibbia nell'Alto Medioevo. Spoleto: Presso la Sede del Centro, 1963.

Bible et Informatique: "Materiel et matiere." L'impact de l'informatique sur les etudes bibliques. Paris: Honore Champion, 1995.

Biblical Intepretation in the Early Church. Trans. and ed. Karlfried Froehlich. Philadelphia: Fortress Press, 1984.

Bilezikian, Gilbert. *The Liberated Gospel: The Gospel of Mark Compared with Greek Tragedy.* Grand Rapids, Mich.: Baker Book House, 1977.

Bloom, Harold. *The Book of J.* Trans. David Rosenberg and interp. Harold Bloom. New York: Grove and Weidenfeld, 1990.

Bodenstedt, Sister Mary Immaculate. *The Vita Christi of Ludolphus the Carthusian.* Washington, D.C.: Catholic University of America Press, 1944.

Boff, Leonardo. *Jesus Christ Liberator: A Critical Christology of Our Time.* New York: Orbis Books, 1980.

Bonnard, Jean. *Les Traductions de la Bible en Vers Français au Moyen Âge.* Paris: Imprimerie Nationale, 1884. Rpt. Geneva: Slatkine, 1967.

Bonnardiere, Anne-Marie. Ed. *Saint Augustin et la Bible.* Paris: Beauchesne, 1986.

Boomershine, T. "Mark, the Storyteller: A Rhetorical-Critical Investigation of Mark's Passion and Resurrection Narrative." Ph.D. diss., Union Theological Seminary, New York, 1974.

Boyle, Leonard. "Innocent III and Vernacular Scripture." In Walsh and Wood, eds., *The Bible in the Medieval World.* 97–107.

Boyle, Marjorie O'Rourke. *Erasmus on Language and Method in Theology.* Toronto: University of Toronto Press, 1977.

Brown, Peter. *Augustine of Hippo.* Berkeley: University of California Press, 1969.

Bruce, F. F. *The English Bible: A History of Translations.* New York: Oxford University Press, 1961.

Brueggemann, Walter. *Texts under Negotiation: The Bible and Postmodern Imagination.* Minneapolis: Fortress Press, 1993.

Bryan, Christopher. *A Preface to Mark: Notes on the Gospel and Its Literary and Cultural Settings.* New York: Oxford University Press, 1993.

Bultmann, Rudolf. *Die Erforschung der synoptischen Evangelien.* Giessen: Töpelman, 1925.

———. *The History of the Synoptic Tradition.* Trans. John Marsh. New York: Harper and Row, 1963.

Burridge, Richard A. *What Are the Gospels? A Comparison with Graeco-Roman Biography.* Cambridge: Cambridge University Press, 1992.

Camery-Hoggatt, Jerry. *Irony in Mark's Gospel: Text and Subtext.* Cambridge: Cambridge University Press, 1992.

Chartier, Roger. *Forms and Meanings: Texts, Performances, and Audiences from Codex to Computer.* Philadelphia: University of Pennsylvania Press, 1995.

Childs, Brevard. *The New Testament as Canon: An Introduction.* Philadelphia: Fortress Press, 1985.

Coates, Wilson H., Hayden V. White, and J. Salwyn Schapiro. *The Emergence of Liberal Humanism: An Intellectual History of Western Europe 1: From the Renaissance to the French Revolution.* New York: McGraw Hill, 1966.

Collins, Adela Yarbro. *Is Mark's Gospel a Life of Jesus?: The Question of Genre.* Milwaukee: Marquette University Press, 1990.

Coogan, Robert. *Erasmus, Lee and the Correction of the Vulgate: The Shaking of the Foundations.* Geneva: Droz, 1992.

Copeland, Rita. "The Fortunes of 'Non Verbum pro Verbo': Or Why Jerome is Not a Ciceronian." In Ellis, ed., *The Medieval Translator.* 1:15–35.

———. *Rhetoric, Hermeneutics, and Translation in the Middle Ages.* Cambridge: Cambridge University Press, 1991.

Corley, Bruce, ed. *Colloquy on New Testament Studies: A Time for Reappraisal and Fresh Approaches.* Macon, Ga.: Mercer University Press, 1983.

Crossan, John D. *Cliffs of Fall.* New York: Seabury Press, 1980.

———. *The Dark Interval: Towards a Theology of Story.* Niles, Ill.: Argus Communications, 1975.

———. *Four Other Gospels: Shadows on the Contours of Canon.* Minneapolis: Winston Press, 1985.

Cuendet, Georges. *L'Ordre des Mots dans le texte grec et dans les versions gotique, armenienne, et vieux slave des evangiles.* Paris: Librairie Ancienne Honore Champion, 1929.

Deanesly, Margaret. *The Lolland Bible and Other Medieval Biblical Versions.* Cambridge: Cambridge University Press, 1920. Rpt. 1966.

Dekkers, Eligius. "L'eglise devant la bible en langue vernaculaire." In Lourdaux and Verhelst, eds., *The Bible and Medieval Culture.* 1–15.

Delegue, Yves. *Les Machines du Sens: Textes de Hugues de Saint-Victor, Thomas d'Aquin, et Nicolas de Lyre.* Paris: Editions des Cendres, 1987.

de Poerck, Guy, with Rika Van Deyck. "La Bible et l'activite traductrice dans les pays romans avant 1300." In Jauss, ed., *La Litterature Didactique, Allegorique et Satirique,* 1:21–48.

Devreesse, Robert. *Essai sur Theodore de Mopsueste.* Vatican City: BAV, 1948.

de Waard, Jan, and Eugene A. Nida. *From One Language to Another: Functional Equivalence in Bible Translating.* Nashville: Thomas Nelson, 1986.

Dibelius, Martin. *From Tradition to Gospel.* Trans. and rev. ed. Bertram Lee Woolf. Cambridge and London: James Clarke, 1971.

Documents for the Study of the Gospels. Ed. and trans. David R. Cartlidge and David L. Dungan. Philadelphia: Fortress Press, 1980.

Donohue, John R. *The Theology and Setting of Discipleship.* Milwaukee: Marquette University Press, 1983.

Eden, Kathy. "Rhetoric in the Hermeneutics of Erasmus' Later Works." *Erasmus of Rotterdam Society* 11 (1991): 88–104.

Elliott, John H. *Home for the Homeless.* Philadelphia: Fortress Press, 1981.

Ellis, Roger, ed. *The Medieval Translator: The Theory and Practice of Translation in the Middle Ages.* 2 vols. London: Center for Medieval Studies, 1989–1991.

L'Evangile selon Marc: Tradition et Redaction. New edition, augmented M. Sabbe. Louvain: Louvain University Press, 1988.

Essays on the Diatessaron. Kampen, The Netherlands: Kok Pharos Publishing, 1984.

Evans, G. R. *The Language and Logic of the Bible: The Earlier Middle Ages.* Cambridge: Cambridge University Press, 1984.

———. *The Language and Logic of the Bible: The Road to the Reformation.* Cambridge: Cambridge University Press, 1985.

Farmer, William R. *The Last Twelve Verses of Mark.* Cambridge: Cambridge University Press, 1974.

———. *The Synoptic Problem: A Critical Analysis.* New York: Macmillan, 1964.

Farmer, William R., and Denis M. Farkasfalvy. *The Formation of the New Testament Canon.* New York: Paulist Press, 1983.

Fedwick, Paul Jonathan, ed. *Basil of Caesarea: Christian, Humanist, Ascetic.* Toronto: PIMS, 1981.

Ferguson, Everett, ed. *The Bible in the Early Church.* New York: Garland, 1993.

Fiorenza, Elizabeth Schussler. *In Memory of Her: A Feminist Theological Reconstruction of Christian Origins.* New York: Crossroad, 1983.

Fischer, Bonifatius. *Beitrage zur Geschichte der lateinischen Bibeltexte.* Freiburg: Verlag Herder, 1986.

Fishbane, Michael. *The Garments of Torah: Essays in Biblical Hermeneutics.* Bloomington: Indiana University Press, 1989.

Fowler, David C. *The Bible in Early English Literature*. Seattle: University of Washington Press, 1976.

Fowler, Robert M. *Let the Reader Understand: Reader-Response Criticism and the Gospel of Mark*. Minneapolis: Fortress Press, 1991.

Franceschini, Ezio. "La Bibbia nell'alto medio evo," 15–37. In *La Bibbia nell'Alto Medioevo*.

Frei, Hans W. *The Eclipse of Biblical Narrative*. New Haven: Yale University Press, 1974.

Frend, W. H. C. *Rise of Christianity*. London: Darton, Longman, and Todd, 1984.

Frere, Walter Howard. *Studies in the Early Roman Liturgy: The Roman Lectionary*. Oxford: Oxford University Press, 1934.

Friedrichsen, G. W. S. *The Gothic Version of the Gospels: A Study of Its Style and Textual History*. London: Humphrey Milford, Oxford University Press, 1926.

Frye, Northrop. *The Great Code: The Bible and Literature*. New York: Harcourt Brace Jovanovich, 1981.

Funk, Robert. *The Poetics of Biblical Narrative*. Sonoma, Calif.: Polebridge Press, 1988.

Gamble, Henry Y. *The New Testament Canon*. Philadelphia: Fortress Press, 1985.

Gay, Peter. *The Enlightenment: An Interpretation*. New York and London: W. W. Norton, 1977.

Glunz, H. H. *History of the Vulgate in England from Alcuin to Roger Bacon*. Cambridge: Cambridge University Press, 1933.

Greer, Rowan A. *Theodore of Mopsuestia: Exegete and Theologian*. London: Faith Press, 1961.

Gros Louis, Kenneth R. R., ed., with James S. Ackerman. *Literary Interpretations of the Biblical Narrative*. Vol. 2. Nashville: Abingdon, 1982.

Gunkel, Herman. *The Legends of Genesis*. Trans. W. H. Carruth, intro. William F. Albright. New York: Schocken, 1964.

Hadas, Moses, and Morton Smith. *Heroes and Gods*. New York: Harper and Row, 1965.

Hagendahl, Harald. *Augustine and the Latin Classics. 1: Testimonia*. Stockholm: Almquist and Wiksall, 1967.

Hardisson, O. B. *Christian Rite and Christian Drama in the Middle Ages*. Baltimore: Johns Hopkins University Press, 1965.

Hudson, Anne. *The Premature Reformation: Wycliffite Texts and Lollard History*. Oxford: Clarendon, 1988.

Hug, Joseph. *La finale de l'Evangile de Marc* (Mc.16, 9–20). Paris: J. Gabalda, 1978.

Hunningher, Benjamin. *The Origin of the Theater*. New York: Hill and Wang, 1955.

Jauss, Hans Robert, ed. *La Litterature Didactique, Allegorique et Satirique*. Vol. 1. Heidelberg: Carl Winter, 1968.

Johnson, Alfred M., ed. and trans. *The New Testament and Structuralism*. Pittsburgh: Pickwick Press, 1976.

Johnson, Sherman E. *The Griesbach Hypothesis and Redaction Criticism*. Atlanta: Scholars Press, 1991.

Jordan, Mark D. "Words and Word: Incarnation and Signification in Augustine's *De Doctrina Christiana*." *Augustinian Studies* 11 (1980): 177–96.

Kealy, Sean P. *Mark's Gospel: A History of Its Interpretation.* New York: Paulist Press, 1982.

Kelber, Werner H. *The Oral and the Written Gospel.* Philadelphia: Fortress Press, 1983.

Kemp, Wolfgang. *The Narratives of Gothic Stained Glass.* Trans. Caroline Dobson Saltzweld. Cambridge: Cambridge University Press, 1997.

Kermode, Frank. *Genesis of Secrecy.* Cambridge, Mass.: Harvard University Press, 1979.

Kieckhefer, Richard. *Magic in the Middle Ages.* Cambridge: Cambridge University Press, 1990.

Kirby, Ian J. *Bible Translation in Old Norse.* Geneva: Librairie Droz, 1986.

Krentz, Edgar. *The Historical-Critical Method.* London: S.P.C.K., 1975.

Kugel, James L., *The Idea of Biblical Poetry.* New Haven: Yale University Press, 1981.

Kugel, James L., and Rowan A. Greer. *Early Biblical Interpretation.* Philadelphia: Westminster Press, 1986.

Kustas, George L. "Basil and the Rhetorical Tradition," 221–79. In *Basil of Caesarea: Christian, Humanist, Ascetic.* Ed. Paul Jonathan Fedwick. Toronto: PIMS, 1981.

Le Goff, Jacques. *Medieval Civilization.* Trans. Julia Barrow. Oxford: Basil Blackwell, 1988.

Levy, Berard S., ed. *The Bible in the Middle Ages: Its Influence on Literature and Art.* Binghamton: State University of New York, 1992.

Lightfoot, R. H. *The Gospel Message of Mark.* Oxford: Oxford University Press, 1950.

Lønning, I. *"Kanon im Kanon": zum dogmatischen Grundlagen problem des neutestamentlichen Kanons.* Munich: C. Kaiser; Oslo: Universitetsforlaget, 1972.

Lourdaux, W., and D. Verhelst, eds. *The Bible and Medieval Culture.* Louvain: Louvain University Press, 1979.

Louth, Andrew. *Discerning the Mystery.* Oxford: Clarendon, 1983.

Luderitz, Gert. "Rhetoric, Poetik, Kompositiontechnik im Markusevangelium." In *Markus Philologie,* ed. Hubert Cancik. Tubingen: J. C. B. Mohr, 1984.

Mack, Burton L. *Rhetoric and the New Testament.* Minneapolis: Fortress Press, 1990.

Mack, Burton L., and Vernon K. Robbins. *Patterns of Persuasion in the Gospels.* Sonoma, Calif.: Polebridge Press, 1989.

Malbon, Elizabeth Struthers. *Narrative Space and Mythic Meaning in Mark.* San Francisco: Harper and Row, 1986.

Marrou, Henri-Irenee. *Saint-Augustin et la fin de la culture antique.* Paris: Editions E. de Boccard, 1958.

Marxsen, Willi. *Der Evangelist Markus: Studien zur Redaktionsgeschichte des Evangeliums.* Gottingen: Vandenhoeck and Ruprecht, 1956.

———. *Mark the Evangelist: Studies in the Redaction History of the Gospel.* Trans. James Boyce. Nashville: Abingdon, 1969.

Massaux, Edouard. *Influence de l'Evangile de saint Matthieu sur la litterature chretienne avant saint Irenee.* Louvain: Publications Universitaires, 1950. Rpt. Louvain: Louvain University Press, 1986.

Mastrelli, Carlo Alberto. "La Tecnica delle Traduzioni della Bibbia nell'Alto Medioevo." In *Bibbia nell'Alto Medioevo.* 657–81.

Matera, F. J. "The Incomprehension of the Disciples and Peter's Confession (Mark 6:14–8:30)." *Biblica* 70 (1989): 153–72.

Mazzeo, Joseph. *Renaissance and Seventeenth-Century Studies.* New York: Columbia University Press, 1964.

Mazzotta, Giuseppe. *Dante's Vision and the Circle of Knowledge.* Princeton: Princeton University Press, 1992.

McKnight, Edgar. *Postmodern Use of the Bible: The Emergence of Reader-oriented Criticism.* Nashville: Abingdon, 1988.

McNally, Robert E. *The Bible in the Early Middle Ages.* Westminster, Md.: Newman Press, 1959.

McNamara, Martin. *Studies on Texts of Early Irish Latin Gospels (A.D. 600–1200).* Dordrecht: Kluwer Academic Publishers, 1990.

Meeks, Wayne. *The First Urban Christians.* New Haven: Yale University Press, 1983.

Meershoeck, G. Q. A. *Le Latin Biblique d'apres Saint Jerome: Aspects Linguistiques de la Rencontre entre la Bible et le Monde Classique.* Utrecht: Dekker and Van de Vegt N.V. Nijmegen, 1966.

Metzger, Bruce M. *The Canon of the New Testament.* Oxford: Clarendon, 1987.

———. *The Early Versions of the New Testament: Their Origin, Transmission, and Limitations.* Oxford: Clarendon, 1977.

Momigliano, Arnaldo. *The Development of Greek Biography.* Cambridge, Mass.: Harvard University Press, 1971.

Moore, Stephen D. *Literary Criticism and the Gospels.* New Haven: Yale University Press, 1989.

———. *Mark and Luke in Poststructuralist Perspectives.* New Haven: Yale University Press, 1992.

Morey, James H. "Peter Comestor, Biblical Paraphrase, and the Medieval Popular Bible." *Speculum* 68 (January 1993): 6–35.

Murphy, G. Ronald. *The Saxon Savior: The Germanic Transformation of the Gospel in the Ninth-Century Heliand.* Oxford: Oxford University Press, 1989.

Neill, Stephen, and Tom Wright. *The Interpretation of the New Testament 1861–1986.* Oxford: Oxford University Press, 1988.

Neirynck, F. *Duality in Mark.* Louvain: Louvain University Press, 1972.

Neusner, Jacob. *Canon and Connection: Intertextuality in Judaism.* Lanham, Md.: University Press of America, 1987.

Nida, Eugene A. *Toward a Science of Translating.* Leiden: E. J. Brill, 1964.

Orchard, Bernard, and Harold Riley. *The Order of the Synoptics: Why Three Synoptic Gospels.* Macon, Ga.: Mercer University Press, 1987.

Orlinsky, Harry M., and Robert G. Bratcher. *A History of Bible Translation and the North American Contribution.* Atlanta: Scholars Press, 1991.

Pagels, Elaine. *The Gnostic Gospels.* New York: Vintage, 1979.

Perrin, Norman. "The Christology of Mark: A Study in Methodology." *Journal of Religion* 51 (1971): 173–87.

———. *The New Testament: An Introduction: Proclamation and Parenesis, Myth and History.* New York: Harcourt Brace Jovanovich, 1982.

Pesch, Rudolf. *Das Markus-evangelium.* 2 vols. Freiburg: Herder, 1976–1977.

Petavel, Emmanuel. *La Bible en France ou les Traductions Françaises des Saintes Ecritures.* Paris, 1864. Rpt. Geneva: Slatkine, 1970.

Peterson, Norman. *Literary Criticism for New Testament Critics.* Philadelphia: Fortress Press, 1978.

Peterson, William L. *Tatian's Diatessaron: Its Creation, Dissemination, Significance, and History in Scholarship.* Leiden: E. J. Brill, 1994.

Pope, Hugh. *English Versions of the Bible.* Rev. and amplified Sebastian Bullough. London: B. Herder, 1952.

Press, Gerald A. "The Subject and Structure of Augustine's *De Doctrina Christiana.*" *Augustinian Studies* 11 (1980): 99–124.

Prickett, Stephen. *Origins of Narrative: The Romantic Appropriation of the Bible.* Cambridge: Cambridge University Press, 1996.

Quispel, G. *Tatian and the Gospel of Thomas.* Leiden: E. J. Brill, 1975.

Reinhardt, Klaus, and Horacio Santiago-Otero. *Biblioteca Biblica Iberica Medieval.* Madrid: Consejo Superior de Investigaciones Científicas, 1986.

Rhoads, David. "Narrative Criticism and the Gospel of Mark." *Journal of the American Academy of Religion* 50, no. 3 (1982): 411–34.

Rhoads, David, and Donald Michie. *Mark as Story: An Introduction to the Narrative of a Gospel.* Philadelphia: Fortress Press, 1982.

Rice, Eugene F., Jr. *Saint Jerome in the Renaissance.* Baltimore: Johns Hopkins University Press, 1985.

Rico, Francisco. *Alfonso el Sabio y La General Estoria.* Barcelona: Ediciones Ariel, 1972.

Ricoeur, Paul. "Interpretative Narrative." Trans. David Pellauer. In Schwartz, ed. *The Book and the Text: The Bible and Literary Theory.* 237–57.

Robbins, Vernon K. *Jesus the Teacher: A Socio-Rhetorical Interpretation of Mark.* Philadelphia: Fortress Press, 1984.

Robinson, James J. *The Problem of History in Mark.* Philadelphia: Fortress Press, 1982.

Rummel, Erika. *Erasmus' Annotations on the New Testament: From Philologist to Theologian.* Toronto: University of Toronto Press, 1986.

Sauvanon, Jeanine. *Les metiers au Moyen Âge: Leurs "signatures" dans les vitraux.* Le Coudray: Houvet, 1993.

Schildgen, Brenda Deen. "Augustine's Answer to Jacques Derrida in the *De Doctrina Christiana.*" *New Literary History* 25 (Spring 1994): 382–97.

———. *Crisis and Continuity: Time and Narrative in the Gospel of Mark.* Sheffield: Sheffield Academic Press, 1998.

———. "The Gospel of Mark as Picaresque Novella." *Genre* 29 (1996): 297–323.

———. "Rhetoric and the Body of Christ: Augustine, Jerome, and the Classical *Paideia.*" In Brenda Deen Schildgen, ed., *The Rhetoric Canon.* Detroit: Wayne State University Press, 1997. 151–73.

Schmidt, Karl Ludwig. *Le probleme du Christianisme primitif; quatre conferences sur la forme et la pensee du Nouveau Testament.* Paris: E. Leroux, 1938.

Schwartz, Regina, ed. *The Book and the Text: The Bible and Literary Theory.* London: Basil Blackwell, 1990.

Selvidge, Marla J. *Woman, Cult, and Miracle Recital: A Redactional Critical Investigation on Mark 5:24–34.* Lewisburg, Pa.: Bucknell University Press, 1990.

Smalley, Beryl. *The Gospels in the Schools c.1100–c.1280.* London and Ronceverte: Hambledon Press, 1985.

————. *The Study of the Bible in the Middle Ages.* Oxford: Clarendon, 1941.

Smeets, Jean Robert. "Les traductions, adaptations et paraphrases de la Bible en vers." In Jauss, ed., *La Litterature Didactique, Allegorique et Satirique,* 1:48–57.

Smith, Morton. *Clement of Alexandria and a Secret Gospel of Mark.* Cambridge, Mass.: Harvard University Press, 1973.

————. *The Secret Gospel: The Discovery and Interpretation of the Secret Gospel According to Mark.* San Francisco: Harper and Row, 1973.

Sneddon, Clive R. "The 'Bible du XIIIᵉ siecle': Its Medieval Public in Light of Its Manuscript Tradition." In Lourdaux and Verhelst, eds., *The Bible and Medieval Culture.* 127–40.

Sobrino, Jon. *Christology at the Crossroads.* Trans. John Drury. New York: Orbis Books, 1978.

Sourcebook of Texts for Comparative Study of the Gospels. Society for Biblical Literature, 1973. Later published as *Documents for the Study of the Gospels,* ed. and trans. David R. Cartlidge and David L. Dungan. Philadelphia: Fortress Press, 1980.

Sparks, H. F. D. "The Latin Bible." In Ferguson, ed., *The Bible in the Early Church.* 342–69.

St. Mark and the Coptic Church. Cairo: Coptic Orthodox Patriarchate, 1968.

Stamm, Friedrich Ludwig. *Ulfilas oder die uns erhaltenen Denkmaler der gotischen Sprache.* Ed. Moritz Heyne and Ferdinand Wrede. Paderborn: Druck und Verlag von Ferdinand Schoningh, 1903.

Stevens, W. P. *The Theology of Huldrych Zwingli.* Oxford: Clarendon, 1986.

Stock, Brian. *The Implications of Literacy: Written Language and Models of Interpretation in the Eleventh and Twelfth Centuries.* Princeton: Princeton University Press, 1983.

Talbert, Charles H. *What Is a Gospel?: The Genre of the Canonical Gospels.* Philadelphia: Fortress Press, 1977.

Theissen, Gerd. *The Social Setting of Pauline Christianity.* Ed. and trans. John H. Schutz. Philadelphia: Fortress Press, 1982.

Thouzellier, Christine. "L'Emploi de la Bible par les Cathares." In Lourdaux and Verhelst, *The Bible and Medieval Culture.* 141–56.

Tolbert, Mary Ann. "The Gospel in Greco-Roman Culture." In Schwartz, ed., *The Book and the Text: The Bible and Literary Theory.* 258–75.

————. *Sowing the Gospel: Mark's World in Literary-Historical Perspective.* Minneapolis: Fortress Press, 1989.

Tollington, R. B. *Clement of Alexandria II.* London: Williams and Norgate, 1914.

Turner, Victor. *The Ritual Process.* Ithaca: Cornell University Press, 1969.

Via, Daniel Otto. *Kerygma and Comedy in the New Testament.* Philadelphia: Fortress Press, 1975.

Votaw, Clyde Weber. "The Gospels and Contemporary Biographies." *American Journal of Theology* 19 (1915): 45–73, 217–49. Rpt. Philadelphia: Fortress Press, 1970; intro. John Reumann.

Waetjen, Herman C. *A Reordering of Power: A Socio-Political Reading of Mark's Gospel.* Minneapolis: Fortress Press, 1989.

Walker, William O., Jr., ed. *The Relationship among the Gospels.* San Antonio: Trinity University Press, 1978.

Walsh, Katherine, and Diana Wood, eds. *The Bible in the Medieval World: Essays in Memory of Beryl Smalley.* Oxford: Basil Blackwell, 1985.

Weisse, Christian Hermann. *Die Evangelienfrage in ihrem gegenwartigen Stadium.* Leipzig: Breitkopf und Hartel, 1856.

Wengert, Timothy J. *Philip Melanchthon's Annotationes in Johannem in Relation to Its Predecessors and Contemporaries.* Geneva: Librairie Droz, 1987.

Wilder, Amos N. *Early Christian Rhetoric: The Language of the Gospel.* Cambridge, Mass.: Harvard University Press, 1971.

Williams, James G. *Gospel against Parable: Mark's Language of Mystery.* Sheffield: Almond Press, 1985.

Willis, G. G. *A History of the Early Roman Liturgy: To the Death of Pope Gregory the Great.* London: Boydell and Brewer, 1994.

———. *St. Augustine's Lectionary.* London: S.P.C.K., 1962.

Index

Africa, 40, 52
African-American, 30
Africana, 102
Aichele, George: *Jesus Framed,* 169n. 27; *Postmodern Bible,* 169n. 27
Aland, Kurt, 27, 100, 123; *Synopsis of the Four Gospels,* 25, 141nn. 21, 22
Albertus Magnus, 65, 77, 79, 81–82, 90, 153n. 9
Alcuin, 86, 104, 114
Alexandria, 40, 41, 44, 56, 103
Alfonso X el Sabio: *General Estoria,* 66, 77, 108, 154n. 15
Alighieri, Dante: *Comedy,* 31; *De vulgari eloquentia,* 108, 164n. 87
allegory, 53, 72, 78–79, 81, 89, 94, 103
Alter, Robert: *Art of Biblical Narrative,* 170n. 75; *Art of Biblical Poetry,* 170n. 45; *Literary Guide to the Bible* (with Frank Kermode), 169n. 27
Amalarius Episcopi: *Liber Officialis,* 74, 155nn. 45, 46
Ambrose of Milan, 39–41, 57, 63, 144n. 29
annotations, 17, 22
Anthony, 57
Anti-Marcionite Prologue, 35
Antioch, 39, 40, 44, 56, 83

"anxiety of influence," 18, 29, 140
apocrypha, 32, 70–73
Apollinaris of Laodicia, 58
apostolic period, 12 passim
Aquinas, Thomas, 81, *Catena Aurea,* 65, 81, 94, 153n. 10
Arabic, 45
Aramaic, 66
Aristotle, 12, 19, *Aristotle on Rhetoric,* 139n. 4, 140n. 12; *Rhetoric,* 19
Arnobius, 56, 58
Arnold, Duane W. H., 160n. 42
Asia, 40
astronomy, 64
Athanasius, 37, 57
Auerbach, Erich, 133, *Literary Language and Its Public in Late Latin Antiquity and in the Middle Ages,* 146n. 2; *Mimesis: The Representation of Reality in Western Literature,* 146n. 2, 169n. 26
Augustine, 19, 21, 25, 28, 35–40, 54, 60, 63, 67, 72, 78, 80, 82, 90–91, 94, 102–3, 112, 117–18, 122, 126–27, 131–32, 138; *City of God,* 41; *Confessions,* 41, 48, 59, 133, 145n. 47, 150n. 62; *De Consensu Evangelistarum,* 21, 46–49, 79, 119–20, 143n. 2, 147nn. 13, 14,